Praise for *Quitting America*

"Randall Robinson is very much alive,
keen-eyed, and very much a force to be reckoned with, and
has a record that can be double-checked."
—*Newsday*

"This is a well-constructed book that gives in-depth insight into
why Robinson and his family departed his native homeland."
—*Upscale*

"Sitting in the Caribbean, a safe distance from the demons
which evidently once frustrated his tortured soul, Robinson
has managed to craft his best work to date."
—*Caribbean Life*

"Required reading."
—*The New York Post*

Randall Robinson is the founder and former president of Trans-
Africa, the African-American advocacy organization he established
to promote constructive and enlightened U.S. policies toward
Africa and the Caribbean. The author of *The Debt, The Reckon-
ing,* and *Defending the Spirit* (all available from Plume), Mr.
Robinson lives with his wife and daughter in St. Kitts.

Visit www.RandallRobinson.com.

Also by Randall Robinson

The Debt
Defending the Spirit
The Reckoning

QUITTING AMERICA

THE DEPARTURE OF A BLACK MAN
FROM HIS NATIVE LAND

RANDALL ROBINSON

A PLUME BOOK

PLUME
Published by the Penguin Group
Penguin Group (USA) Inc., 375 Hudson Street, New York, New York 10014, U.S.A.
Penguin Group (Canada), 10 Alcorn Avenue, Toronto, Ontario,
Canada M4V 3B2 (a division of Pearson Penguin Canada Inc.)
Penguin Books Ltd., 80 Strand, London WC2R 0RL, England
Penguin Ireland, 25 St. Stephen's Green, Dublin 2, Ireland (a division of Penguin Books Ltd.)
Penguin Group (Australia), 250 Camberwell Road, Camberwell,
Victoria 3124, Australia (a division of Pearson Australia Group Pty. Ltd.)
Penguin Books India Pvt. Ltd., 11 Community Centre,
Panchsheel Park, New Delhi – 110 017, India
Penguin Books (NZ), Cnr Airborne and Rosedale Roads, Albany, Auckland 1310,
New Zealand (a division of Pearson New Zealand Ltd.)
Penguin Books (South Africa) (Pty.) Ltd., 24 Sturdee Avenue, Rosebank,
Johannesburg 2196, South Africa

Penguin Books Ltd., Registered Offices: 80 Strand, London WC2R 0RL, England

Published by Plume, a member of Penguin Group (USA) Inc.
Previously published in a Dutton edition.

First Plume Printing, January 2005
1   3   5   7   9   10   8   6   4   2

Excerpts from "Statement of a Return to the Country Where I Was Born" by
Aimé Césaire, © Présence Africaine, 1975, used with permission from the author.

Ⓟ REGISTERED TRADEMARK—MARCA REGISTRADA

The Library of Congress has catalogued the Dutton edition as follows:
Robinson, Randall, 1941–
Quitting America : the departure of a Black man from his native land / by Randall Robinson.
p.   cm.
ISBN 0-525-94758-2 (hc.)
ISBN 0-452-28630-1 (pbk.)
1. Robinson, Randall, 1941–   2. African American political activists—Biography. 3. Political
activists—United States—Biography. 4. African Americans—Saint Kitts and Nevis—
Biography. 5. Expatriation. 6. Saint Kitts and Nevis—Description and travel. 7. National
characteristics, American. 8. United States—Social conditions—1980–   9. United States—
Race relations. 10. United States—Politics and government—2001–   I. Title.
E185.97.R665A3 2004
973'.0496073'0092—dc22   2003019226

Printed in the United States of America
Original hardcover design by Leonard Telesca

For Hazel
and for the gracious people of her native land,
my adopted new country—St. Kitts and Nevis

This is a testament of leave-taking,
a single candle guttering in an angry wind
of national hysteria.

Contents

PART THREE: THE INNOCENCE OF GUILTLESS SMALL PLACES

PART ONE

FIVE HUNDRED YEARS OF WHITE CRIMES AND SELF-ABSOLUTION IN THE AMERICAS

Chapter One

Jewel

You must listen to a place before you can know it, before you can know it even a little. Be quiet and listen. The place, the people, the peculiar textile of the culture will tell you all about itself, by and by, if you, hard though it may be for an American, manage to be respectful enough to shut up for a time and listen.

You know this and it is still all but impossible to achieve, particularly here where you are distracted at first so completely by the mesmerizing otherworldly look of the place.

Just this morning shortly after six I observed a miles-wide plate of clouds, washed red on the flat underside by the rising sun and balanced on a spit of cotton that appeared to coil up from the depths of a shimmering sea—a sea that triangularly glistened varieties of red fanning forward from the fulcrum cloud's foot to the distant shores that welcomed the sea's ageless return. The mountain beside which the sun rose appeared purple on its shadow face, a deep green toward the coming day. The vista was animated by the swaying palm fronds of slender coconut trees that clustered in small sandy bays along a pristine coastline. This is St. Kitts.

The early first-century Christian authors of the *Gnostic Gospels* must have seen a place like this while developing the philosophical conviction that God indeed was *in* us and *everywhere* around us. For how else could such matchless natural beauty be possible?

The artist Georgia O'Keeffe lamented the modern human's compromised ability to *see* natural beauty and thus be spiritually renovated by it. Rendered insensible by steel girders and concrete-surround, what chance have the eyes of the soul to rest upon a bird-of-paradise blossom on a verdant hillside? But here still on this tiny Caribbean island where there is a surviving sanity of scale, where the quaint wood and stone-face buildings decline to dwarf their makers, where traffic is directed by a person and not a machine, where on narrow streets the rules of vehicular behavior are recited solicitously to drivers by every man, woman, and child afoot, here I think, yes, in a small place like this, the soul, the spirit, has a fighting chance.

Of course what size chance may depend on the gravity of one's wounds. America is a big place. Everything about it is big. It has big buildings, big streets, big guns, big money, big power, big hubris, big wounds. Everything about America is big except its people, who, unbeknownst to most Americans, are mere human beings, no bigger or smaller than human beings any place else in the world. They only look smaller, or behave smaller, because they come from a country where everything else, besides them, is so lethally big, so crudely antagonistic to the naked human's social requirement.

Recently at the Ocean Terrace Inn, an American white father was heard saying over dinner to his family and forty-nine fellow dinner guests, waiters, and a maître d' that he "couldn't wait to get out of St. Kitts and back to Trenton."

Trenton?

It seemed not to matter to the unhappy American that he had offended the maître d', all of the waiters, and most of the dinner guests on racial grounds alone. He was an American with big hubris. He had noticed in his short stay that the weather was "nice." He had not noticed, except as backdrop, the people of the country—least of all, apparently, those bringing him his food—and he would return to Trenton without knowing what a bird-of-paradise was.

Both the personality type and its ideas are an American commonplace abroad, oozing like a contagion throughout a resort-mad world, replicating resentment toward America by a factor of what? Ten, twenty, thirty, forty, fifty percent of white Americans who vacation in the black and brown world? There is no way to answer this. The evidence is anecdotal. But ask any cab driver in the long lines that begin to form throughout the Caribbean at 5:00 A.M. at the deep-water ports on cruise-ship days.

Make no mistake, the people who live here and elsewhere along the archipelago of the eastern Caribbean very much want American economic partnership. No island economy can afford to be cut adrift by so powerful a regional neighbor. The governments of these islands have met every reasonable test for friendship. They all rank high in the global community of civilly well-run democracies. They all score high marks in the areas of human rights, literacy, health care, and general quality of life. They are all well-disposed toward the United States.

Why then have America and Americans behaved so callously toward governments and peoples who present them with no threat but only proffers of friendship? Perhaps Americans, or more specifically, white Americans, have behaved such because they only really value or respect what they either crave or fear: money or might, all else to be belittled, disdained, dismissed, even desecrated. Could it be that in America, the unexcelled bigness of all *things* material has resulted in the concomitant relative smallness of all *values* nonmaterial? Moribund ethics. The death of the spirit. An unexamined and withering national soul. The commercialization of everything from school to pew.

I am not suggesting that most Americans behave abroad like the white father from Trenton. He not only was possessed of a malignant purpose, but of an absence of manners to cloak his boorishness, as well. Most white Americans in their dealings with black, brown, and all other varieties of nonwhite people are altogether well-mannered and are often all the more damaging for it. For indeed fine manners and America's national opiate of choice, chauvinistic narcissism, combine to immunize white Americans *en masse* from self-knowledge, self-doubt, self-criticism. *If they don't like us, it is only because they are jealous of us.*

So cut off are most white Americans from self-knowledge, that one could publicly present a typical example of American high-office churlishness aimed at a foreign black head-of-state without causing so much as a ripple in the American press, while the same insult aimed at, say, a clerk of the exchequer of Liechtenstein, would result in windy umbrage taken in a rumble across the American body politic.

Dr. Denzil Douglas is the prime minister of the two-island nation of St. Christopher and Nevis (known more widely as St. Kitts-Nevis). Dr. Douglas, a medical doctor by training, is black, as are the vast majority of the forty-five thousand citizens of his stable democratic country, which is located not terribly far east of two islands that are better known to Americans: St. Thomas and St. Croix. Dr. Douglas (who heads the island's Labor Party) and leaders of the opposition party, the People's Action Movement, have agreed, if on little else, that the small economy of the country must be diversified away from a reliance on sugar production, which lately has been losing money due to falling prices across the world. Thus, efforts have been undertaken on St. Kitts and other Caribbean islands to expand the tourism and offshore banking sections of their economies, the latter of the two efforts frustrated significantly by the United States.

It was in this connection that an official of Ross University, an offshore American veterinary school operating in St. Kitts with a virtually all-white American faculty and students, sought to arrange a meeting in the United States between Dr. Douglas and Congressman Curt Weldon, a Republican from Pennsylvania. It was during this meeting, after listening to Dr. Douglas discuss what he thought was the sole item on the agenda, that Congressman Weldon proposed what he thought Dr. Douglas's tiny country might do for the United States.

Contemporaneous with the meeting between Dr. Douglas and Congressman Weldon, all hell had broken out on Vieques, an island parcel of Puerto Rico, a possession of the United States. The United States has been using parts of Vieques as a test site for American military weapons. Our boys bomb it, shoot it, pulverize it. Blow it up to watch its dust dance hither and yon on the poisoned wind. As a result, Puerto Ricans living in the vicinity of the tests have over the years developed cancer at an alarming rate. Massive protests, joined in by prominent U.S. mainlanders, were begun on Vieques calling upon the U.S. Navy to end its bombardment of the island. Congressman Weldon thought the Navy might be forced to move its operations to another venue. This realization caused him to invite Prime Minister Douglas to consider allowing the United States to bomb *his* beautiful, peaceful, stable little island nation. Our boys had to play with their ordnance somewhere.

No regional small-country leader can afford to brand a proposal from a U.S. congressman as stupid, no matter how absurd the proposed idea. Congressman Weldon had spoken, as Republicans are wont to speak, with no trace of irony. Prime Minister Douglas had little choice but to say that his government would take under advisement the congressman's politely rendered proposal to destroy his country. It should surprise no one that Congressman Weldon's proposal, gotten wind of by the local press, provoked quite a tempest on the island and died aborning. Not a line about any of this appeared anywhere in the American press.

Many, if not most, Americans will read this and no doubt sigh a "what's the big deal, and where is this place you're talking about, anyhow?" As a practical matter maybe it *wouldn't* be such a big deal, were not such coarse little bricks being hurled willy-nilly across the world daily by brainless, insensate white Americans, high and low, numbering in the thousands. And no, I have not suffered an inexplicable lapse of language judgment. I use the words *brainless* and *insensate* advisedly, if perhaps somewhat desperately. White people around the world insult black people, brown people, everyone-but-them people, regularly and gratuitously, without even the bitter, dubious flattery of conscious intent. From overbearing congressmen, to wide-eyed cruise line steerage, to fuzzy-cheeked Ross veterinary students who somehow cannot bring themselves to walk amongst the locals without a flank of attack dogs.

In any case, it is not a fair fight to contest coarseness of power with coarseness of language. No chance of winning. But it might make a handful of Americans—no let's be blunt here, white people—

see themselves if for the briefest of moments self-critically, particularly in a world churning dangerously out of anyone's clear control.

Americans believe that their country is the *greatest* country in the world. I have never known what this was supposed to mean. If however it was meant to suggest that America is the best place in the world to live, Americans might be a little annoyed to learn that another group of white people, presumably not Americans, had decided that Norway is the *best* place in the world to live, this despite Norway's frigid 2:00 P.M. winter nightfall, which might well explain the country's high alcoholism and suicide rates.

I am just guessing here, but I think when Americans say that America is the greatest country in the world, they mean only that it is the richest and most powerful, that their country meets all the *bigness* tests, that Americans have more stuff than anybody else, and that they can just flat shoot everybody else's lights out. This is what they must mean. I don't think they can mean that Americans are the happiest people in the world, or the most well-adjusted people in the world, or the most moral, or anything like that.

In Idaho, a U.S. senator running for reelection is being called a fraud by his opponent because the senator hasn't been making maximum use of his hunting license. The thinking goes that the incumbent senator can't be reliably pro-gun if he hasn't been using his own gun regularly enough to shoot animals. The incumbent's opponent has been hammering away on this point in a television campaign ad, with reason to believe that the good citizens of Idaho are coming to share his view that the senator has indeed not been shooting enough animals.

CNN squeezed the Idaho campaign story in between live news segments about the serial snipers who had been terrorizing the Washington, D.C., area. The snipers had shot and killed ten people at range with a high-powered rifle poked through a hole in the trunk of a two-hundred-and-fifty-dollar Chevrolet Caprice. A talking-head psychologist said on CNN that the snipers were killing because snipers "enjoyed" killing. The CNN interviewer then asked the talking-head psychologist to give a profile of the snipers. The talking-head psychologist said among other things that a very reliable predictor of psychopathic adult behavior is a childhood enjoyment taken in the killing of animals. When I was twelve, I saw a boy named Mordecai Harris impale a frog on his scout dirk. This was long before the talking-head psychologist was born, long before CNN even. I thought then on that weekend camping trip in July 1953, before I had ever heard the word *psychopath,* that Mordecai Harris was crazy.

Most people in the world who hunt do it to eat, to survive. But in the "great" nations with the great surpluses of *stuff,* hunters hunt not to eat but for the "sport" (a euphemism for joy) of it. Get the glorious beast (the proud buck in New Hampshire, the lolling lion in Kenya) in the crosshairs of the scope's reticle and blow the beast to kingdom come. Sever the head. Stuff it. Ship it home. Bolt it onto the family-room wall above mantle and hearth. And regard one's own proud countenance reflected in the dead beast's glassy eyes.

Mordecai Harris stabbed a frog that happened across his path. It was plain enough that he enjoyed it. As I have said, I thought he was crazy, really crazy. But there must be degrees of crazy here. If Mordecai had been required, in order to kill the frog, to go to some bureau downtown to buy a license, and then on to some gun store to buy a hunting rifle and other gun paraphernalia, and then pile into a car with two or three other guys at four in the morning, and then shiver in the woods waiting maybe hours for the frog to show itself. . . .

Well, I just think if Mordecai had had to go to all that trouble to have a little fun killing a frog, he'd have foregone the pleasure. And Mordecai bore all the signs, according to the CNN talking-head psychologist, of a born psychopath. The whole point that the CNN talking-head psychologist was laboring to make was that it was a very short developmental leap from Mordecai Harris to psychopath to serial sniper.

Well if Mordecai was crazy, and he certainly was, what does that say about all the others who kill for the joy of it—not frogs, but big, good-looking mammals out for a stroll in their own habitat, warm-blooded vertebrates that nourish their young with milk just like we humans do? Animals with hair like humans, not bothering anyone, animals whose meat the shooter doesn't need and won't bother to eat? God, what a beauty moving with balletic grace in the glass circle of the big scope.

Look at the thing, will ya?

Jesus, there's two of 'em. Which to take down?

Just standing there.

Do you see 'em Jack? Do you see 'em?

Hol-ld still now, baby.

Blam!!

I got 'em. I got 'em, Jack.

Look at that thing.

Neck blown open. Antlers askew. Surprised eyes, wide and sightless. Blood, red and spumy, bubbling up from the large, ragged hole in the graceful neck.

Aah, that was great.

That was sick, was what it was. Real sick. Way sicker than Mordecai Harris, the born psychopath, ever was. But that's a good chunk of Idaho, most of the membership of the National Rifle Association, and a sizable section of American men.

Fanny Kemble, an actress on the English stage in the nineteenth century, married a wealthy Philadelphian, Pierce Butler, during her tour of America in the 1830s. After living on the Butler family's slave plantation in the Georgia Sea Islands, Kemble described her impressions of American life in journal entries in 1838–1839 that were later published upon her divorce and return to England in a book entitled *Journal of a Residence on a Georgian Plantation*:

> The profusion of birds here is one thing that strikes me as curious, coming from the vicinity of Philadelphia, where even the Robin Redbreast, held sacred by the humanity of all other christian people, is not safe from the gunning prowess of the unlicensed sportsmen of your free country. The Negroes (of course) are not allowed the use of firearms, and their very simply constructed traps do not do much havoc among the feathered hordes that haunt their rice fields. . . . no day passes

that I do not, in the course of my walk, put up a number of land-birds, and startle from among the gigantic
sedges the long-necked waterfowl by dozens. It arouses
the killing propensity in me most dreadfully, and I really
entertain serious thoughts of learning to use a gun, for
the mere pleasure of destroying these pretty birds as
they whirr from their secret coverts close beside my
path.

On the matter of the "humanity of all other [C]hristian people,"
Ms. Kemble's research falters:

> Henry VIII, early in the sixteenth century, on more than
> one occasion had two to three hundred deer rounded
> up from his royal forests, penned, and set upon by his
> hunting; an admiring observer of a wild-bird hunt wrote
> that "sometimes they take a pretty feathered army pris-
> oners, two or three thousand at one draught and give
> no quarter"; the Duke of Henneberg in 1581 is credited
> with shooting "no fewer than 1003 red deer" in a single
> afternoon, and the elector of Saxony and his party
> killed 1,532 wild boar on one hunt in 1585.
>   —Kirkpatrick Sale
>   *The Conquest of Paradise*

Practically no one shoots animals in St. Kitts. At least not for the
sheer fun of it. There are no serial killers. There are murders, but
they are of the ordinary stripe.

Trevor Isaac, the man who built our house here—wonderful
craftsman, sound aesthetic judgment, calibrating mind and all
that—says to me one day, "You know, Mr. Robinson (I had tried
on and off for two years to get him to address me by my given
name, but to no avail), I've never lived off St. Kitts. I've been to
some other islands but never to America. Tell you the truth, I've
never been interested in living anyplace else but here." He paused
and looked out toward a sea that was blue-green under a sun sparkle
with whitecaps tossed about by a strong northeasterly trade wind.
He was one of those people who appeared taller than he actually

was, which looked to be about six feet. He was athletically built, with a contractor's deeply sun-burnished skin. He was a very smart man who had overcome an impoverished start that might have diverted him from a career in quantum physics. As it was, he was an on-the-job genius with his quantities. No miter-cut missed, no board wasted, no wedding of material miscarried.

"I've seen a number of news stories on CNN about people stealing children in America. Do things like that really happen there?"

Through some no doubt costly magic property of the unconscious, the human animal can habituate to virtually any condition and read the condition as endurable, even normal.

"When Hazel and I would take Khalea to a shopping mall in America, we would tell her never to get more than fifteen feet from one or the other of us and never out of our line of sight." I told him what had happened to the Lyon sisters, white preteen sisters who had disappeared from a Wheaton, Maryland, shopping mall nearly twenty-five years ago with no indication then or since what had happened to them.

"This happens frequently in America. It has for a very long time, although I can't recall that it happened quite so often when I was a child."

He looked as astonished as a manly sort will allow. Kidnapping is unheard of in St. Kitts.

It is 6:30 in the evening as I write this and growing dark. It is late October 2002, and the days are shortening, though not by Washington lengths because of our relative closeness to the equator. Khalea is downtown at a meeting of her school's Young Leader's Club. She is serving her second term as president. The club of twelve-year-olds is meeting over dinner at a restaurant up from the Bay Road near the center of Basseterre's small business district, which is five miles or so along the main island road from our home. We will pick Khalea up at seven. It will be dark by then. The other children live in town nearby. They will walk home. No one will have reason to worry about their safety.

Trevor said, "America seems to be a very dangerous place."

"I guess it is, although I never thought about it as much when I lived there as I do now."

Hazel and I park our Honda CRV on the Bay Road a half block shy of the restaurant, which is situated on a corner just up from the bay waters of the Caribbean Sea, quiet now save for the soft rhythmic lapping of the resting tide. Not far from the restaurant and into the bay runs the ghaut, a street carved into a V-shaped basin to evacuate the torrent of water that pours down from the mountain during hurricanes.

We turn off the engine and settle down to wait for Khalea to finish her meeting. We are early. The sun shows to the west a parting sliver that spreads out onto the sea like mercury on a mirror and then dissolves slowly into the shining surface of the water.

Across the Bay Road and down from the restaurant, there are some fifty people either sitting or strolling about on the Port Zante courtyard. About fifteen men dressed in blue denim shirts and trousers begin to climb up onto the back of an open bed truck parked just inside the courtyard. They have only just finished delivering chairs for an evening social event of some sort on the courtyard. The men all appear to be in their twenties, with the exception of three who looked middle-aged. They pull each other aboard laughing and talking in an idiom that I can hear but not understand at a distance.

Several of the men waiting in the vicinity of the truck talk with others around them who are dressed more conventionally. One of them, carrying a razor-sharp machete with which he has been pruning coconut fronds, brings a sprig of purple bougainvillea and presents it to a little girl of four who is standing with her parents. The girl smiles. The man who walks with a slight limp joins a line of four others waiting to be pulled aboard the truck. All boarded, a tall erect man dressed in a service cap and starched cottons secures the truck's rear gate and walks toward the driver's side door on which are stenciled the letters H.M.P. On his belt are a clutch of keys and a nightstick that he removes and places on the seat beside him. Slowly the truck belonging to Her Majesty's Prison pulls out of the Port Zante courtyard and heads north on Fort Street toward the Cayon Street Prison.

I have witnessed this intermingling of prisoners and civilians many times now, enough times to know that I am the only one present who feels anything close to fear. In America, we have been conditioned with good reason to be wary of prisoners. Their wardens keep them away from civilians and under armed control, behind and beyond the prison walls, for fear that they will hurt us. We see them as alien and dangerous people, former human beings. America has more than two million such people now, half of them black. America, believed by its people to be the greatest country in the world, accounts for a quarter of the world's prisoners, although it represents but a twentieth of the world's population.

During my last year of law school, thirty-two years ago, I spent time helping convicted felons prepare appeals pleadings. It was in this connection that I on several occasions visited Walpole State Prison, the maximum security state penitentiary in Walpole, Massachusetts. I can still feel the tower guns and lights trained on my back as I strode what seemed an interminable distance from the prison wall to the cell block. I can still hear the closing of the steel doors, the echo of the first preternatural sound giving way grudgingly to the chilling clang of the next. Men, for all the middle years of their manhoods, pent in small sunless chambers, black, white, Hispanic, locked in, locked out, scorned, scuttled, heaped together in mutual disaffirmance, producing together finally for the outside society a price higher by far than the crimes of which they had originally been convicted.

I saw something here last week that brought the Walpole memory back in fresh relief. The Springfield Cemetery sits on a rise just to the west of a section of Basseterre called Greenlands. The old burial ground, dating back to 1855, is square-shaped, running three city blocks to a side with a small chapel at its center constructed of ancient limestone walls under an anterior steeple and a sharply pitched roof. Just north of the cemetery square is the official residence of the governor general, Sir Cuthbert Sebastian, a retired physician of some distinction and a great friend of Hazel's late fa-

ther, Esbon Ross. Around the cemetery's perimeter stretches a faltering, wrought-iron fence featuring the elaborate fretwork of a
long-dead island craftsman. Lining the fence to the south are very
old, very rare trees that can best be likened in appearance to what
giant bonsai trees would look like were they bowing under crowns
of orange berries.

Running between the cemetery's southern perimeter and the William Connor Primary School situated directly across from it is upper
Cayon Street, down which I was headed when I saw what startled
me. There were at least twenty prisoners deployed loosely on the
cemetery grounds, all flailing machetes against errant patches of
guinea grass. Standing with his back turned to at least half of his
charges, some of whom were working at a distance hard against
the four-foot fence, was a lone policeman, again armed only with a
slender nightstick.

I took in this sight from a crosswalk at which I had been stopped
by a uniformed woman crossing guard who was shepherding a
large group of Connor School six-, seven-, and eight-year-olds
across Cayon Street. The children were on their way home by way
of the cemetery and the machete-wielding prisoners. There were
several pedestrians on the sidewalk. Two people in a late-model
Toyota had stopped on the other side of the crosswalk. I looked at
them as they distractedly watched the children climb the steps and
move onto the paved path leading through the cemetery grounds.

No one did anything. The policeman. The crossing guard. The
onlookers. The children. The prisoners. Well, no one did anything
unless you count the pleasantries that two machete-wielding prisoners exchanged with a lead group of three six-year-old girls clad
in gaily colored blouses and plaid jumpers.

I had never seen anything like this before and had difficulty
understanding its meaning. Of course, serious crimes are committed here just as they are in any country in the world. And those
who commit them here are not working with machetes on public
works details. Still one feels remarkably safer here than one does in
virtually any part of the United States, where a postal stamp cannot
be purchased without anxiety. People had always robbed people in

America. And sometimes the victims were hurt or killed. Indeed that happens here, not frequently, but still more than it once did.

Still, the majority of the people who commit crimes here appear to do so largely for material gain and seem not to have lost their basic humanity. They have not been turned into creatures of universal dread, which seems to be very much the case in America, where some general unparticularized anger has metastasized throughout American society, producing in its wake a new generation of Americans who kill people whom they do not know for no other reason than the sheer sick satisfaction of killing them.

You can't imagine what the "greatest" country in the world looks like from here. A nursing student in Arizona shoots two of his teachers to death in front of students, presumably because he was barred from taking an exam. A prostitute murders a string of customers. Two little blond brothers murder their father. In the Northwest, an employee murders most of his coworkers. In the Midwest, students who are not part of the "popular" group murder the students who are. Nationwide, children are kidnapped, molested, and murdered. Then there are the robbers who methodically murder everyone on the target premises. The killer who buries his victims in the yard. The killer who buries his victims under the floorboards. The killer who entombs his victims in concrete. The killer who chops his victims up, refrigerates them, and eats them. The young handsome killer who decapitates his victim and flees to Israel with his father's blessing.

I had begun, while in any public place in America, to watch everyone, every gesture, every motion, every hand retrieved from every pocket. I had begun to map out escape routes from post office lines, movie theaters, and fast-food stores. I had begun to do a quick security recon on even the smallest crowds I encountered. I had even begun to give winos a wider berth.

From here, where prisoners do their chores cheek by jowl with the populace, America appears a very troubled place. It wasn't always like this. When I was a child in the forties and fifties people left house doors open, keys in cars, and no one had ever heard of an alarm system.

The truth put squarely is that I am spent, having fought too many American social battles that should never, in a more decent society, have presented themselves as such to begin with. I am no longer a normal person, as it were, preoccupied, as I have been constrained to be, with *race* and all the wearying baggage that rakes heavily in its train. But, of course, America had scarcely noticed *me*, not least that I was weary, preoccupied as America was with the taxing obsession of its unrelenting self-adoration. All along, I hadn't really needed all that much. Once it may have been enough to know only *who* was responsible. An official confession of all the lurid details, a report, for once, of brutally candid self-investigation, a *book* from on high of awful truths about what all had been done to me and why. A compendious volume replete with the beneficiary's moldy detailed records, journals, charts, graphs, ship manifests, U.S. Treasury receipts, contracts, balance sheets, pictures, plans, pen-and-ink drawings, memoirs of my 346-year-long legal destruction. The long overdue mea culpa that a nation like Brazil, riven with the freight of its own ugly racial past, is brave enough to issue, but America is not. Write the thing, damn it! Explain my stolen story and give it back to me, to the world and, indeed, to that quarter in as much need of it as I, *yourself*. Ask yourself: Would you have done any better, had you been in my place and I in yours?

I no longer grind my heart against the cold rock of a sightless soul. I know now that this America, that I am, at last, reclaimed to have left, uncoupled, at last of its glittering spiritual anchorage, could never confess any wrongdoing, small or large, old or new, the powerful feeling, now more than ever, no need to learn, in the nation's middle age, the painful craft of moral honesty.

But still you must understand that I, like any other human being, needed to know things about who I was. A need felt in an earnest child's breast all the more pressing because *you* had metronomically instructed my parents, and theirs, and theirs, that they and I had originated in a dark forest of savages. I hadn't believed this. Quite. Maybe. Not all of it anyway, my tender child's spirit fighting for its life much too early, before my bones had finished forming, before I scarcely knew what *race* was, before, long before, I learned that some would never even notice my humanity. Who could have done such a thing? What had I done to anyone on high by the small age of five?

Chapter Two

Man-Boy

I was in Rochester, New York, for a speaking engagement when I walked smack into them not two blocks from my hotel, its gleaming glass facade mocking them, their circumstance. No other course open to me now, threading my way through them, people I used to *know,* they me, but no longer. The faces are adolescent but too knowing, old from unnatural experience, at once expressionless and quietly menacing. The eyes, empty of light, evidence the dissociation of battered souls that had given up and left home long ago. Floppy caps turned backward over black rags, pants bagging low over haute hood sneakers. Milling, dispersing, clumping, talking in low English pieces behind the bus shelter's dirty brown fractured glass. It is February and deathly cold on this downtown street over which everything appears to move purposelessly except the wind that gusts about with an owlish howl.

I happen into their midst while looking for a drugstore. There are more than twenty of them, these Man-boys, trudging in and out of the damaged little bus shelter, moving a few feet this way, then that, not going anywhere this sunny school day afternoon. Not going anywhere, period.

They are the children of long-sown seed, old burned Civil War cannister packed with live grapeshot, marked: DANGEROUS IF NOT TREATED.

They are slavery's harvest.

They look at me blankly without connection. I can mean no more to them than they manage to mean to themselves.

I am mildly ashamed of my reaction. This fuguelike feeling, however, is overtaken by another more selfish emotion. I—man of the people, race man, foundering activist, aging pan-Africanist—I—after a lifetime of the work *they* forced those of us who cared to do—I—an escapee, a lucky victim with lucky loving victim parents—I on this cold, flat desolated street in Rochester, New York, navigate the slouched ranks of our future and feel *fear* of the small, privately humiliating kind, and then fear's firstborn, utter hopelessness.

Difficult but simple enough were the problems that obstruct my course soluble by money alone.

No, money ain't the real problem. Not by a long shot. But even should I try, I cannot explain this to Man-boy looking at me, for we are not joined to each other by any common memory, old or new. Nor can I find a common language with which to speak to his spirit, because some committee of the nation ordained long ago for such talks has killed it. Has killed his spirit and buried it under the rubble of the nation's more pressing business.

Man-boy once had a family but it was dismembered by slavery like a life-giving river dammed generations before, many lifetimes upstream. He had a house that wasn't much to speak of, but his homelessness is spiritual in any case. He had a father but his father was run off without his manhood centuries ago. And he had a mother (which was about all he had left) for whom mothering under the weight of America could be likened to the futility of a salmon struggling spastically to swim up a parched arroyo to spawn.

He had a history, a story of his people, that began on a plain in Ethiopia when humans pulled themselves upright thousands upon thousands of years before. But he had not been told his story, thus he believed, unlike the people of other races, that he had no story to be told, no tapestry of ageless accomplishment. He had been, millennia before the birth of Christ, produced of an oral tradition that had carried like an eternal stream all of the vitals of his spiritual identity forward—the names of his ancestors treed out well into the mists of Africa's glorious antiquity, the rituals of a timeless familyhood, the ancient practices of religious ceremony, the embrace of a time-honored culture that shielded his soul from outside assault as the skull would protect the human brain. But that was long ago. And he doesn't know a damn thing about anything except that he is cold in Rochester and feels the near-tactile grip of the biting wind.

How pointless it would be to tell him now at this late stage of his death that the ancient Ethiopians were Christians when Europeans were pagans in idolatrous worship of their old gods, Pan and Diana. How could he possibly, so long after his social malformation, benefit now upon learning of the ancient manuscripts in the library at Timbuktu.

It is painful to look at him now without a language with which to tell him who he was and who he was supposed to become before *it* happened. And now he has been caused to forget even that there had been an *it*, except as a mouthed academic refrain or the wall-side work of a graffiti activist.

I do not know what to say to him because I know of no other example in the modern world where millions of people from a single racial group had been stripped of everything save respiratory function—mother, father, child, property, language, culture, religion, freedom, dignity, and, sometimes, even genitalia.

Now he is a menace to society. He knows this but not how he became this. He really doesn't give a fuck, either. He knows his name but not who he is. He simply cannot remember. His memory was stolen from him. Not his memory of cultural contemporary facts but his memory of a cultural tradition to which he, before *it*, once belonged in the long stream of time. Even if he knew he had lost something or had something taken from him, he would have thought a measure more of himself. As it was, he thought nothing of himself because he was, he concluded, nothing.

But somebody gon pay. Maybe even this old mothafucka coming up da street lookin' at me.

"You know I never thought about that before," Phil McConnaughay had said to me. Phil is the dean of Penn State's Dickinson

Law School. He is tall, fortyish, self-assured, well-educated, and white. As far as I know, his background is marked neither by wealth nor social prominence. He had invited me to speak at his law school about reparations and I had told the students that even worse than stealing the value of a people's line is the theft of a people's memory of themselves. "No people can survive that intact. Property can be recovered. The damaged self cannot be so easily fixed." Penn State had only recently acquired the faltering law school and Phil had been hired away from the University of Illinois Law School to fix it. You sort of knew that in his quiet, competent way he would do just that.

Driving me back to my hotel in Harrisburg, Phil said to me, "I can trace the McConnaughays back two hundred to three hundred years. I know where and how they lived. I think about it often. It gives me kind of a kick." Enough, I bet, to generate the confidence and capacity to fix Dickinson Law School. "I never thought before about what it would be like not to have that." He meant a memory of something from the past—family, culture, custom, religion—to which to moor a brand-new fragile human being. Indeed it has to have been that memory that enabled Phil's mother to mother, his father to father, Phil's promise to flower so predictably.

As predictably as a Man-boy's whose important poverty had never been of the material stripe. What I hated most was that I could talk to Phil, an innocent tangential beneficiary of *it,* and not to Man-boy, *its* breathing victim who looks vacantly at me without connection on this blustery school day afternoon in Rochester, New York.

So now, I have left, and begun to know, all too late, what social normalcy can feel like. In the sight of God, now, make your statement. Dedicate it to Man-boy. Tell him who he *was.* Tell him who he is. Tell him *why* who he *is* is not who he *was.* Tell him the five-thousand-year story of his people. Tell him where and how you *entered* his story. Why you lied to him. Why you blighted his one bequested memory, invented another, implanted it and scrapped him, standing dull-eyed on a frigid Rochester corner in mid-afternoon. Tell him. And tell me, too, while you're at it. For how am I different from Man-boy, save that I am the same machine with rationed opportunity's optional equipment: Man-boy-eloquent, Man-boy-educated, Man-boy-funded? But off the very same white, Western-world assembly line that has produced Man-boy for 346 years.

I have never been one to view the past through the cracked lens of nostalgia. There is very little rosy about the public past of a black man who grew up in the old segregationist South. It was awful. Nonetheless, it is indisputable that America then was generally a great deal safer to walk around in than now. That is, of course, if one, particularly a black one, knew where to walk. The grisly crime had not yet become something one could liken to a competitive sport, a sport played with advancing vogue in every neighborhood of every state in the country. There are no safe harbors left, not even a nursing school classroom in sunny Arizona.

Seen against all other societies that, like living organisms, surge and ebb, the deterioration of American society has been alarmingly rapid, although it may not seem so when measured with the short ruler of one subjective, adaptive life. People generally have little ability to compare a current social condition to a previous condition from which they have gradually been extruded, or not known at all. They have even less ability to compare a current social condition to conditions of life in distant cultures about which they know little to nothing of anything accurate.

Swallowed up by the urban animal named *development,* one feels walled up, increasingly and inexplicably discontented, unhappy, anxious, uncounted, psychically undernourished. Or perhaps city lovers *feel* none of this. Perhaps they disdain the paceless quiet of reflection, the unobstruction of nature's offer, the conducive simpler space for human interaction.

In the last analysis it makes no difference what people *want* or *choose* or are caused even to believe they *need.* These are all trained elections, trained by those who over time have created for themselves and the rest of us new and material appetites that may have put the human species off its natural course and onto a course of eventual self-destruction. *Things,* for which we have all cultivated an insatiable hunger, but provide no spiritual sustenance to the human animal. Blinkered thus, we've come to *want* things, *need* things to the virtual exclusion of all else. The culture that makes and measures, measures and makes, like no culture in history before it, and, yes, sells, sells us the stuff we, God yes, *need*, need I tell you—buildings and cars and excursions to Mars, planes and trains, tunnels and chunnels, the CD, the OD, greener grass, a brand-new ass—and all this upon the head of the vain lost primal animal whose spiritual requirement has not altered from the day it climbed upright.

Could it be that *big* will be the death of us all, that it cannot feed us and keep us healthy, that it has obstructed an interior knowledge of our essential human selves? Perhaps it was in the contemplation of such that the poet Robert Duncan remarked, "The drama of our time is the coming of all men into one fate." For what is the value of democracy if our opinions are formed, our appetites manipulated, our values shaped, our decisions made, our most fundamental human needs camouflaged by the puppet-masters of politics and profit? Could it be that the cultivated obsession of *firstness* that makes America a rich and powerful country also makes it a sick society under homicidal siege to the enlarging ranks of its alienated and forgotten? Could it be that lost in the deafening noise of excessive pride, wisdom of public course has become all but impossible to come by?

Many years ago when I lived in Boston, I recall for reasons I can't remember that city officials on Saturday afternoon closed the entire downtown business district to vehicular traffic and gave the city for a day over to pedestrians. The space sounded, smelled, looked, and felt dramatically differently. So much so that the sudden absence of noise and danger shocked the senses, causing people to behave toward each other much more communicatively than ordinary. Everything slowed down. People staked out the middle of Tremont Street with the zeal of irredentists. They talked, laughed, stood about in aimless contentment. They seemed a different species.

I don't relate this story to suggest that cars should be banned. It's a little late in the day for that. We should, however, be more thoughtful about how we define *progress* and *development,* not just in terms of broadened material wealth but also with an understanding of how indispensable social arrangements are compromised when the market becomes the only voice listened to, its barometer the only measure of a nation's health.

The Kasidah of Haji Abu el Yesdi, a Persian philosopher, wrote: "The truth is a shattered mirror strewn in myriad bits, and each believes his little bit the whole to own."

Truth is elusive, even when vigorously searched for, and America can clearly make no pretense to such. For it has tricked itself and preserved its self-adoration by mistaking wealth for worth.

Indeed America is the wealthiest country in the history of the world. Tiny, modest-living St. Kitts, however, is a healthier society. The suicide rate is nearly always higher in the mansion than in the bungalow. The mansion dweller can ill afford not to ask why.

Fanciful philosophical exertions notwithstanding, life for the human animal has no purpose other than the quest for a relatively pleasant trip through it, en route to that murk-shrouded province of the great unknown, that mysterious and fathomless after-space. Because the human animal is spiritual and instinctively social, the essential art that humans, over the relatively short course of life, must cultivate in order to arrive at a modicum of interior ease is the art of simply *being*, first alone contentedly inside one's own skin, and then with others whose self-found ease we compound by the pairing of it with our own. Is not this *ease*, this absence of psychic pain, this interior contentment elevated periodically by the exhilarations of demonstrated love and beauty and empathy, the only useful definition of *happiness*, that elusive emotion necessarily trivialized by the language of description? If we can't know *why* we live, can't we at least discover what we must, at the very least, do within ourselves and for others to make our existence, at the very least, bearable? Existence as a proposition, justified by something more than the fear of death?

Since the age of Columbus, the ends of European materialist cultures have not served well the deeply private emotional requirements of the modern but still fragile human animal. The suffocating preoccupation with the acquisition of *fame and fortune* has directed untold numbers of helpless unreflective unfortunates to search down the wrong streets for psychic sustenance, resulting in a rabid competition of the lost between the unhappy *failures* and the unhappy *successes,* the former comparing its troubled insides to the latter's well-varnished outsides.

One sure measure of a society's relative health is its suicide rate. If a society produces large numbers of people who destroy themselves, that society cannot be described as successful under any reasonable definition of the term. Well-adjusted people, people who culturally *know,* ever so unobtrusively, how to simply *be* don't kill themselves.

Norway, a nation, as I have indicated of some apparent envy, has, according to the World Health Organization, a suicide rate of 18.2 for males and 6.7 for females per 100,000 people. The United States has a slightly higher rate for males (18.6) and a somewhat lower rate for females (4.4). St. Kitts has a suicide rate for both males and females of zero. The same is true for St. Kitts' English-speaking neighbors of Antigua and Barbuda and St. Vincent and the Grenadines. Perhaps there is indeed something special about what Dr. Ralph Gonsalves, the prime minister of St. Vincent and the Grenadines, calls "Our Caribbean Civilization." To put a converse face on the point: Does Donald Rumsfeld look happy to you? Squint if you have doubts.

Don't you think Americans need to step back and attempt a broad inventory of what is happening to them within?

Does it frighten Americans to even contemplate that American society may well be slowly but inexorably disintegrating due to some diffuse and complex social disease eating away at its foundation?

Is there for Americans any realistic alternative to behaving like the dead sap who believed to his last anguished breath that if he refused to acknowledge the cancer eating out of his gut and into his spine, he wouldn't have a problem?

When serial snipers John Williams and John Malvo were arrested, ending their killing spree, the national capital area breathed a sigh of relief.

Why?

Did the people pouring out of their houses into the weekend sunshine for the first time in three weeks believe that these particular killers were mutant life forms?

Wouldn't an obvious logic compel the conclusion that these killers are the products of the peculiarly American social forces that impelled them?

Wouldn't the same straightforward logic tell us that the Jeffrey Dahmers and Timothy McVeighs of America do not mark the end of a short line but, rather, stand somewhere near the beginning of what looks from here to be a very long line?

Three days ago, my son Jabari, during his lunch break, walked up ritzy Wiltshire Boulevard and into his bank scarcely five feet behind two guys with dead eyes and gleaming pistols who proceed to heist the place, scaring the hell out of my son and everyone else who no doubt breathed a sigh of relief thinking upon the robbers' departure that these two L.A. bad guys would be the last to plunder the tony *miracle mile*.

Only countries rent by civil war or fresh political upheaval are more violent than the United States. Yet we look at each event of violence as if it were *sui generis,* as if it really matters who the killers, robbers, psychopaths, rapists, kidnappers, homegrown terrorists are as long as an unacknowledged, unidentified, untended, social pathogen is left free to generate exponentially their replacements.

Americans only ask: *who?* Never: *why?* Why the galloping plague of impersonal violence that outstrips many times over law enforcement's capacity to contain it? It has never been the mission of law enforcement to stop *crime* but to apprehend criminals. Why a focus on the latter and not the former? Why does this plague appear to afflict industrialized societies like America's more than middle-income societies like St. Kitts or poor societies like Sri Lanka? Has it something to do with the climate of the North? The personality of race? Capitalism's by-product of insensitivity to human suffering? The decomposition of the family in materialist societies? From whence does all the generalized anger spring?

*   *   *

J. N. France, the much revered labor leader, walked everywhere he went. Having elected not to own a car until those poorer than he could do so, he walked by choice. His house had no indoor plumbing for the same reason. Virtually everyone on the island had indoor plumbing but still some did not, and that was enough for J. N. France.

To Americans, J. N. France seemed for his self-imposed sacrifice eccentric to some, crazy even, but to the people of St. Kitts, for reasons that distinguish this national culture from America's, he was a universally admired man. One measure of this regard is the national hospital that bears his name.

On New Year's Eve, Hazel and I took Khalea to the J. N. France Hospital to have her looked at. The waiting room is not a room at all but an airy concourse just off a sun-bathed courtyard landscaped with date palm trees. Across from us sat three children who, we learned, were sisters and brother. The oldest, ten-year-old Cheryl, had deep chocolate skin, a bright smile, and engaging eyes. She wore a sleeveless tiger-skin print dress. Her eight-year-old sister, Barbara, looking like a smaller twin, wore a bright orange dress with an African print. Their brother was five and charged with energy and playful mischief. His name was Edward.

"Edward," Hazel asked him, "do you like school?"

"I like to play."

"What do you want to be when you grow up?"

"A doctor."

Then Edward gave his most mischievous smile, looked at Hazel and went, "Psst, Psst" which, translated from the argot of the working class, meant the two-foot-tall five-year-old was flirting with my forty-six-year-old wife. Edward, encouraged by laughter all around, repeated this twice before turning his attention to Khalea, who was ten and twice his size. "Girl, I like you." Everyone on the concourse laughed.

Cheryl asked Hazel, "Where are you from? From America? You see a lot of shooting up there right? Hear a lot of shooting?" And then she made a statement. "And there is lots of killing right in the home."

These were children not unlike those that Hazel offered rides to along the island road on school days. Tiny children without reason to fear climbed into cars with complete strangers every morning to be dropped off near their primary schools—children who watched nightly, on the local cable television system, American public service announcements that warned American children never to talk to strangers.

Khalea, ill for two days, had become dehydrated. On the evening of New Year's Eve, not long before the merrymaking was to begin, Hazel called the hospital's chief of surgery, Cameron Wilkinson, at home where he had been making preparations for the evening with his wife, Pat, and their three children. Hazel and Dr. Wilkinson had not seen each other since they were small children thirty-five years before.

Edward was regaling us with his view of the world when Dr. Wilkinson arrived not thirty minutes after we had. By then Khalea had been seen by the emergency room physician, who talked with Dr. Wilkinson beside a corridor wall before Dr. Wilkinson undertook a second examination of our daughter. He then ordered nurse Phipps and nurse Williams, both dressed in starched caps and white uniforms gathered at the waist by four-inch red belts, to put Khalea on intravenous drips of fluids and medication.

After three hours of intravenous treatment, a third doctor, a diminutive woman who had trained at the University of the West Indies in Jamaica, examined Khalea to find her much improved. She called Dr. Wilkinson at home to ask whether Khalea could be released. Dr. Wilkinson recommended two hours of further observation, at the end of which, all told, five hours in a private room, Khalea was cleared to be taken home.

I asked nurse Williams where we were to go to pay. In a kind, calm voice, she said, "You don't." Befuddled, I asked, "You don't what?"

"You don't pay."

She smiled slightly. I was confused. I said nothing for moments. Nurse Williams said nothing. Kittitians are not loquacious.

Sensing, I think, a confusion borne largely of my foreignness, nurse Williams said, "Our job here is to get your daughter well." She turned to leave before we could thank her adequately.

We left the hospital with Khalea just after eleven and drove through streets festooned with holiday lights draped from light post to light post. Our progress was slowed by a crowd of people dancing at the Circus roundabout behind a big truck with a payload of huge speakers facing outward and laid in two lines of five abreast, stacked four layers high. Musicians wedged between the speakers boomed calypso music into the warm, high night as a celebrated local calypsonian singer sitting atop the stack of speakers lampooned with rhythm a universe of politicians, some of whom were in attendance and seemingly enjoying the skewering to no end.

This was the very different place of a people who had not lost to the slaver's torment all of Africa's cultural bequest and, thus, not all of themselves. From these few living within themselves on this verdant rock, I had much to learn. As did America.

But the forty-five thousand people for their own protection needed to learn something about America as well. The cultures of the two countries are so radically different as to give rise to disastrous misunderstandings. An unspoken code of honor appears to govern commercial relations here.

I say, "How much will it cost?" The taxi driver, the housekeeper, the landscaper, the customs broker, the cook, the contractor is likely to answer, "Suppose I just do the job for a week and we'll see," or, "Don't worry about that now," or, "We will work it out later."

I say later, "I haven't received your bill yet." They say, "Oh that. I'll get around to it soon. Were you pleased with your work?" I *was* and they *will* get around to it in time.

For two hours every Saturday afternoon, Kittitian teenagers study advanced mathematics at Fitzroy Bryant College with Mr. Stephens, one of the country's finest math minds. Hazel asked him at the beginning about his fee. "Oh I couldn't accept a fee. I'm a teacher. I get paid." But not for sacrificing his Saturdays.

On another occasion, Hazel called the taxi stand at the Circus roundabout and asked for Sadie. Another taxi driver, a man, said, "She's not here." Hazel had had Sadie transport small packages for her before. Hazel said, "I need Sadie to go by Laws Bookstore and pick up a book to take up to my daughter at school." The taxi stand was four blocks from Laws and another ten from Khalea's school.

"I'll do it."

"But I don't know how much the book costs."

"Don't worry. I'll get it and take it up to school. You can pay Sadie when you see her. She'll give it to me. What's your name and what's your daughter's name?"

"I'm Hazel Ross-Robinson."

"You're Ross from Orchid Villa up by the Moravian Church?"

"Yes."

"I went to school with your sister."

And so these things so often go here. Oh, people trust with reason that they will be fairly compensated. But more often than not, talk of money in the initial discussion is looked upon as gauche. Money is simply not the main thing, to put it colloquially. In America money is the only thing. It is the value system clad heavily with unpleasant behaviors that Christopher Columbus brought to the New World. Kindness read as weakness, decency as opportunity.

Chapter Three

Progress

On his way home in 1493 from his initial New World voyage of discovery, Christopher Columbus wrote what is commonly known as the *Santangel Letter* for the eventual benefit of King Ferdinand and Queen Isabella. In the letter Columbus describes his impressions of the Caribbean islands and the Taino Indians he found living there.

> But it [the *Santangel Letter*] fairly throbs with great promises of all kinds of wealth, "great trade and profit," streams and "great mines of gold," spices of cotton and mastic and aloes and "a thousand things of value," harbors beyond compare, lands "rich for planting and sowing and for livestock of every sort," and "all are more richly supplied than I know or could tell" . . . and the people simple and untainted, who "all go naked, men and women, as their mothers bore them," without weapons or irons or even private property, it seems, "well-built people of handsome stature" and "keen intelligence," but "timid beyond cure" [this he says four times], exceedingly generous and friendly, "so artless and so free with all they possess, that no one would believe it without having seen it." . . .
>
> God, gold, and glory, then, were the stuff of this man's dreams, as they were the motivations for the millions who would follow him.
>
> —Kirkpatrick Sale
> *The Conquest of Paradise*

Columbus sailed from a fifteenth-century Europe that was by Sale's measure "steeped in an ardor of wealth, the habit of violence and the pride of intolerance . . . why would one suppose that a culture like Europe's . . . dispirited and adrift after a century and more of disease and famine and death beyond experience, would be able to come upon new societies in a fertile world, innocent and defenseless, and not displace and subdue, if necessary, destroy, them? Why should one suppose such a culture would pause there to observe, to learn, to borrow the wisdom and ways of a foreign, heathen people . . . ?"

Montaigne was to despair in the sixteenth century "that we shall have greatly hastened the decline and ruin of this New World by our contagion."

In the nineteenth century, Henry Harrisse opined, "As to the sum of happiness which has occurred to humanity from Columbus' discovery, philosophers may deem it light and dearly purchased. . . . It is even a mortal question whether the two worlds would not have been far happier had they remained forever unknown to each other."

Columbus, a product of a renaissance materialism that put self above and outside all else, had not the smallest evident inclination to understand or learn from the indigenous people he encountered on the islands of the Caribbean. There is scant evidence to suggest that he harbored even the merest regard for these people and their fashion of seeing themselves as one with nature—nature from which they believed themselves inseparable, nature seen as biocentric and ecocentric with functions and transitions measured in circular, not linear, time. That the Taino people believed, not in "progress," but in renewal and restoration, and in a sacred rather than a material interpretation of *things,* caused Columbus to describe them contemptuously through the prism of his own obsessively materialist value-construct as "generous." In time, Columbus and his heirs would, either directly through slaughter or indirectly through the transmission of disease, destroy the whole of them and what Calvin Martin called "their biological outlook on life." An Earth-friendly people wiped virtually from the face of the Earth by a ruthless force with superior weaponry bent upon an insatiable quest for gold and wealth.

It can be asserted with the considerable weight of a multidisciplinary scholarship that the origins of modern America's terminal social infection can be traced to the cruel and insatiable greed of Christopher Columbus and to a white-world culture, soaked in rapacious arrogance, that produced him.

It is indeed sadly ironic that the white man (who knows much about the science of nature save simply how to *live,* owing to that very science, without doing massive harm to nature) has come through the instrumentalities of unprecedented global power to instruct all of us by dint alone of that power on how precisely *not* to live. And now the awful harvest of technological America's, all-powerful America's, irreversible disintegration from within.

Twenty-seven years ago, Doris Melliadis, an Arokwa woman in New York, said:

> Now they come to gather for the coming disaster and destruction of the white man *by his own hands,* with his own progressive, technological devices, that only the American Indian can avert. Now the time is near. And it is only the Indian who knows the cure. It is only the Indian who can stop this plague. And the unheard will be heard. And we will be seen and we will be remembered.

I don't believe this. Though the Indian had the metaphysics of it right all along about the timeless place of the human animal in the seamless space of nature, the Indian will neither be seen nor listened to now. The powerful, the heirs of Columbus, the makers, the measurers, the sybarites, the *things* people, the owners, the one-realm thinkers, the *matter* laureates, the price-knowers, the patriots—no, they will not listen because they cannot. They hear the world only on the frequency of *their* tribe, and no outsider has that frequency. They will not hear the Indian or the black or the brown or the poor or the prescient or the wise. They will only hear the sound of guns, their own guns, aimed at them from without,

aimed at them by them from within. But even then they will listen
to no voice but their own same voice. They were built a long time
ago to do only this. To kill themselves, to kill us all, not crudely,
but very efficiently, with science.

> Even if I did speak Irish I'd be an outsider here, wouldn't
> I? I may learn the password but the language of the
> tribe will always elude me, won't it? The private core
> will always be . . . hermetic, won't it?
>
> —Brian Friel
> *Translations*, 1981

Tribe upon tribe, strangers each to the next, lost in a killing
field, angry and armed all by one amongst them. Only the technology of the quantitative fool could have set the world on a course
of such utter madness. This indeed is the *progress* with which the
big have saddled the small, the *progress* with which the antagonists
hold hostage the antagonized. When nuclear devices go to school in
lunch boxes, as they inevitably will, is it not likely that it will happen first in America, the home of *progress*?

Will not the law of constant extinction, the so-called Red Queen
hypothesis, have been proven, sadly, once again in a fashion:

> The idea is that an evolutionary *advance* by one species
> represents a deterioration of the environment for all re-
> maining species.

Has not our vaunted *progress* threatened the future existence of
every living thing on earth?

Chapter Four

Theft

No civilization prior to the European had occasion to believe in the systematic material progress of the whole human race; no civilization placed such stress upon the quantity rather than the quality of life; no civilization drove itself so relentlessly to an ever-receding goal; no civilization was so passion-charged to replace what is with what could be; no civilization had striven as the West had done to direct the world according to its will; no civilization has known so few moments of peace and tranquillity.

—William Woodruff
Impact of Western Man

He bore the same name, Taino, by which his people were called. In his language, the word meant *noble* and *good*. He stepped outside his commodious round dwelling and drew the new morning into his lungs. In spite of his advanced age of thirty-six, he felt robust and optimistic. The dawn seldom failed to fill him with euphoria, and this dawn seemed no different from the thousands he had seen before. He had no way of knowing that within a matter of minutes, the lives of his people on the islands and those of their ethnic relations on the mainland, numbering in the millions, would change forever.

His island, Guanahani, northwest of modern St. Kitts and southernmost on a coral necklace, was relatively flat, with broad white-sand beaches bathed by a sea of luminescent green. From the vantage point of his house he could see the fields of knee-high mounds called *conucos*, which regularly produced bumper crops of manioc, sweet potato, and a variety of squashes and beans.

He was the hereditary leader, or *paseke*, of his village of twelve families. It was a position from which he functioned more as a conciliator and a spokesman than as an arbiter. The system had worked well for them since his people, arrayed across the island in villages not unlike his own, had arrived from the mainland fifteen hundred years before and to the island of Guanahani five hundred years later.

While he was a respected elder and steward, his was a station, owing to their cooperative way of life, for which he had not needed to fight his way through adversity and jealous opposition. Things were done as they had always been done, collectively, and not just with his fellow villagers, but within a physical environment to which they believed themselves spiritually and indissolubly joined. Thus, their farming methods were gentle to the living soils, their natural, round houses resistant to hurricanes, their *canoa*, or canoes, carved in one piece from the silk-cotton tree and crafted for trade with ethnic relations living in places as distant as the one later to be known as Florida.

Theft and violence were unknown to them. They had no word for war and no experience with intratribal or intertribal conflict. They weren't plagued by greed, inasmuch as one could no more *own* the land than the air they all breathed. They played sports. They danced. They made love. They practiced basketry and wood-working. They turned pots and made jewelry. Poverty, hunger, and serious disease were strangers to them.

Taino's wife and two adolescent sons joined him outside the door of their home, which was constructed of conical walls made of joined cane poles covered by a roof of interwoven vines. They were an attractive family, tall, brown-skinned, and in obvious good health. Because they lived in a warm climate, they dressed sensibly in the lightest possible accord with the modesty honored by custom. Taino had painted his body black to protect it from the sun's rays. His wife and sons had not done so. Unlike his wife, whose hair was jet-black and long, Taino's hair, the texture of a horse's tail, reached over his eyebrows in front and, in back, well down in a flat, narrow shaft toward his waist.

The day, Taino had reason to believe, would unfold as a village enterprise of work and discussion, like all other days. Just as the sun broke over a line of coconut trees to the east, Taino's family heard the loud call of a fellow villager coming from the direction of the sea a half mile to the south. When the family reached the line of coconut trees set back seventy-five yards from the surf, they saw nineteen villagers looking out silently toward three boats anchored, prows to the east, and floating taller in the water then any boats they had ever seen.

Taino's wife asked him what he thought. Taino said only that the boats must have come from a place very far away. The odd-looking, bulky boats had mysteriously materialized. The only sound heard from them was caused by the swells that slapped against the planked hulls. Eyes under the boats' gunwales watched the villagers through square, black sockets. The villagers had no idea how long the boats had been there. Perhaps they had come in the night. Though they were completely unarmed, having devised only the bow for small-game hunting, the villagers had no frame of reference for fear, and thus were merely curious, as one might reasonably expect after roughly a thousand years of placid uneventfulness.

While the three moored boats appeared larger than the villagers' *canoa*, the taller, three-masted craft carried fewer passengers than the low-slung canoe, which could carry up to one hundred and fifty.

After an hour of waiting, the villagers saw a man with colorless skin climb down from one of the two smaller boats and board a long, low boat. The long boat then moved on to accept a man with the same strange skin from the second small boat before collecting a larger party from the lead craft, which looked a little like a large wooden tub under sail.

The sun was behind the long boat when it washed aground and

discharged ten backlit silhouettes into the foamy surf. Wearing metal on their heads and around their torsos while trailing long, shiny implements attached to the waists, the strange men jangled as they lumbered forward.

The first man ashore was the captain general of the small fleet of boats, which included two caravels, the *Pinta,* and the *Nina,* and the flagship, a nao, named the *Santa Maria.* The captain general was about forty years old and taller than average, with white hair, deeply lined reddish skin, and a beard.

He was the Jewish wool-weaver's son from Genoa who would become known to the world as Christopher Columbus. Flanking the captain general were Martin Alonzon Pinzon, nearly fifty years old and the captain of the *Pinta,* and his younger brother, Vincente Yanez Pinzon, who was the captain of the *Nina.* Behind them trudged several bearers of royal standards and banners, two representatives of the royal court there to serve as witnesses, and a scribe named Escobedo, who was equipped with parchment and inkpot with which to record the captain general's oaths.

The captain general, having scarcely sloshed onto dry land and without looking at Taino, his wife, his sons, or the villagers whose people had lived on these Bahamian reef islands for nearly one thousand years, said to his party alone (for the villagers could not understand a word of his language) that "he before them all was taking possession of the said island for the King and Queen."

Columbus then buried a cross in the beach for the Roman Church, the significance of which the natural heirs to the place could not possibly have fathomed. Although Columbus had just arrived, and did not know even roughly where in the world he was, he began a practice that he would pursue with a frenzy over the next ninety-six days of naming all manner of things that had had names for centuries.

The island of Guanahani would thereafter be known as San Salvador.

It was October 12, 1492, the very first morning for Christopher Columbus, the "Great Discoverer," on the far side of what was then called by Europeans the "Ocean Sea." The ceremony that fateful morning, unintelligible to those who rightfully belonged there, foreshadowed the end of their pacific and holistic way of life. Indeed it was to portend the virtual extirpation of a whole people (and the humane cultures they had created) from the face of the very *Old World* that the Great Discoverer had not known existed before stumbling upon the island he thought to be near Marco Polo's Cipango in the Sea of China, some seven thousand miles to the west.

The villagers, practicing the customs of their cultures, lavished gifts upon Columbus. Columbus, evincing the prejudices of his culture, saw "naked people" of inferior status who could make "good servants" and help him to find all that he yearned to find: gold.

Columbus wrote in his journal:

> They bear no arms, nor are they acquainted with them for I showed them swords and they grasp them by the blade and cut themselves through ignorance. . . . Gold is most excellent . . . whoever has it may do what he wishes in this world . . . It was my wish to bypass no island without taking possession . . . in order not to lose time I intend to go and see if I can find the island of Cipango. . . . There may be many things that I don't know, for I do not wish to delay but to discover and go to many islands to find gold.

The ongoing era of the globalization of greed had begun. Columbus had set out from a Europe ravaged by poverty, violence, famine, and the Black Death to find a hospitable, forthcoming people whose wisdom for living he, in doltish condescension, could not rise to credit. In the *Santangel Letter,* Columbus had said of the Taino, "They even took pieces of the broken hoops of the wine casks and, like beasts, gave what they had." By common assessment, he was a bigoted, grasping, vainglorious, deceitful man whose overweening preoccupation with titles, honors, profits, and privileges threatened for him at his advanced age a last-chance mission that presaged five centuries of suffering for nonwhite peoples the world over. But for all his flaws, his values were emblematic of the Europe that dispatched him westward.

He had set out with ninety men on August 3 from the small port village of Palos, Castile, having never before captained anything larger than a rowboat. The day before his departure, the deadline had arrived that resulted in the expulsion of all Jews (120,000–150,000) from Spain. In their flight the Jews lost everything—homes, land, currency, gold, silver, jewels—their most personal possessions.

By the morning of his second day on Guanahani, Columbus had wearied of the gifts he called "trifles" (cotton and parrots) that the friendly Taino people had given him. He wrote in his journal that he "worked hard to know if there was any gold." Although he could not communicate with them, he took a number of villagers captive on board his ship to help him search nearby islands for gold.

> I believe that they would easily be made Christian because it seemed to me that they had no religion. Our Lord pleasing, I will carry six of them at my departure to Your Highness in order that they may learn to speak.

Columbus himself confessed that he had been involved as a slave trader in Africa. Never a man of noble intent, the machinery of his thinking ran only on the fuel of material ambition. Writes Sales: "No clothes, no arms, no possessions, no iron and now no religion—not even speech: hence they were fit to be servants, and captives. It may fairly be called the birth of American slavery."

Columbus put it bluntly in his journal: "They are fit to be ordered about and made to work, to sow and everything else that may be needed . . . nothing was lacking but to know the language and to give them orders because all that they are ordered to do they will do, they will do without opposition."

Columbus undertook a feverish hunt from island to island while naming as many as ten topographic features a day—ports, points, capes, mountains.

The second small island he visited he named Santa Maria, the third, Fernandina, for the king, and the fourth, Isabella, for the queen. He named a large island Juana and then another Española. It was on Española, or Hispañola, somewhere within the territory of modern Haiti, that Columbus established the new colony of La Navidad and, with the help of the ill-fated Tainos, built what Sales calls, "the first structure erected by Europe in the New World," a fortress. Of course the Great Discoverer did not discover the so-called *New World*. Nor was he Europe's first building contractor there. That distinction would likely go to the Viking Leif Eriksson, who established a colony with permanent structures in Newfoundland in the eleventh century. With respect to the matter of "discovery," Columbus never set foot on or, for that matter, even caught a glimpse of North or South America. Thinking the world a third smaller than it actually is, he died without knowing that the Americas existed at all, and that he was not in the Indies in the vicinity of Asia. If discovery means at the very least a sighting, then we should tell our schoolchildren that Bjarni Herjolfsson, en route from Greenland, probably saw North America first on a trip he made in 986. And then upon urging our cloistered pups to seat themselves, tell them that a host of learned scholars, including Ivan Van Sertima and Eric Williams, believe that "Africans had reached South America before Columbus sailed for the Indies in 1492."

Well, if all this is the case, why does the white world (and derivatively the rest of us) celebrate Columbus Day and Columbia everything else five hundred years later? Why would Columbus, met only with friendliness, first build a fortress?

Unlike the Africans and the Vikings, Columbus wasn't sailing around the Ocean Sea for edification's sake. He was sailing for the virtual salvation of a self-absorbed white world, Europe, which found itself in desperate straits, its lands and waters depleted after thousands of years of dedicated abuse—a Europe sick to distraction with gawk-eyed love for the *machine*.

Lewis Mumford writes: "Only Europe saw fit to adapt the whole mode of life to the pace and capacities of the machine." The white world, drunk with technophilia and gazing hypnotically at the sharply accurate swinging metal timepiece of its beloved *progress,* was seized with an addiction that craved to be fueled. There was little left in the lands of Europe with which to do so. Thus, Europe introduced itself to the people of Africa and Asia, to the Tainos, Arawaks, Caribs, and their kinspeople of the *New World,* as conscienceless takers. Thus, Columbus was Europe's steward, and for his trouble, he was empowered by Ferdinand and Isabella to take for himself 10 percent of all the riches his men could plunder. According to the Spanish scholar Ramon Iglesia, Columbus could be measured in a single word: "businessman." But say what you will of the greedy mariner from Genoa, his was a troth of purpose to which all Europe was pledged: the prince; the privileged; the pauper; the Pope. For he was the shining groundbreaker like none before him, the multifaceted pioneer whose imprint still reads clear upon modern world economic relations. His *business* trips opened a naive but viable world to European exploitation and devastation. Unlike his peers and predecessors, he kept a meticulous record of his *business transactions.* He could as well fairly be called the father of modern public relations, so effective was he in the art of self-promotion. Murder and plunder would be known for centuries to schoolchildren as heroic exploration. Slavery and colonialism would costume in their time as "civilizing missions" and Columbus' great, great, great, great grand offense, transnational corporate avarice, would find modern expression adorned in an array of diverting garments, *industrialization* for a season, *development* for another, *free trade* and its alias *globalization* for still another. He hailed from the home of *progress* where the *product* was king. (The Chinese may have invented the firearm but Europe on the wings of *business* gave it to the world.)

For all this (save possibly the Fijians, who have not to this moment fallen under the electron spell of television) the black and brown of the world have Europe to thank: for Columbus (the poster boy for all that has happened), for his linear successor (the CEO, the profit raker, the art taker, the Bible hawker, the snake-oil salesman, the ordnance senator and, yes, his lovely wife); for the death of our culture; for the yet to be acknowledged disappearance of our *self*; for changing out the old outmoded values of communalism and sharing for the more modern robotic values of competition and scorekeeping; for evangelizing us away from the religions we knew; for Billy Graham; for new diseases and old clothes; for showing *us*, the fruit of millennia, how to talk, how to dress, how to forget ourselves, how to forgive those who had us do so; for teaching everyone in the world, including yourselves, how to live by Europe's product and how to die by Europe's product.

Bang. Bang.

And, yes, for your seemingly contagious and boundless greed, against which I am constrained to accept that the spirit can make no contest.

> To be rooted is perhaps the most important and least recognized need of the human soul.
>
> —Simone Weil

And lastly the tortured black and brown of the earth have Queen Victoria, the Spanish conquistador, King Leopold, and all the other white-skinned heirs to Columbus to thank for the bloody turmoil that is Kashmir, the unsolvable dilemma that is the Middle East, the suffering that is Haiti, the political instability that is Africa, the lethal poverty that is Latin America, and the sickness of splintered identity that is black America.

It is hard now to imagine the world before Columbus, the progenitor of the downtrodden's wretched condition, a condition *celebrated* amongst the privileged by facility of their relentless homage to themselves via a man who introduced into much of global society a sadist's serving of enduring pain. Is it too late to fantasize a world in which Europe had never ventured out its front door?

Before the captain general from clockwork Europe dropped anchor on that fateful October 12, 1492, the indigenous people of the Americas had known only of *living* and nothing of *winning*, not even the word for such. By now, five hundred years thence, *they* have long since killed all the innocents and turned the rest into warring, competing liars, even those of us who believe themselves possessed of the victim's virtue. *They* have justified all crimes now to hide theirs in the mosaic of the mess they inspired with greed and arrogance. Now no truth remains except that which survives as a disembodied ideal floating off, cowering from contamination at the hands of the clever liars we have all learned to be. God let me camp unnoticed at the end with the last of the naive before they too are found to have something of value: For theirs is the last refuge of decency in human relations. Theirs is the world of *sharers* giving way to the *winners*, whose nature it must be to take, always and everything.

Chapter Five

Extermination

Researchers Woodrow Borah and Sherburne Cook of the University of California at Berkeley have estimated the population of Tainos living on Española when Columbus arrived at eight million people. Within twenty years there were less than twenty-eight thousand. By 1542, fifty years after Columbus set foot on Guanahani Island, two hundred Tainos were alive on the colonized island of Española. As far as we know, they were all that remained, throughout the archipelago, of the Taino people, who, within two decades, would be extinct. Most of them died from diseases that the Spaniards brought from Europe to the Americas. The rest were slaughtered by the Great Discoverer, his brothers, Diego and Bartolome, Spanish colonists, and soldiers armed with crossbows, pikes, lances, arquebuses, and killer dogs.

On November 13, 1493, in his second voyage, Columbus sailed past a small, cone-shaped island with a grassy peak wrapped in a fluffy white cloud. Moments later he reached the peninsula of an elongated and mountainous gourd-shaped island that its Carib Indian inhabitants called Liamuiga, or "fertile land." Pressing on a westward course along the main mass of the island, the Great Discoverer veered sharply to port to avoid foundering upon a string of huge, black, volcanic, Carib-inscribed boulders that warned of the shallows. Reposing like funerary monuments to a dispossessed and murdered freeholder, these boulders, which memorialize the beginning of the end of Carib Indian existence in the world, still rest in the sighing sea below my family's home.

Swinging his arm like a wand, Columbus called out the island's new name, St. Jorge, to his scribe. The Great Discoverer did not stop there, just as he had not stopped at the cone-shaped island he had only moments before dubbed San Martin. Thus the Carib Indians who lived on the two islands would not know for sometime that they no longer lived where they thought they had lived for hundreds of years. As if to mock the Caribs further, Spanish sailors not long after renamed the islands still again, and by the early sixteenth century they were known on Spanish maps as San Cristobal and Nieves or St. Christopher (Kitts) and Nevis.

Having no earthly recourse against the marauding European settlers who would invade their lands over the ensuing centuries, the Caribs appealed to their wrathful god, Hunrakan, to unleash against the pallid metal-clad interlopers the terrifying storms that bore his name.

Owing to spotty recordkeeping, we know little of Hunrakan's performance before the year 1623. But after the fall of that year, the settlers began to chronicle the viler fortunes of nature rather more meticulously:

> On 29 September 1623, a hurricane destroyed the first tobacco crop planted in St. Kitts by the English settlers who had arrived only in January of that year, and caused great hardship.
>
> Three hurricanes struck in 1642. During the second one, a very powerful storm blew for twenty-four hours. Merchant ships loaded with tobacco from both St. Kitts and Nevis were blown ashore between Basseterre and Old Road in St. Kitts. They broke up and the tobacco poisoned the water, killing thousands of fish. These vessels were almost all of a convoy of 23 ships under the control of the famous Dutch Admiral Michiel de Ruyter, riding off Basseterre ready to sail to Europe. All but one vessel, including de Ruyter's flagship, were driven ashore and wrecked. "Along the coast of Basseterre, one did

see nothing but the dead bodies the tempest had thrown on the sand. . . ." The one vessel which escaped destruction was commanded by a Captain Volery, who cut his anchor cables and ran helpless before the storm for a distance of six hundred miles to the south of St. Kitts.

—Vincent K. Hubbard
A History of St. Kitts: The Sweet Trade

Storms and primitive weapons, however, proved woefully insufficient to the challenge of Carib survival. In the years leading up to 1626, French and English settlers poured into St. Kitts. They claimed. They cleared. They farmed. They fenced. They killed to defend. Tensions between Caribs and Europeans swelled to a menace point.

Recognizing that the Europeans were on the verge of taking over the island, the Carib chief Tegremond in 1626 decided upon the only course of action that remained open to him: eliminate the Europeans completely while there was still a chance to do so. But his plan to surprise the Europeans with a region-wide united front of armed Caribs was leaked by an Indian woman named Barbe to the French and English settlers, who paused long enough in their mutual hatred of each other to join in a well-laid, premeditated massacre of the Caribs.

In the pitch of night, Chief Tegremond was run through with the rapiers of English soldiers while sleeping in the royal hammock (a Carib invention). All one hundred and twenty Indians found in the village were immediately put to the sword.

On the following day, French and English soldiers drove four thousand Caribs into a deep ravine near the coast not far west of where I live. Over two thousand Caribs were murdered there, including those who tried to surrender. The rest fled into the lush mountains. For two days the stream at the ravine's bottom ran red and viscous with the blood of the slaughtered Caribs. The ravine soon came to be called Bloody Point, and the stream Bloody River, and they remain so-named to this very day.

Chapter Six

Race

Is it race, because of its conspicuous characteristics, that confuses us? Could it be that race is merely incidental to some more compelling but less palpable determinism? How separate and several are the causal tributaries that variegate the great streams of human culture, setting one off irritably against the next with predictably disastrous results? I have never wanted to be master of the universe. I have never wanted to visit the moon. Why would I? Why would anyone? Isn't it perfectly obvious that every such incremental know-how draws us all closer to the end of *everything*? Isn't the simple knowledge of *that* more important than the advanced quantum physics of mass self-destruction? Is it some inexplicable spiritual emptiness that sends the progeny of one culture, and not the next, questing—ever unremittingly, blindly, suicidally questing? Looking out, never in, where the small decencies wither in bad light unpraised? Isn't the most essential achievement the achievement of learning how to *be*?

Do I reveal here the bias of my cultural compass as starkly as Frances Anne Kemble, the great lady of the English Industrial Age stage reveals hers?

How invariably have the inhabitants of Southern countries, whose teeming soil produced, unurged, the means of life, been cursed with indolence, with recklessness, with the sleepy, slothfulness which, while basking in the sunshine, and gathering the earth's spontaneous fruits, satisfied itself with this animal existence, forgetting all the nobler purposes of life in the mere ease of living? Therefore, too, southern lands have always been the prey of northern conquerors; and the bleak regions of Upper Europe and Asia have poured fourth from time to time the hungry hordes, whose iron sinews swept the nerveless children of the gardens of the earth from the face of their idle paradises: and, but for this stream of keener life and nobler energy, it would be difficult to imagine a more complete race of lotus-eaters than would now cumber the fairest regions of the earth.

Do souls freeze in the cold?

In any case, the conqueror gets to decide who has won. And not just the battle, but the story of the battle and the social values spawned from it as well. I think that I may hate them for this alone. They had me root for Jim Bowie and Davy Crockett at the Alamo. I should have rooted for Santa Anna. I should have screamed for Santa Anna. But I did not. Well, why in the hell didn't I?

After all, he was defending his country, and Texas was a part of Mexico. Mexico prohibited slavery in all its provinces, including its province of Coahuila and Texas. The American "heroes" of the Alamo wanted to wrench Texas from Mexico, in part to institute slavery in Texas a day later. This wasn't covered in the John Wayne movie. They canted the tale so as to have me root against Santa Anna, and I remain embarrassed by my stupid sympathies.

They separated me out and left my condition unexplained. They made a child grateful for unwilling mercies. Old Dr. Baxter, a staunch segregationist, was an astringent Southern white man in a white suit with white hair who saw his "colored" patients on Thursdays—colored health days in Richmond, Virginia—and vaccinated us as we sat in a worn, white, cane-back chair beneath the same likeness of Confederate General Robert E. Lee, that appears today, fifty-five years later, on a St. Kitts postage stamp. (Dr. Baxter wouldn't have understood this. Certainly Lee wouldn't have. But

Lee was a famous American and that's about all anyone here knows about him.)

To each tender Thursday child who sat in the white, cane-back chair beneath the likeness of the slave-owner's idol, old Dr. Baxter would say in his tribal drawl of day-long vowels: "Now I'm gonna give you some good old white medicine in your arm so as you won't catch smallpox. You know what that is, don't ya?"

And Thursday's child, spared thus of agony and disfigurement, would nod mutely in self-destructive appreciation.

In the early 1700s, as America was being ravaged by smallpox, Onesimus, an African slave who belonged to Cotton Mather, told of a technique, long practiced in Africa, to prevent smallpox by introducing the "pus from the ripe pustules" of a smallpox patient into a small incision on the arm of an uninfected patient. The technique resulted usually in a mild case of smallpox but prevented the full-blown disease. Dr. Zabdiel Boylston (a great-uncle of John Adams), who had gotten the idea from Cotton Mather, tried the technique in America—first in Boston—with great success.

The winners control the story of everything, but hardly conspiratorially. I would doubt seriously that Old Dr. Baxter had ever heard of Onesimus, who, himself owing to his very bondage, was in no position, had he any mind to, to speak either to Cotton Mather or to Dr. Boylston about patents or any other eighteenth-century notion of intellectual-property-rights protection. And Onesimus is not likely to have had the mind to, in any case, even were he free to act on the thought. Such notions of material selfishness would have been alien to the African culture that had shaped his way of engaging the world. (This perhaps explains why Louis Armstrong fell prey to unscrupulous forces and lost the rights to virtually all of his brilliant early work.)

This cultural disinclination of blacks to measure the value of every quantifiable good and service with a price appears to be a great deal more alive in the Caribbean than in the United States, where we've been beaten into a whitish powder of reflex cynicism.

I have the black man's disease: high blood pressure. An off-duty nurse, who works at the J. N. France Hospital, comes across town to our house to check my pressure.

So she does this. Twice to be sure. I'm reading one twenty over eighty. My medication is working. She tells me this and shares that she has "pressure" as well. She describes the measures she has taken (diet, stress reduction, and so forth) to wean herself from the medication.

She appears ready to leave when I ask, "How much will that be?" Instantly, "Oh, nothing."

A little surprised even. That, or maybe the question was gauche. They see Americans, even black Americans, I suspect, as, well—yes, gauche. Americans see them and their "generosity," they see opportunity. Lower still, perhaps, for Americans are suspicious of selfless generosity.

Onesimus lives. Everyone knows here that white periwinkle is good for "pressure," that stinging nettle will "clean" the bladder, and that nothing manages "sugar" like yellow elder. No one here, however, would think to tabletize, bottle, price, and market what nature provides fecundly as the foundation of the Western pharmaceutical industry.

Paul Prince is our gardener. He lives with his wife and three-year-old son in a neat, modest house built and sold by the government for a modest sum. His family fills out the small house nicely. A sister he has never met is sending her daughter, whom also he has never met, to live with him and his family in their small home while she attends college. He describes the plan to us with an air of celebration. They don't make his model of person anymore in America. It was discontinued following the urban death of the extended family.

This is a very different place, which, unbeknownst to its decision-makers, is mixed-blessedly unready for a commercial marriage to Frances Anne Kemble's "northern conquerors." These people actually *trust* people. Until recently, they've had little reason not to. In the Value Mart Grocery Store a clerk accepted a personal check, as always, without proof of identification, at the same time a television monitor at the TDC home products store beams a CNN account of young American filmmakers paying homeless Americans to beat each other senseless on camera. The story's tincture of the absurd is deepened by a commercial that follows it about a potty song training video for diaper-clad toddlers:

When you feel that feeling way down below
Hey, Hey, Hey. I gotta go

The customers in TDC watch this, incredulous.

At the service station, an attendant pumps gas for Hazel (no one pumps their own gas here). She forgot her money. Not to worry. Drop it by when you can. I phone Mitchell Gumbs at TDC to tell him that I need fifteen lengths of one-inch PVC pipe to irrigate a line of yellow bells.

"Can you send it over today?"

"I can do it within the hour." I have no credit account with TDC but they know me and honor is everything here. At Delisle Walwyn's wine store, they do not know me. I request a case of Buena Vista Sauvignon Blanc and present my American Express card on a Saturday afternoon just before closing.

The clerk says: "The manager has already left with the charge card machine." I say: "What can I do?" The clerk says: "Take the wine and come in sometime next week," which I do the first thing Monday morning. This *trust* business, something new in my adult commercial experience, I feel an urgency to handle like filigreed crystal.

The steel pan (you may know the instrument as the steel drum) is the only wholly new musical instrument developed in the twentieth century. A poor black factory worker in Trinidad cut up an oil drum and turned it into something that sounds like a marimba, not struck, but sung sweetly by an exotic coloratura. A voice-box marimba from which the sounds seem to undulate on trade winds wafting through coconut fronds.

Calypsonians and reggae artists give about as much consideration to stealing away the "rights" to the steel pan as they give to taking stock options on air. Not the Mighty Sparrow. Not David Rudder. Not the legendary Bob Marley. The thought of "owning" the rights to the pan simply would not occur to a Caribbean. It did however occur quite naturally to the affable global entrepreneur, Columbus America. Last year, Columbus America applied for a patent on the steel pan, the Caribbean's signature instrument. This provoked a considerable measure of consternation. In the conflux of regional emotions that roiled to a boil, surprise (the one emotion that history could not be expected to forgive) was not represented.

There is no such person as Columbus America. He does *live* however somewhat displacingly in the cramped space of our uncertainty about ourselves. He has a personality. He has a spiel and a damn good one. He has heft and chutzpah. And a long string of victories against the "southern lands" inhabitants he has beguiled silkily of their trust. The face is as featureless as a police artist's composite drawing. Little matters but that it is white. It speaks and says that it has come to *help* us. We believe it even when history warns. The white skin has that sort of addling magic. The face need not even speak. The white skin speaks for it. It stays us with a little subcutaneous thrill that those of us who think about such things loathe but somehow cannot quite free ourselves of.

This morning I listened to a public affairs discussion aired by the new radio station here, WINN-FM. Panelists were fielding questions from listeners about the mammoth new Marriott hotel that is months away from opening its doors, but from whose shuttered royal suite the prime minister nevertheless made his Christmas address to the nation three weeks ago. The Kittitians calling in to the public affairs discussion seemed measurably less impressed by Columbus America than were the panelist-policymakers who had occasion to deal with Columbus America "up close," so to speak.

One of the panelists said that "if we want foreign investment we have to make concessions." As I had tuned in while the discussion was already in progress, I had not heard the listener's comments that provoked the panelist's defense of the Marriott hotel chain. Just guessing, it may have been one of a host of things, large and small. If it was anything like what I had been hearing around the island, there would have been complaints about common water sources being used to service the huge hotel and its golf course, complaints about restrictions on locals' access to beaches, local cab drivers losing out to foreign-owned systems of transporting tourists, local builders being passed over, local haulers being shoved aside . . . well, it could go on and on.

". . . Marriott is good for my country," says the panelist.

The island's farmland drapes the lower, less severe slopes that fall just below an expanse of gorgeously green glady terrain, which then rises steeply to join the bands of coconut and date trees that wrap around and cover the sharply sculptured upper ridges of Mount Liamuiga. The farmer looks up from his labors and braces against his mountain to see from one vantage point the peaks of Nevis and Montserrat rising sharply from the glistening blue-green seafloor, and from another, the day-end reddening silhouettes of Saba and St. Eustatius against the setting sun. Perhaps it is the sheer beauty of his space that provides the farmer edge enough to win a decent living from a small, well-used parcel of land. Perhaps it is the filter press wrung from stalks of harvested cane and used by the farmer to reinvigorate weary soils. We should know something here soon enough. This year it was very difficult for local farmers to secure a filter press for their crops. The lot of it went to Marriott for use on its grounds and golf course.

"The Marriott has donated sheets and other items to our new J. N. France Hospital . . . ," and moments later, ". . . has offered to build a police station at Frigate Bay, including a holding pen."

This last reference to a Marriott offer to build a police station and holding pen near the new hotel produced a storm of concern from callers and panelists alike. The germ of that concern was this: If Marriott wishes to make a contribution to the government, fine. But the government should not accept a contribution that can only be used to build a police station near the Marriott.

A holy ranter of a call comes in—I can't remember whether it came before or after the talk of Marriott having its own police station and holding pen. (Technically and in all fairness, this wouldn't, of course, be Marriott's own police station. *Note: I must never forget, even though it may seem excessive, to add the phrase "holding pen" or you'll miss much of the temperature of the calls.* The facility would be the government's, but built on Marriott's doorstep to reassure its guests.)

In any case, the call that came in had to do with the Marriott people closing roads that had provided unrestricted beach access. The caller pointed out that the Building Board had not approved this.

Another caller who may well host the reincarnated soul of the first Taino to welcome to the "New World" the "Great Discoverer" said that foreign investors come here to "help" our island.

On another occasion in a press conference, a Marriott representative, an American who seemed tickled pink to *help* the island, encouraged every Kittitian within earshot of his broadcasted voice to greet every tourist with a "big bright shiny smile" and sallied on to diagram the smile's mechanics: "It's got to have a laserlike focus." Oh boy. This was new. This everybody everywhere smile business. Wide, wide, wide. Now, hold and lock. This hadn't been tried in Paris or anywhere else. Laserlike, huh? The otherwise busy citizenry would need to practice, wouldn't they? How to effect this laserlike "smile" without looking demonic and scaring the tourists back into the sea?

Fat chance. As far as I can see, the citizens of this very small country are as centered as any I've encountered anywhere. They recognize well enough that theirs is a tiny economy that must tie itself to the outside world. They follow the price of sugar. They see Fidel Castro, the oldest surviving doyen of economic self-sufficiency, cutting ribbons on glossy, new joint-ventured tourist traps on big island Cuba. They know the country has to bring in outside income. These are courteous, solicitous people, but they're not going to line the pier and laser-grin at docking cruise ships.

In his book, *The European Tribe,* St. Kitts's most celebrated writer, Caryl Phillips, warns from abroad of the dangers of tourism as he writes about the cost of it to the communities of southern Spain:

> All along the Costa del Sol what were once pretty little villages have now, like Estapona, been abused by commercial demands. I saw old Andalucians looking bewildered as men and women in skimpy beach wear cavorted past. Old styles and new clashed in the streets and in bars. The older Spanish women turned their heads away in shame and disgust as the semi-naked tourists lolled around what used to be peaceful and closed communities.

I saw this look on the face of a Kittitian woman as a rented motor scooter driven by an American girl in halter top and high-riding shorts sped along Cayon Street.

Chapter Seven

Money

Jobs and money are as important here as they are in any country. You must have them to live. All the same, it would appear that the people of St. Kitts have a radically different idea than Americans about the role of money in the social equation of their society. Dignity would seem here to be of greater importance than money.

Quite frequently the price for a service is not even discussed until after the service is rendered. I would say: "How much will it cost to do this?" And the service renderer will say, "Let me do the work first and then we'll see what's fair."

This made me uneasy at first, but it works well enough when the parties to these routine daily commercial understandings know and comply with the local, unspoken precepts of ethical expectation. They trust because trust is a natural social state, and because trust is practicable in a small place where most know and live by the rules.

But of course, none of the foregoing applies when big price tag services are contracted for. The numbers in those cases are discussed and agreed to in advance. This would be the case, as well, for ongoing employer-employee wage relationships.

Having said this, the central point stands. You pay a fair price here for goods and services. But what you pay and when and how you arrive at that *what* is pleasantly unlike anything I've ever known. Money is not the only thing and it is never the first thing.

Singer Whitney Houston came here once on a private jet with her husband, Bobby Brown, who, upon emerging from customs, whipped out a roll of one-hundred-dollar bills and began passing them out to Kittitians outside the terminal. Many, if not most, of them gave the money back. Americans would find this odd, as I'm sure Mr. Brown did. He no doubt meant well, but he couldn't have had ample opportunity to understand very much about how the culture works here.

Americans wrap themselves so tightly in the coarse cloth of their own *everything* that they can see little else beyond the shores of their own unmarked, unseen cultural insularity. This condition stewed in a pot laced with a pepper of deeply socialized racial assumptions can cause Americans (virtually all of whom are white here) to behave quite awfully.

A young Kittitian man that I know was asked by an American innkeeper here to clear unsightly weeds and thicket from a perimeter of the family's sprawling and exquisitely landscaped hotel property. The young man, twenty-two, had not finished high school and performed jobs of this sort to eke out a living.

The innkeeper asked: "How much do you want for the job?"

Wary of Americans from experience, the young man, who is very poor but impressively well-known to himself, said to the innkeeper: "Two hundred dollars." The innkeeper quickly agreed to the price, and the next morning, the young man, armed with machete, pick, and hoe, began hacking away in the hot tropical sun at the root systems of the prickly *cacia,* bastard vines, and guinea grass that had infiltrated and spoiled the showy red bougainvillea bracts that covered the sloping perimeter's long fence. In two days the work was completed. The young man applied to the innkeeper for his wages. The innkeeper forestalled his request by inviting him to work an additional three days performing similar tasks on another flank of the vast property. The price for the additional work was not discussed. The young man reasonably assumed that because he was doing more than twice the work that he had initially agreed to do, he would receive at the end of the week not two hundred dollars but five hundred dollars. On Friday, with the work finished, he applied for the second time to the innkeeper for his wages. He was told to pick them up at the office.

In the office, the young man was given an envelope that contained twenty-seven dollars. He said to the office clerk: "There must be some mistake."

She said: "No, I have it right here, twenty-seven dollars is what I have been authorized to pay you."

The young man turned to leave. The clerk said to the young man's back, "Don't forget your money."

The young man is spare of frame. The *white*s of his small eyes are not discernibly whiter than the muddy dun color of his irises. His short working life has already taken the measure of him. He is speckled with fragments of plant matter and tired. He has worked a full week for Friday, the day, as in America, when the nameless people who make all societies function get their packets.

The impecunious and grave young man turned and faced the clerk: "Tell her to keep the twenty-seven dollars." He walked out and was never paid a cent for his week's work by the Americans who own and operate the upscale retreat for the very well-heeled.

My guess is that most American day laborers would have taken the twenty-seven dollars. Either that or done grievous bodily injury to the dear lady. Though such reckonings are impressionistic, I strongly believe it greatly less likely that the matriarch would have tried such a mean-hearted stunt in the United States. But that is lateral to my central point. A young man whose mother and father are dead, and who has no means of support beyond the uneven scratchings of day labor, left money, the eastern Caribbean equivalent of twenty-seven U.S. dollars, on the table. He had his dignity.

On an adjoining patch of land, an old Kittitian man lived alone in a small cottage with his dog. The dog's barking was said to have disturbed the peace of the American family's resort guests. After being authorized by his boss, a staff member at the resort killed the old man's dog with Futan, a granular poison that caused the dog's intestines to explode.

Vydate L is an insecticide that destroys a variety of plant enemies. When it comes into contact with the skin, it also results in serious neurologic damage to humans. The granular form is no
longer allowed for use in the United States and the liquid form is
acutely poisonous. The United States does, however, export it for
use in St. Kitts and Nevis, where agricultural workers know little of
its potential hazards.

The dangerous insecticide may or may not be used by black
workers on the rolling lawns of a resort in Nevis. When I asked
someone who had once been a gardener there, I was told, "I don't
know whether we were using Vydate L or not. The managers removed all the names and warning labels from the packaging of the
chemicals that we used."

On one occasion after a morning session of spraying, the same
gardener developed a painful itch that covered the entire surface of
his body. When he asked his American supervisor for permission to
shower and change his clothes, he was told to wait until he reached
home after work.

These are two of the most beautiful parcels of earth on the
surface of the globe. The people on the whole seem neither ostentatiously aware of this, nor of their increasingly uncommon, unprepossessing civility. Compared to America, these are very safe places
to live, but not so safe as they once were. Contact with the colossus
of the north, contact that a tiny nation like this must cultivate and
husband to survive, comes at a high price to the health of its society. Like the rich American neighbor and the old man's dog, *contact* with America has slowly begun to poison the rich wellspring of
Caribbean life and culture.

Incipient gangs imitate the American archetype. Criminals, born
here, but socialized in America, are exported back here by the United
States to a country ill-prepared to cope with them. Drugs and drug
money, skulking north from South America, stain every island culture they touch en route to the bottomless markets of America. "Pray
for the Police," poignantly reads the bumper sticker here. Ever so
slowly, their job gets harder by the day.

Press Release
From the Nevis Christian Council

The Nevis Christian Council wishes to inform member churches and the general public of a number of social concerns affecting the community, and which the council has taken steps to address at the highest level.

Following discussions, both at Denominational and Council levels, a special committee from the Nevis Christian Council was appointed to bring these concerns to the attention of the Nevis Administration, and for clarification on the same.

The Special Committee, which was led by the Chairman of the Nevis Christian Council, Rev. Canon Dr. Alson B.H. Percival met with the honorable Premier on November 28, 2002, and discussed the following topics:

1) Prostitution
2) The Electricity Rates
3) The Telephone Rates

Prostitution: On the issue of Prostitution, the Honorable Premier confirmed that his Administration was aware that there is a growing problem with prostitutes, and the establishment of "Houses of ill Repute" at five different locations on Nevis, which are serviced mainly by the women who are foreign nationals and who come to our country, pretending to be tourists; some action has already been taken via the Immigration Authorities, and the Immigration Authorities have been advised to keep a close watch in this area.

The Council's Chairman informed the Honorable Premier that when the matter was first brought to the Council's attention, a letter was sent to the Commissioner of Police on April 29th, 2001, informing him of the situation and requesting assistance in dealing with the matter. In his reply the Commissioner stated that the police were not aware of the situation but they would investigate. No word has been received since on that matter. Yet however, public mention has been made concerning the gravity of the situation on the popular radio programme, *Doc Talk,* by the island's Medical Officer of Health. The drug problem was discussed, particularly among teenagers of school age. The Honorable Premier said his Administration was saddened by it, based on the number of incidents reported, and every effort is being made to bring it under control.

Except by sporadic informal avocation, prostitution did not exist here before the arrival in large numbers of northern tourists. Now, prostitutes from the north have arrived to service them, hunkering down in five *houses* on tiny Nevis.

Chapter Eight

Courtesy

The low, early-morning sun angled its rays through a light, fragrant rain shower and painted a rainbow, with one foot resting in the sparkling sea and the other diffusing iridescent colors against a lush foothill below the summit of Mount Liamuiga. Directly beneath the high point of the rainbow's arch stretched the Main Island Road, which encircled the kidney-shaped trunk of St. Kitts. To the east, at Frigate Bay, it junctioned with the Kennedy Simmonds Road, which took drivers, hikers, and bikers along a six-mile mountainous peninsula that at its terminus pointed directly toward Nevis, two miles away across the volatile channel that joined the Atlantic Ocean to the Caribbean Sea.

The rain borne along on the morning wind vectored aslant and gently, like the orange rays of the new sun. It was eight o'clock and the new grocery store situated just below Mattingly Heights on the mountainside of the Main Island Road, was just unlocking its double glass doors. "Best Buy," open only months and still paint-fresh, bore no corporate kinship to its American namesake. It was said to be owned by Seventh-Day Adventists, either because it, in fact, *was,* or because it was open every day but Saturday. Whichever was the case, the small store was immaculately clean and well-stocked, its double insulated glass-fronted coolers filled with beverages, dairy products, and a melange of frozen goodies that lined a length of the store from floor to ceiling. Of the three checkout registers, only one was clerked, owing to the time of day. The young woman looked to be in her late twenties. She was dark-skinned with a strong, open face. Her hair was woven into intricate corn-rows that dressed out into robust braids. African in its inspiration, it was a variant of a hairstyle seen frequently here.

The store, like most commercial establishments and all government buildings, was air-conditioned and, thus, among the hermetically sealed buildings on an island whose citizens were generally cooled nicely enough by trade winds that never seemed to pause.

The clerk heard the voice of a dog whose hawking bark was muted by the closed windows of a nearby car. She turned on a wooden, three-legged stool to see the door being opened by a white man, whose small son preceded him into the store. When I was a small boy in grammar class, I developed the diversion of grouping people by the cut and arrangement of their facial features. Some faces were constructed of eyes, mouths, noses, chins, cheeks, and skulls that were vowels. A smaller number of faces bore only the shapes, planes, and angles of consonants. The vast majority of faces, however, fell sway to nature's vast and comical disposition to mix and match. Vowels were roundish shapes, while consonants were straight lines that cornered. Vowels were warm. Consonants were cold.

The man, tall with straight brown hair, wore a face of round friendly vowels. His eyes were blue and earnest.

The clerk said, "Good morning."

The man bent to say something to his son as if he had not heard her. He rose and looked straight in front of him down aisle two, where canned goods, batter mixes, jarred spreads, and cookies were stacked on shelves that rose to within four feet of the low ceiling. Her face now an expressionless mask, the clerk looked at his profile and said nothing. Beginning his motion and discovering what he was looking for before saying anything, the man reached across the checkout surface down into the knee-well of the clerk's space and deposited a brown paper bag into a small open trash basket.

Without looking at the clerk, the man said "trash." That was all. It was not a question. He then picked up an express-line basket and walked with his son down aisle two. Before completing his selection from aisle two, the clerk said sotto voce to a fellow worker standing nearby, "What is that smell?" Again the man gave every appearance of not hearing her and continued to read from the label of a large can of Del Monte sliced peaches.

The clerk then directed her question to the man, "What did you put in my trash can?" The man did not answer immediately, or, in any case, had not answered before another female clerk, who had been applying price stickers to the beverages on aisle four, arrived and removed the brown paper bag from the trash can behind the first clerk's checkout counter.

"You put dog mess in her trash can!" The voice was controlled but angry. The white man, who had begun to walk farther down aisle two, then said evenly in an American accent and over his shoulder, "I thought it was all right." He then gave a slight, bitten-off smile of dismissal.

I told this story recently to a group of students and faculty at Reed College in Portland, Oregon. The story served my larger conviction that America's most important enemy, at least the first in line in the causal chain of such, is America itself, this being the result of an ever-present cocksureness that our runted ruinous social values are like everything else about America, the *very, very best* in the history of civilization. There were three blacks around the table, an English professor and two students. There were roughly twenty whites, including the school's president, Colin Driver, with whom I long ago attended law school, five professors, and fourteen or so students. Just two nights before, the president of the State University of New York at Brockport had told me that "in academic circles, Reed College is seen to be the Ivy League of the Northwest."

Well, the assembled group acquitted itself quite admirably indeed. They were a smart bunch, self-examining and delightfully unafraid of thinking critically—well, that is, save one whose face was literally chiseled in consonants, giving me an early-warning heads-up.

I recall saying that St. Kitts's society compared well with the general health of America's.

Chuckling his words in a pompous romp, and proving, altogether inadvertently, every point I had tried to make, professor something-or-other asked with mock incredulity: "But you're talking about an island. What could that have to do with Americans?" I suspected that he was thinking not *island* but *black island people*, but I shouldn't always assume the worst in people.

I should have been silent for a while but I have never mastered the competitive value of silence, damn it. I should have looked at the faces of the others who were hearing this from Professor Consonants because they had gotten it, gotten it quite well. The professor had tripped and fallen quite gracelessly on his own self-sharpening sword of hubris. And more, much more, I suspect, but I won't say it.

This is what I did say, repeating myself: "All indications are that their island society is healthier than our *great* society. We can learn a great deal from them."

I don't recall that he said anything by way of response to this. It must have sounded to him so nutty as to not warrant a response. Then, the non sequitur that for him wasn't a non sequitur at all. He said, "St. Kitts is a tourist economy." I lived there. He'd never been there, but he *knew* more about it than I did.

The only thing most Americans see of the Caribbean are television commercials of beaches with themselves splayed supine on them. Add a taste of the lilted accent and a dash of reggae so that they can know they'd be going somewhere different, somewhere warm, and that's about all that Americans know about the entire region. In America when I say "St. Kitts," well-educated Americans say, "Is that a country?" Moderately well-educated Americans say, "Is that a beach?" All the rest, which represent the overwhelming majority, say, "What is that?" Professor Consonants was very well-educated, and thus wasn't in the habit of asking anything because he was in the habit of *knowing* everything, or, if that's a little strong, at least knowing everything about some tropical island that nobody who was anybody had ever heard of.

I said, "St. Kitts is not a tourist economy," while thinking *it is trying its damnedest to be one,* and at the same time *what other options do the managers of its small economy have?* Professor Consonants smiles a mildly weary this-isn't-worth-my-time smile and the exchange between us dies. He is to be forgiven. He is what he has no choice but to be, an American. When he thinks of St. Lucia, he simply cannot visualize Nobel Laureate Derek Walcott or Nobel Laureate Arthur Lewis, but only, at the very top of his cognitive powers, a Grand Piton–framed stretch of sand. He simply has not been prepared to imagine for "island people" the serious enterprise of democratic governance, education, economic self-management, and the higher arts of artistic expression. He is not just an American, but a white American, and thus more likely than his black countrypersons to see the people, like the flora, of the Caribbean as little more than exotic, backstage props to the theater of his winter vacation.

Meanwhile, another member of the American family (which owns and operates the sprawling resort, orders the execution of a neighbor's dog, and pays a day laborer nothing for a week's work) has discovered the letter K carved in an old wooden chair sitting in the hotel's laundry room. It is an old and rickety chair, and has been placed in the laundry room for workers to sit on.

The proprietor, no longer a young man, is nonetheless garrulous and vital. He confronts the "suspect," a black worker who is only seventeen but short and slight. The patriarch says with the boom of a blunderbuss, "Kenneth, did you carve this K in the chair?" Kenneth says, "Yes."

The proprietor strikes Kenneth in the chest with both hands and pushes him backward. The proprietor follows this with a looping roundhouse right that misses its mark because Kenneth, regaining his balance, has moved deftly out of range. For reasons that are not known, Kenneth does not retaliate with the hammer he has in his hand, but leaves the employ of the American family that very day.

Why didn't Kenneth pop the fellow a good one in the chops? His forbearance explains much about the incompatibility between the two cultures, an incompatibility that heavily favors white Americans who come here to make money.

There are several elements involved here. First, there is the disadvantage of honor and honesty that Caribbeans bring to the negotiating table. Americans and Europeans believe that in business dealings, nothing is a matter of honor. The ghosts of Columbus and the Taino haunt still.

I came across a passage recently in the novel *Half a Life* by V. S. Naipaul that delimits a degree of the great cultural space that separates Kittitians and Americans, even though Naipaul was not writing about the Caribbean but about a meeting in London between an English book agent, Richard, and a talented writer, Willie, who was an Indian from India. Naipaul, a native of Trinidad, describes the dilemma of a culture's beleaguered honor-bound people painfully well, with Richard beginning the exchange

> "This is the contract for your book."
> Willie took up his pen.
> Richard said, "Aren't you going to read it?"
> Willie was confused. He wanted to look at the contract, but he didn't feel he could tell Richard that. To want to read through the contract in Richard's presence would be to question Richard's honour, and that would be such a discourtesy that Willie couldn't do it.

Indeed, officials here study and discuss the contracts meticulously. But I suspect they have neither lawyers, economic cushion, nor greed enough to negotiate evenly with their American counterparts.

It cannot be denied that the government did not or could not negotiate out to the nth degree with the management of the yet-to-open Marriott the small, dull contract language that would protect the local small-business people: the cab drivers, the bus drivers, the truck drivers, the heavy-equipment owners, the contractors, the maids, the masseuses, the masseurs, and defenseless workers like Kenneth. Such matters were left to honor. But American business practice here respects no such constraints of honor.

A representative of the Johnson & Johnson company swept through the schools here recently giving lectures on hygiene, or at least, school officials were given to believe that hygiene would be the subject of the representative's talks. Turned out the talks were little more than marketing spiels: *For acne, use Johnson & Johnson this; for pimples, use Johnson & Johnson that; for all else that ails your sweet little adolescent faces, use just about all of everything on the good old Johnson & Johnson product list.*

Now, this goes only a small piece of the way toward explaining why Kenneth forbore to pop the man who put his hands on him. Perhaps a bigger part of Kenneth's discretion was that he feared what the man could and would do to him. After all, the resort owner was white, and one errs on the safe side in assuming that all white Americans here are rich and powerful. This business of a *white mystique* is something more than a baseless notion. It is real and supported by a painful history of unequal relations and the abuse of privilege.

Kenneth had seen locals of influence eating beside the pool in the man's five-star restaurant beneath languidly turning fan blades. He had seen the man chatting up the big guys that Kenneth didn't know, would never know. My God, the man had even put a stop to loud music in the neighborhood. Yes he did. Went to court and silenced the calypso and the reggae that lilted up the slope from a tiny local club down toward the sea on the island road. Jesus, how did the white man do that? Music is everywhere on this island, *nuh* this is the culture, man, the loud celebratory story of it, the percussive sweet rhythm of it, borne along for miles, lifted up to *Jah* by the night wind. This is *our* culture, eh? But the big white man went to court and stopped the music. Up North, the black Americans got the blues. We got no blues here. Our music is our tonic for blues. How did the white man do that on this island, our island, eh?

If truth exists as anything more than a phrase-maker's rumination, it can only be found in the whole of the mosaic that spans the infinities of human experience. How can I or anyone else, viewing alone the enterprise of life, *know* even the smallest social truth about anything? Perhaps as Michael Ondaatje suggests in *Anil's Ghost,* there is no truth, but only opinion. Indeed, all social reporting is subjective. The difference here is that I readily confess this. My opinion, my measure taken, is but a small bit of what could resolve with other bits into a collective and useful truth about anything. Or perhaps all of this business of truth-seeking is just so much bullshit, just so much palaver to disguise the ugly, ongoing, atavistic tension between egos and classes and genders and ethnic groups and races. Thus I can only do my best to describe things to you as I, this race-victim shaped in America, *see* them in a country markedly different from the America I have left, in every likelihood, for good. Of course, like everyone else, I can only *see* through the prism of my own experience, through the pain of what happened to me, what happened to me in America at the hands of white Americans, whom I believed I know well enough, and they are here smiling, hardly laserlike, but smiling in any case, and investing and acquiring. They are courted and cultivated and trusted.

Just recently an American had been pushing aggressively here to buy a five-hundred-acre parcel of land that reached from mountain to sea. The buyer, who described himself as a developer, operated out of a tiny jerry-built structure situated on the back lot of a Las Vegas industrial site. He proposed to build a resort hotel, and toward that objective presented a minimalist boilerplate drawing so unoriginal and environmentally thoughtless that it might have been torn from a grade-B trade magazine on a drugstore rack. The "developer" could not make good on his financial commitment and the project collapsed of its own weight, which for the country seemed a fortunate turn of events, inasmuch as the "developer" had never in his life built a hotel, much less a resort facility that bestrode a green dimpling sea, a sculptured, tree-clad mountain peak, and a majestic slope that carried from one arresting vista to the next. But the "developer" was from America and he had *sounded* good—always and everywhere, the most important thing.

PART TWO

THE UNREMARKED
DISINTEGRATION OF
AMERICAN DEMOCRACY

Chapter Nine

Leader

The Maximum Leader had a little forehead creased with furrows that horseshoed around impish eyes that were wide with some remembered adolescent mischief. He walked with an exuberant little hop that reminded one of a child in an oversized cowboy suit on Christmas morning, slowed by a bullet-laden gun-belt that sagged under twin six-shooters that bounced along the living-room floor. The Maximum Leader flashed a smile that betokened a condition the old folks had a name for: *soon.*

Maximum Leader's father, who was very rich and had once been Maximum Leader himself, knew that his son was no great shakes, but gave him his home state to play with anyway because he loved him. Averse to favoritism, he gave his other son another state, while making sure that the other son would not play with his state in a neighborhood near the Maximum Leader's state.

The boys were never known to be terribly bright, but giving the boys a couple of states to play with was all in good fun and, looka here, where's the harm anyway? It's just the kind of joke white folks play to see how long it will take people to catch on. Sorta like the joke that white folks played years ago on Native Americans when they named the Lone Ranger's sidekick "Tonto," which is the Spanish word for "stupid."

The show ran on national television for years.

How many people caught the joke?

Christ, who was hurt by it?

Even now, a white student at Dickinson Law School says to me, "I knew about *Tonto* and I knew 'tonto' meant 'stupid' but I never made the connection."

See?

Nobody's out to hurt anybody.

A joke's a joke.

But people never get it anyway.

One thing Maximum Leader loved to do when he had his state to play with was strap guys who looked like Man-boy down in the old buzzer chair and watch them fry up like center-cut bacon when the bye-bye button was pressed. Maximum Leader did this more than anyone else in the land.

I first became worried when Maximum Leader grew bored with his toy state and asked his father if he could play with the whole country.

"Get a holt of all those bombs and missiles, Dad. Geez! We've got the most powerful country in the history of the universe, right Dad?"

Remember when that Aeroflot pilot left the two kids alone in the cockpit of a big Russian-made Tupolov jet at thirty thousand feet?

Passengers cruising along, their heads in the clouds.

Kids flew the thing smack into a mountain.

Killed everyone aboard.

Whe-e-e-e-e!

Honest to God, this was the first thing I thought about when the Maximum Leader got his hands on the largest concentration of *weapons of mass destruction* in the history of the universe to play with.

Frightening man.

First thing the Maximum did was bring on some black people who agreed with him, because he knew that black people liked to see black people in high places no matter what you did to them or didn't do for them. Most black people are like this, and the Maximum Leader knew it. Took one of his blacks to a black church with him, an experience as freaky for his black as it was for him, and got a standing ovation.

What can you say about those blacks, huh?

The Maximum Leader had once read something somewhere about the *Crusades* and got the idea that you could be a Christian and a mean sonofabitch at the same time. He had a guy like that from his toy state sitting in the U.S. Congress. Guy had snake eyes in a flat cold face. Loved the Lord. Mean as hell.

It was then that the Maximum Leader got the first glimmer of an idea for his first little joke as Maximum Leader. Take a big God-guy who had had his toy rudely snatched away from him and make him what? The head of—this is too beautiful—the *Justice* Department.

Americans won't get the joke, though. A few of the pointy-headed bastards that I never could stand but not the rest of them, because they're stu-u-pid.

Frank A. Jung, an assistant state attorney general from Missouri, U.S. Attorney General John Ashcroft's home state, appeared before the Missouri Supreme Court to oppose an attempt by a death row inmate to have his conviction reopened on the basis of new evidence.

Judge Laura Denvir Stith asked Mr. Jung, "Are you suggesting that even if we find [that] Mr. Amrine is actually innocent, he should be executed?"

Mr. Jung answered, "That's correct, your honor."

With just one-twentieth of the world's population, America has, living behind bars, one-fourth of the world's prisoners, over two million and counting. Half of them are black. Of those on death row, half are black, another quarter are Hispanic.

America does not care about them. It does not care about the circumstances of their predicament, how they got where they are, or America's long- or short-term responsibility for their dilemma. The country has turned its back on the past, and in so doing, destroyed its domestic future.

Man-boy will see to that.

America does not know this yet.

For now, it is preoccupied, stricken with a homogenizing patriotism of the type that chills free expression and frightens the thoughtful. Could Germany in the early going after the Versailles humiliation have felt like this? Before all the public blaring of marshal music. Before German patriots surrendered their minds to the fatherland on flat planes of straight numberless lines that stretched as far as the eye could see across the urban landscapes of Berlin.

Man-boy, the domestic time bomb of modern America, was created by the Founders. The Founders were smart, visionary, if racist, limited men. Could as much be said about George W. Bush? In this new era of rampant impersonal e-tardism where the prosperous have little range of knowledge and the suffering are shunt from the view, could such a man as George W. Bush come near to thinking the thoughts that could save American society from itself?

I have lived well in America. But my core needs are essentially spiritual and run well beyond the material. I am joined indissolubly by the tragic *it* to Man-boy.

I do not want to live in a country that made the boy who looked through me in Rochester, New York.

Chapter Ten

Insiders

Who holds title to America? No. *Title* is not the word I'm searching for. *Title* is a legal term. It only measures the surface of a thing, a legal fact of the season. At best, the term *title* is two-dimensional in its descriptive reach. The question *Who owns America?* would get me closer but not *there* to the core of my conundrum. Who *possesses* America? Giving *possesses* heft: Who or what unidentified group of somebodies really runs the machinery of the thing, crafts its macro-machinations, writes its domestic information, decides which sheep go where, which get the abattoir? Is there some school, some club, some nineteenth hole, some underground where cult numbers of the *select* chant passages from *The Prince* and learn how to make poor white truck drivers vote for rich white Republicans? Could this have been the post-slavery role planned for freed blacks? To be decoys? To be the spellbinder's watch swung before the glazed gaze of poor white trash? *Let your mind rest now—relax. Keep your eyes on the swinging blacks. Watch them go up. Watch them fall down. You're getting sleepy. Very, very sleepy. When I snap my fingers, you will wake up and have only subliminal memory of our little talk. There, there. You will do what your leaders tell you to do. Watch the blacks. They are your enemies.*

I don't believe working-class whites ever understood democracy. They were never taught to. It wasn't in some group of somebodies' interest to do so. Who and where are these geniuses, these brilliant puppet-masters, these clever, silent dictators? (I should have known something was up when ostentation lost its footing.)

Louis Brandeis wrote that "the most important office in a democracy is the office of citizen." Brandeis wasn't writing about voting but about thinking, thinking critically, thinking independently.

You will do what your leaders tell you to do.

It is hard to miss the message printed on the board in oversized letters at the front of every class.

Another voice, quieter, somewhere under the watch-master's, deep down from the pit of white trash's beleaguered soul: *Think, think, try hard to think. I'm trying goddammit, I'm trying* (which comes out like *crying*) *but I can't hear myself in here. And I work hard, you know, really, really hard. Where's the time to think?*

That ubiquitous portrait of Robert E. Lee lends a rather noble impression to the man, don't you think? It's all over the South, country maybe. On walls of grade schools, universities, on the recommended reading display stands of major bookstores. Who hasn't seen it? Guy looks more honorable than all but a few members of the U.S. Congress. Guy tried to overthrow the U.S. government and led hundreds of thousands of men to their deaths in defense of slavery, an American institution no one denies but, nonetheless, has been somehow bleached of its moral horror. Did the geniuses do this or does racism flow naturally and unimpeded through the chambers of the white heart? I don't know the answer to this, despite a lifetime of trying to know it.

Did the Jews construct *for* America a little holocaust corner of its national conscience? Given our experience with slavery, it is hard to believe that Americans would have made a big deal of the Nazi holocaust of their own free will. Or perhaps the club saw that some strategic purpose could be served by keeping Germany on the defensive long after the war. In any case, unlike slavery, the holocaust was not America's doing. Thus, America had no need to deny the consequences.

I'm not in the club, that diaphanous assemblage with no office, that somehow meets and decides everything. I can't burrow in. I shot my mouth off, destroyed my chances as a mole and now I can't even find the club—and my forebears literally built the country. Henry Kissinger, an immigrant with a heavy German accent, is in the club, although he doesn't look happy about it, or anything else for that matter.

Saw a picture of Lee once, posing with Confederate General Nathan Bedford Forrest, the man who helped found the Ku Klux Klan. Lee is in the club, however, voted in by the Veterans Committee. Another American who fought against the United States (much less effectually, less lethally than Lee by the way) was John Brown. He was never in the club. In fact, the club has made him into something of a raving lunatic because he fought against slavery and not for it. Brown paid with his life for his treason at the end of the rope. Lee, who three days before the war ended sent thousands to an unnecessary death at Sayler's Creek, became the president of a university after the war.

There is also the ubiquitous portrait of John Brown around and about. In it, the antislavery crusader actually *looks* like a raving lunatic.

The invisible guys who decide these things must be geniuses. Where the hell are they and how do they do it?

Blood thirst unslaked, *they,* in the name of variety, had begun to pull their razor fangs out of Michael Jackson and plunge them dripping into Susan Sarandon and Martin Sheen, actors who knew who Louis Brandeis was and took the cerebral jurist seriously on the matter of the obligations of democracy. The actors had publicly critiqued American foreign policy, which is what all American citizens are obliged to do, I think.

You will do what your leaders tell you to do.

A half-mad-looking commentator on CNN, resting from spearing Michael Jackson, nearly sprayed spittle upon his shirt front, so agitated was the poor man about the actors having expressed "opinions" to which they were not entitled, in his view, because they were "actors" and thus apparently not citizens, as Mr. Brandeis, the learned constitutional scholar, had somehow assumed all American-born people to be. The actors were using their "celebrity" to tell a crowd of demonstrators how they felt. And the CNN coronary candidate used his camera to tell millions around the world just what he thought about the "actors," in no uncertain way.

FOX has jumped ahead of CNN in the ratings war. FOX knew its audience could be found at the book-bare bottom and went there right off the bat to join it. CNN, which once upon a time was a news organization, finally smelled the coffee, pinched its nose, and plunged.

Increasingly, I am having trouble distinguishing "news" commentators from actors. "News" commentators often tell us what *is* but *ain't*, while just as often, actors tell us what *ain't* but *is*. Because they readily identify themselves as "actors," and the *ain't* is their art, I believe actors are usually rather less harmful to the public interest than "news" commentators. I believe this even when I am completely fooled by an actor. After all, the actor warned me up front.

Let's take Robert Duvall for example. I have always liked Robert Duvall with his short, bandy legs, small cryptic smile, and funny little arm-hand gestures that move his head in odd directions. *Tender Mercies* was little known but one of my favorite movies. I thought Duvall's work in the movie was a tour de force.

Virtually everyone on the planet saw Duvall's work in the *Godfather* pictures. *Mr. Corleone likes to hear bad news right away.* The guy was great in a gimpy, understated sort of way. I formed a small admiration for the man, or actor (it's hard to know which), even while hearing a voice in my head that always warns me about people I don't know: *Don't put your weight on that limb, boyo.*

Not long ago, I turned on CNN and caught Robert Novak interviewing Duvall about Duvall's portrayal of Robert E. Lee in a picture that was soon to be released.

Novak was smiling. That in itself was frightening, both the smile—which seemed an ill-fitting mask that had been borrowed from someone else—and what the smile connoted. Novak liked what he was hearing. The interview was a gush 'nough of a love fest to raise the Ole South. You could nearly see the two of them in dress grays cantering aboard bays behind an erect and resplendent

Lee aboard his handsome white horse trotting back into the loving arms of dear ole slaveholding Virginny. To them, Robert E. Lee was a man of unexcelled character and integrity. That the enslavement of human beings stood at the center of Lee's treason against the United States never found a moment's expression in their exchange.

I have never heard the choleric "news" commentator say anything, unkind or otherwise, about Robert Duvall.

I ask myself, where does that leave me, a black man armed only with a figment of citizenship? I mean where the hell does that leave me, stranded in a society where Robert E. Lee can be publicly admired without consequence, or even remark.

White folks say: *Oh, that.* Yeah. *Oh, that.*

In his initial statement, Senator Tom Daschle, a liberal democrat, couldn't see how Senator Trent Lott had made anything more than a *mistake* in his praise of the Dixiecrat hate mongerings of Senator Strom Thurmond.

Oh, that.

Was Clarence Thomas the biggest joke white America ever played on black America? *You want one. We got one for ya.*

No matter how many go-along-to-get-along blacks land seats in the president's cabinet, America will always be a society of antagonistically opposed racial awarenesses. We will always be the majority's afterthought, modified Americans, parentheticals, February's public service announcement, history's orphans, memory's inconvenient burr in America's saddle. America will always leave Man-boy unexplained, won't it? *I may learn the password but the language of the tribe will always elude me, won't it? The private core will always be . . . hermetic, won't it?*

I had always understood the terms of conditional acceptance. Booking passage off the shore of this periphery had always cost more than I had been willing to pay. I had always preferred being ineffectual because of *them* to being ineffectual because of *me*. No passage at all is better than passage to complicity. Thus, I have fought *them* from the shore. On occasion, we have slowed them, curbed them, raised the profile of their ridiculous hypocrisy. But I am convinced now that I cannot *change* them—from within or from without—and even attempting to from within is to run the risk of losing one's soul. America may now be the only country powerful enough to mask its awful sins. Little people in little countries know their sins, know them all too painfully. But they don't matter. No more than the Tainos on the beach mattered to Christopher Columbus.

The hazards of geostrategic course-taking are infinitely greater today than what passed for such five hundred years ago. Then there was space in the world, much of it mutually undiscovered. The weapons were comparatively primitive, the casualties of conflict self-limiting. At the beginning of the twentieth century, there were 1.2 billion people in the world. At its close, there were six billion—living under the long shadow of one hyperpower with weapons abundant and powerful enough to destroy every man, woman, and child on the planet several times over. Run out the numbers to see how short the future could be. Obviously, world population cannot continue to grow indefinitely at its current rate. Malthus wouldn't have known what to make of any of this. The advanced technology of modern weaponry may well have robbed the future of any opportunity to prove his gloomy forecast, which may, in any case, seem less gloomy now in retrospect as we flirt with apocalypse.

Accumulatively developed weapons technology has combined with a static mediocrity of human judgment to narrow our margin of human error to the finest of measures.

Perhaps a cataclysmic population correction is inevitable for us. Sooner or later, one would think this would have to be the result of the course that the white world set for all of us long ago. Their cursed machines. Machines in the hands of upper primates who've neglected to consider the naturally governing limitations of their species.

> Listen to the white world
> its horrible exhaustion from its
> immense labors
> its rebellious joints cracking under
> the pitiless stars

its blue steel rigidities, cutting
        through the mysteries of the flesh
listen to their vainglorious conquests
        trumpeting their defeats
listen to the grandiose alibis of their
        pitiful foundering.

—Aime Cesaire

If you're scared, you should be. The thought of the future charges my thinking with a voltage that is higher than that recommended. Clichés jumbled themselves up. *The pen is mightier than the sword.* Yeah, but who uses swords anymore? *Pride goeth before a fall.* Well, now that one may still have some application.

Here's a new one. *They lied to us.* The world after the demise of the Soviet Union did not become a *less* dangerous place but a *more* dangerous place. Now the powerless have no opposing poles between which to maneuver with any reason for hope. Now, not only is there no surviving balance of global power, but no balance of reason, no discoursing wisdoms, for virtually all decisions of world consequence are now made in Washington, by Washington, for Washington.

This development is disquieting. Not because so much lethal power is concentrated in the hands of Americans, but rather that there *is* so much power, and that it should be *concentrated* anywhere. (This fear is deepened by an image in my mind of a gnat riding a half-blind charging rhinoceros.)

The guys in the club now have us poised for a massive assault on a country that has not attacked us. Tens of thousands of innocent civilians will likely be killed by American bombs. The club guys decided upon this course nearly unilaterally. The club guys, untrammeled now, may end up precipitating a result too horrible to imagine. The club guys do know some things (Il Duce taught them, for example, not to stand out there and rant on a balcony) except that they're still little more than upper primates. The club guys think they are smart, but no upper primate is ever as smart as it thinks it is. If Murphy had it right, sooner or later the club guys will blow up a good part of the world. It just galls me to have my fate determined by a man as patently mediocre as the president.

Perhaps fifty million years from now, some new life species will remember humans as humans now remember *Brontosaurus*—big body, pea brain. Bronty thought he was smart, too.

In 2003 the president had been waving the flag vigorously enough to churn up a patriotic draught of sufficient energy to fever a thirst in our fighting men and women for foreign blood. One of our brave soldiers spoke eloquently of the call to arms (imparted in somewhat more temperate language by the president) to our forces: "We gotta go over there and kick some butt." The president had told the nation, ad nauseam, that the "enemy" had "weapons of mass destruction." Virtually every American knew that if in fact the "enemy" really had any "weapons of mass destruction" it did not have them in sufficient number and sophistication to pose much of a threat to our boys, who had sized up the campaign as "short work." Hence, our boys were antsy for the kill.

Polls had shown that blacks opposed the war by a larger margin than any other section of the population, which, over all, supported our plans to invade the "enemy" even without sanction of the United Nations Security Council. This discrepancy of support was likely due to blacks having languished too long as citizens of "Oh, that" America, and as a result, not seeing themselves as the wrathful avengers of the president's "real" America, although blacks, who were actually *in* the army, seemed to be as gung ho to shoot somebody as their real American compatriots.

Another group, suspicious of the president's objectives, was made up of college graduates, white and black. They apparently did not believe the president when he told them that the enemy posed a threat to "The Homeland" (which smacks chillingly of "The Fatherland"). The college graduates knew that the Tonkin Gulf Resolution that had gotten us into Vietnam had been constructed upon a foundation of untruths. They also remembered the testimony before Congress of a young Kuwaiti woman. Her gripping story had helped to fire up the masses for an earlier war against the same "enemy." The young woman had horrified the assembled Congresspersons when she testified to having seen the "enemy" pull newborn babies from incubators and dash them upon a hospital floor. It turned out, long after the truth could make a difference, that the young woman was the daughter of the Kuwaiti ambassador to Washington and had fabricated the whole story.

Recently, FOX ran a segment of film that purported to show atrocities committed by Al Qaeda. The film had been "found" by members of the Green Berets.

An unfortunate characteristic common to all governments (democracies, dictatorships, hybrids) is that those who speak for them are almost always obligatory liars. Little of what they say to those they govern can be taken at face value. This trait is inherently less detrimental to public well-being in a democracy than in a dictatorship, owing to certain basic rights pursuant to which individuals and groups in a democracy can question the truthfulness of what their government tells them. That is, if such individuals and groups have available to them alternative, independently obtained information upon which to construct a credible public challenge. This inherent advantage that democracies enjoy over dictatorships is now being eroded by the low-road journalism practiced by the new ratings bottom-fishers, FOX and CNN.

The *FOX News Sunday* program on which I saw the film segment on Al Qaeda's purported atrocities serves as a good example of the growing danger to American democracy that can only be described as *imposter* journalism, where non-journalist *announcers,* who do not research, investigate, or write news stories, hold forth in simplistic, incendiary, categorical language on the significance of the footage we are watching, without either authenticating the footage or connecting it to the "enemy," the instant invadee against which they are clumsily and demagogically inflaming us. There are three of them on the panel telling us what we have seen and how to think about it. There are two men and a woman. One of the men is black. The woman, who always sits in the middle, is young and blonde, thus meeting what appears to be an important FOX journalistic standard. The white man speaks with steely conviction but completely without background or nuance. Giving no ground, the black man disparages former President Jimmy Carter's opposition to the war. He then smiles and looks as if the smile is painted over some deep hurt occasioned by the other two, who only talk to each other and seldom even look at him.

The caliber of discussion is shockingly low, which is all the more apparent because I measure it against a London BBC broadcast I had just watched in which journalists (real writers, that is) from France, Britain, the Persian Gulf, and the United States had conducted an insightful, far-ranging exchange that steered clear of the visceral and provided fresh information and contested analysis. I had seen no discussion like it on American television, where the new "news" is served up in dumbed-down abbreviations by the gilded-voice herders of the cresting nationalistic fervor.

A rear admiral in the U.S. Navy spoke icily on CNN through a face that barely moved: "If we are ordered by the president, our attack upon the enemy will be lethal, devastating, persistent, lightning, and precise."

The president has not shown that the enemy has attacked us, or is even planning to do so. It is enough that the enemy doesn't like us and "could" attack us. Prophylactic slaughter. Something new. Who is next? Who decides who is next?

I had to laugh at the Congressional legislation that sought to change the name of french fries and French toast to "freedom fries" and "freedom toast." I have laughed, first stage, at much of what has transpired recently. It is a sad, mirthless, hopeless laugh, the reaction of one who recognizes the absurd while recognizing the faint border that the absurd shares with catastrophe. You see, I had laughed when the president declared himself a candidate for the world's most powerful job. How could so average a man, one so unremarkably endowed with intellect, wisdom, and even, suspiciously, courage, have given over to him charge of the world? Why should courage be a qualification for command of history's most lethal killing machine? Courage is not, of course, the absence of fear in the face of danger. The absence of fear under such circumstances would be symptomatic of a mental disorder of one variety or another.

Courage, rather, has to do with how one manages fear in the face of danger. Courage, further, is that sensitive, raw human condition of character that implies, among other things, a capacity for empathy. If one has not experienced danger or life-threatening risk or catastrophic loss, or even simple suffering, how can one *empathetically* contemplate the sacrifice of innocent women, children, and men who live under a distant enemy's harsh rule? Is it not brutish to exacerbate their existing agony? Is it not cowardly to ignore it?

Is it that we trivialize the suffering of people who don't look and speak like us, somehow flatten them out, mute their wails, deny them the very humanity, that we, safe again (we would like to believe) above it all, have ourselves evacuated? Is this not the fruit of our deepening falseness, now foisted upon the world? Now, at last sadly, the commodification of *life,* the preciousness of which little is spoken anymore by the powerful?

In America, *everything* has become a game. Nothing is real. No topic anymore need be approached searchingly, soberly, thoughtfully. The game rules forbid it.

Some three years ago, I was invited to be a guest on *The McLaughlin Group,* a nationally syndicated television show that was hosted by a former priest with a fierce brow and knitted eyebrows. I declined. The new and dangerously anti-democratic era of *yak-yak* television had dawned. Typical host question—hear it, in your imagination, barked: *Yes or No! Should America leave the United Nations?* Or, picture a decrepit Robert Novak in full growl: *In just moments, our guests this evening will step into the cr-r-rossfir-r-r-re gr-r-r-r.*

Oh, brotha.

And such serves for public discourse in the most powerful nation on earth.

Haitian children are dying for want of clean drinking water because the president has blocked loans approved for Haiti by the Inter-American Development Bank.

Oh, that.

Grown-up, private-school white boys playing games. World-board Monopoly with real guns. White entertainment television passing itself off as news. Infantile jousting passing itself off as informed debate. All reductive. All irresponsible, dangerous even.

The U.S. government is a massive operation. Not even a brilliant president could manage it without broad, anonymous delegation, both of administration and substantive decision-making. A less than *smart* president would become lost quickly, and virtually wholly dependent on others for even the broadest strokes of a reasoned policy.

Foreign policy-making presents still another remove of complexity, borne of a multilayered evolutionary process of engaging a distant world, very different, often combustibly, from our own. Here, even brilliance cannot fully substitute for experience. You simply cannot know that to which you have not been exposed, not even what a frame of reference within which to supervise more experienced subordinates might look like.

Before assuming command of the most powerful killing machine in the history of humankind, the president, a man of middle years and enormous wealth, had ventured outside the United States only once—a short excursion, was it?—to Mexico. Given the absence of some unknown legitimate impediment or disincentive, this failure of the pre-president to explore the world with little more than his big toe would suggest, at least convincingly to me, that the president has neither an interest in nor the aptitude for understanding the many countries and complicated cultures from which our "friends" and "enemies" spring. By way of comparison, my youngest child, Khalea, thirteen, who is not wealthy by the president's standards, has thus far visited twenty-one countries, all of which she researched vigorously before visiting. The world interested her in a way it had never interested the president. Otherwise, he'd have occasionally gone to have a look at it.

Who's running things? I have no idea. Certainly not the necessarily suggestible president who appears to have been given a short script to memorize.

I watched a debate on C-SPAN that was broadcast from a university campus in California. One of the presenters was Christopher Hitchens, whom I had met two years earlier when he came to interview me for a piece he was doing for *Vanity Fair* on slavery reparations. The piece had been sympathetic, and that very leaning gave me to expect that Christopher would oppose the military invasion promised by the president of the enemy's country. Well, Christopher surprised me by throwing his considerable thoughtfulness behind the now imminent American firestorm. He argued that the enemy was a deserving horror that warranted systematic eradication.

One news report had estimated that five hundred thousand people would die in the war that Christopher counseled. This was not mentioned in his presentation. In fact, before C-SPAN's signal was lost some thirty minutes into the program, not one of the four panelists had said a word about the innocent civilian lives that are certain to be sacrificed in the president's invasion. What should have been the most important term of discussion had not been discussed at all, not even mentioned.

What is with these fine, good, *thinking* people? Has some precious and essential gene of theirs gone missing? Has their *feeling* gene been run down in traffic up-lineage by some blue-steel, metallic *thinking* gene of theirs? How do you wage a debate about whether or not to overrun a country with blistering firepower without treating as central the question of the human cost of war? Shopkeepers, nurses, peddlers, teachers, mothers, fathers, toddlers. Life. Life. Aren't people, the welfare of ground-zero human beings, what decent people incline to consider first? How can you start such a discussion from any other point? Smart people with blind spots are more dangerous than dumb people who see the world with the whole sensate being. Yet, I grant that Christopher may have meant well, even in what appeared to be the naive supposition that the president champs only with honorable intention to open up his bomb bays. Notwithstanding what may or may not trace through the president's head, bad acts are never mitigated by good intentions. Justice Brandeis, who has so much to say to us still, has something on point to offer here as well:

> Experience should teach us to be most on our guard to protect liberty when the government's purposes are beneficent. The greatest dangers to liberty lurk in the insidious enroachments of men of zeal, well meaning but without understanding.

There just has to be more information, buried somewhere under the rich smelly soil of interests, on just how the president was put up to all this. Last year, not a dime could be found for public school refurbishment. The economy plummeted. And 1.3 million Americans filed for bankruptcy. Now the president has found a spare one hundred billion dollars to first destroy the enemy—and, perhaps, several times that—then to rebuild the enemy's country, a reconstruction no doubt that will be carried out by some of the president's business patrons during the president's planned two-year military occupation of "democratic" inspiration.

Huh?

If this is not a winning formula for a terrorist breeding school, tell me what is. I'll tell you one thing. The race is on now. The only lesson to be learned here by countries without "weapons of mass destruction" is to either remain essentially defenseless or to work like hell surreptitiously to get as many "weapons of mass destruction" as one can get as quickly as one can get them without getting caught by the president in the process. This is what North Korea has done and all but throws in the president's face. North Korea is not on the president's invasion calendar because nuclear North Korea, openly test-firing missiles into the South China Sea, really *has* "weapons of mass destruction," placing itself on a short list of nonwhite countries that the president must handle with care. Of course the president will not invade completely defenseless countries that he would not, in any case, deign to notice—to aid or to do anything else for, as he and his predecessor have done for North Korea. The countries to be invaded are only the *relatively* defenseless ones that could mount a measure or two of resistance. But not enough, however, to body-bag a second term.

A CIA agent let slip (they seemed a lot less careless during the Cold War) that once the enemy's territory has been captured, the president will need to build American bases from which to operate against other enemies in the region. The forced transplant of mismatched tissue.

The president, I suppose, can fairly easily invade a number of countries in the region while subverting others. He cannot so easily, however, invade the hearts and minds of the region's people, who are growing to hate America with a suicidal fidelity. When governments, the regents of order, falter, terrorism becomes an angry people's war, privatized.

Man-boy is completely defenseless. Owing to his defenselessness, he gets no attention. Should he *defend* himself, he will be crushed, but not before exacting some measure of something from some bystanding body. In his native land, he is closed off into an airless corner of self-destructive choices. The president is busy invading, defending American freedoms, stuff like that, and does not bother to notice Man-boy.

Chapter Eleven

Deal

Look. Here's how I think it went. Either he approached them, or they approached him. Either way, it was done early, very early, before the public could know what was going on, as if the public ever knows what's going on. In any case, Daddy and the money people set up the pre-president early to take the big one, and even then, the pre-president blew the popular vote, the full count of which constituted less than half of a disaffected electorate. Still, with a little chicanery, the son got his hands on the biggest toy of all, the whole damn world. And that's what counted.

I once had a small experience with this preelection odds-fixing business. A black money guy, who was also a friend of mine, asked me to publicly support someone he wanted to back financially as the mayor of a major city. The candidate was hardly venal, but a numbing plodder, nonetheless. My friend, I suspect, was making an investment for which he would expect a return in business opportunity should our plodder rise to power. I met with the plodder. He said all the right things, ploddingly. I gave him my support, misgivingly. The plodder lost the popular vote, and, quite fortunately, the election.

I tell you this story to give you some insight into how money people maneuver people like the president into power; power that no one seems to care whether or not the one who would be king is intellectually, psychologically, or otherwise suited to manage.

The presidency is one of few American professional jobs for

which there are no mandatory qualifications outside of age and place of birth, which are laid out in the Constitution.

Whenever I see a uniformed policeman wearing a government-issue service revolver, I wonder, if for just a moment, if the stressed-out guy is going to go postal the very moment he's looking at me. I wonder this, even knowing that the policeman has been required to undergo a battery of psychological tests before being issued a revolver and a few live rounds to fill it. I wonder this because bad apples sometimes get through the screen. Still, we are better off than we would be with a bunch of unscreened guys walking around with loaded pistols.

To every new American president, we give the keys to the world's most fully stocked nuclear arsenal. No questions asked. We have no way of knowing whether or not the president knows in which direction the equator can be found, drinks to a nightly stupor after dinner, or is otherwise generally insane. We vote for people we have never met and don't know a thing about, save what we can glean from campaign statements and past public behavior.

One simple fact is undeniable about the way Americans go about choosing a president. We perform the quadrennial rite without knowing just what, if anything, the presidential aspirants *really* believe. Even when we *know* they are lying to us to fool us for our votes, we believe them anyway when they say those things that, prudent or reckless, we wish to hear, our emotions crudely played like overstrung ethnic banjos.

What fools they make of all the little millions—the follow-the-leader, In-God-We-Trust, functionally literate, love-my-country, 4-H-Club, flag-faithful, patriotic, red-blooded, American middle-wage toilers—who don't know squat about what is really going on in the *theater-in-the-round* of their own democracy.

. . . *do what your leaders tell you to do.*

It's different, though, with the shadowy money people. We don't know *them,* but *he* does. We don't know who or what class of people own *him,* but *he* does. *They,* early on, bought time-shares in *his* thinking, long, long before *his* presidential campaign stock went public. Now they are quite married, although I could never figure out why *they* would choose *him* to anoint. Perhaps it was for the very reason that had, at first, evoked laughter from me.

The president has a *huh-head* that possibly made him look malleable to the money people, while at the same time it made him look to me, well, just dumb. You may be curious to know that a *huh-head* is characterized by a forehead in which permanent furrows deepen whenever baffling questions are posed, questions to which the audible response, for too many years, to too many teachers, is *"huh?"*

Whatever the sequence, the big Republican money gathered behind the president's candidacy very early, so early in fact that it caught the rest of the field sleeping, which leads me to believe that the idea of his presidency may have occurred to others before it occurred to him, and those others, Daddy and the time-share owners included, virtually constructed a president who wishes on behalf of his nebulous makers to change the map of much of the world. This is the so-called Spice Girl model with a political twist, where candidate and candidacy are invented by unspecified people for unspecified reasons. Whatever else it is, the whole shabby business of it is contrary to the spirit of democracy.

Chapter Twelve

War

In violation of international law and against the judgment of the United Nations Security Council, the president, with an ancestral cousin in tow, invades the enemy with hundreds of thousands of ground forces under cover of missiles fired from guided missile cruisers and submarines that set much of the capital city ablaze, more than three hundred miles to the north. Though the president has assured us that the enemy possesses "weapons of mass destruction," the enemy appears to have no better idea where the weapons are than the president does. Ninety miles into enemy territory, the president's "Coalition of the Willing" is met with white flags of surrender but no enemy resistance to speak of. The president does not offer an explanation of the discrepancy between his claims of the enemy's carnage-wreaking capabilities and the stillborn resistance offered by the enemy to the blitzkrieg of explosions and flames laid down by the president, whose forces rumble unimpeded across the featureless desert floor in the hunt for the enemy's Stalinist leader. The enemy's leader, a would-be modern Nebuchadnezzar, had been holed up with his family in a fortified bunker when the bunker exploded from a Tomahawk missile fired with the president's approval hours *before* the president's ultimatum to the enemy's leader had expired. All the rules of law and diplomacy had long since been thrown out of the proverbial window of unsought opportunity.

The coalition forces have now thrown caution to the wind and are hurdling across the baked earth with abandon, slowing only to avoid terrain obstructions. Videophone cameras send live pictures across the world of dust-trailing tanks and Bradley fighting machines. Journalists from all manner of news organizations ride along with the ground forces and give a running commentary on what we are watching. The newspeople seem calm, unagitated. They are not managing their fear. They have no fear. No one seems to. I think that this does not look right. That the faces of the president's forces invading, say, North Korea would not look like the faces I see on the screen.

There are no weapons of mass destruction, and these faces, faces that cannot fool fear, know it. Maybe the weapons are in the capital. Maybe they are hidden. But from the enemy themselves? It doesn't make sense. The president's people are coming hard now to find and kill the enemy's leader, who has had ample time to have his loyalists prime and fire his weapons of mass destruction at— something, somewhere, somebody—if only to stave off embarrassment, if only to produce just one large, orange, furious fire-cloud of male desperation.

On the second day of the invasion, one of the president's military leaders says on the *Larry King Show* that when the enemy sees our firepower they'll come over to our side, they'll come over or face "massacre." But where was the firepower that the president kept telling us the enemy had, the mantra-speak "weapons of mass destruction" that were said to justify the president's seventy-five-billion-dollar war fandango?

Arrogance is a disabling condition. It renders its host sightless and bereft of regard for the cultural lifecraft of others. In its most extreme form, the condition, disguising itself as pride, robs its victim of any ability for self-diagnosis. The heirs of Columbus, the makers, the measurers, the machine people, appear to be disproportionately affected by the condition that presents amongst its several symptoms a seeming genetic proclivity to underestimate those who put little store in replicating metal to the teeniest of tolerances, a million times over. Machines are conceived in the image of their makers and marked by a certain repetitive invincibility. The machine cannot think, and thus cannot know its limitations. Its maker *can* think, but sadly, inveigled by its clever child, does little better.

Blindness, utter self-destructive blindness.

The president will win his "war," but likely none of the war's ostensible objectives. Understandably, he, inside his blindness, believed that his forces would win, and win quickly, owing to the vast technological superiority of weaponry that he and his tethered ancestral cousin enjoyed. After all, it was not just two against one, but two first-world, white-world, industrialized powers against what Europeans saw to be a midrange mediocrity of a people in sand-beaten robes and sun-bleached turbans; people described to the president by his CIA as hating the Stalinist dictator who had cruelly abused them for thirty years.

Everyone—the president, the prime-minister-in-tow, the generals, the journalists, the talking-heads, the Western experts—talked past the war itself and concentrated on the president's operational plans for the occupation that would follow the war. After all, the white flags waved by some of the enemy's forces on day one of the war had already signaled the beginning of the end. I saw the lines of surrendering enemies. Others, some in uniform and some not, lay about the desert floor in the arid unmistakable rictus of death. The television footage had been commented upon by "journalists" like CNN's Paula Zahn with what seemed a scarcely suppressed satanic elation. One such "journalist" whooped at the sight of the capital under a flame-lit night sky collapsing upon god-knows-whom. Brown and anonymous to be sure.

The "journalists" seemed never to have visualized what it would be like to have their *own* country bombed from above into a landscape of rubble and overrun from below with foreign soldiers wielding lethal machines and speaking an alien tongue. The "journalists" appeared not to even see it as an invasion, but as something or another our guys do as a matter of natural right, which, of course, was anything they pleased to do, anywhere they pleased to do it. It had gotten so that I couldn't imagine a thing, no matter how unconscionable, that our guys could do to another people that our citizens in the main would find morally repugnant.

It was not that the enemy's leader was not a horrific human be-ing. He was all of that. But the president, in his unique stupidity, had done what had been thought all but impossible: He had virtu-ally single-handedly turned the merciless dictator, loathed at home for good reason, into a near-sympathetic figure in the larger non-white world, none of which mattered one whit to the president's core constituents, the majority of whom having never seen either of their country's framing oceans, much less a foreign country.

I've come to accept, somewhat cynically, that the squirreling away of privilege by a pampered few in the close hidden seams of democ-racy is largely made possible and facilitated by the poor and provin-cial public education that the president tolerates for the many.

As cult opiates go, patriotism, a milder but still dangerous form, is most effective when taken in complete and sustained darkness. On the question of just how far the president's writ of authority should run throughout the world and over its diverse peoples and cultures, the president's bungalow peasants had been socialized to literally believe everything that they were told to believe, and to do everything they were asked to do.

They had once been told that the Russian army represented an imminent threat to their *freedoms*. In the darkness of their flawed small information, and with only their flag to mitigate their ac-cepted insignificance, they believed that the Russian army was for-midable enough to jeopardize their freedoms, the same Russian army that would later be humiliated in Afghanistan and stalemated by Chechen irregulars. They had also once been told, and therefore believed, that the Stalinist tyrant, whose country the president was instantly invading, was a reliable friend and worthy of their arm-ing. Now, more recently, they were told to send their sons and daughters to kill the president's daddy's reliable friend, who would defend himself with the arms the president's daddy had provided him. But the arms would be little match for the one-million-dollar, radar-guided missiles that the president's men were firing from cruisers at the president's daddy's erstwhile reliable friend.

A community of the pampered few who skulked in the close hid-den seams of the president's democracy were well pleased with the results of their back-channel exertions. Weapons were being destroyed, weapons that would need replacing—on all sides. (Only one member of the 535-member Congress, which had supported the president's war, had a child in the military. Indeed, the president had evaded serving himself.)

War is always profitable, but never for those called upon to wage it.

The bungalow-peasant-funded CIA had been wrong so many times—on the collapse of the Soviet Union, the fall of the Berlin Wall—that one could safely place little stock in the agency's predictions anymore. Nonetheless the massively funded spy house continued to enjoy credibility in official circles. But even when the agency was right, the advanced technology of its espionage could not penetrate the ranks of the world's largest secret society, the loosely woven fabric of a billion angry hearts into which the CIA could not see. Anti-Americanism was spreading like an epidemic throughout the world, an anti-Americanism of which the president's bungalow peasants had a completely mistaken understanding. Virtually from birth they had been immunized against empathy for the *different,* the different talking, the different dressing, the different worshipping, the different thinking.

They had never seen their own homes or the homes of their neighbors blown up in a rain of ordnance. They had never had a freshly severed, falling human limb stain their upstart white spring tulips. Save for once, they had never heard, in their own voices, the wrenching wails and screams of grief and deranging, maddening anger. They had never had the soil to which they pledged their allegiance occupied by invaders. They had never suffered. Thus, they had never languished in the ranks of the *knowing,* the feeling, the ranks of the world's everybody else.

Lacking any common experience to share with the rest of the humanity, the president had turned our vision of the world upside down, inside out. He had the power, and used it, at least on his own people, to make right wrong and wrong right. Thus it is *I* who is isolated here in my country by the blindness that *his* majority appears to enjoy.

The president plays with his dogs on a manicured White House lawn, and in every sense is much too far away to see or hear the effects of his lethal technology. Two of the president's precision anti-radiation missiles fall on a food market in the enemy's capital, killing civilian shoppers—women and children mostly, seventeen dead at least, scores injured, the remote killers' *collateral damage*. The awful wailing of women, some of whom swoon, can be heard through the black smoke, over the ambulance sirens. The children trance about the scene of bodies and burning tree stumps looking lost, displaced. The men shake their fists at the BBC camera and look into the lens with a chemical hatred. The war is a crusade for the president, the war he fights from his lawn with his two dogs. He is self-assured here. Brave. He knows exactly where he is and why. He and the playful unwitting dogs and the cameras on the green, green lawn.

The president had complained for several days that the enemy (which is quite literally fighting for its life) had violated the Geneva Convention by "parading" prisoners of war before television cameras. This is all terribly confusing to me. I think that my confusion may stem largely from some persistent cultural misunderstanding between the so-called European personality and that of the more exotic emoting peoples of the world, the divide side of humanity on which I fall. There are *laws*, principally the doing of Europeans, that govern how nations are to go about the quite legal business of slaughtering each other's people. I hope you will share with me your views in order to help me understand just how the other side reasons its complaint, assuming that its complaint is rendered with a measure of sincerity. Here are the indisputable facts as I know them:

- In the wake of a devastating terrorist attack carried out against his country on September 11, 2001, the president undertakes a "War on Terrorism."
- The president to date has been unable to find and apprehend the leader of the terrorist organization responsible for the attack that resulted in three thousand deaths.

- The president cannot, or at least has not, proved to the satisfaction of his traditional allies that the Stalinist leader of the country he has invaded had any responsibility for the terrorist attack carried out on September 11, 2001.

- Although his country has them in abundance, the president has been unable to prove to most of his allies, and to virtually all of the rest of the world, that the country he has invaded has weapons of mass destruction.

- The United Nations chief weapons inspector and a team of experts have searched the enemy's country for three months. They find proscribed items unaccounted for, but no weapons of mass destruction. The chief weapons inspector describes the problem as an "accountancy" matter. In any case, he says that he does not *know* that the enemy has weapons of mass destruction.

- The president fails to win enough support in the United Nations Security Council to pass a use-of-force resolution.

- The Secretary General of the United Nations warns that an invasion of the enemy (a United Nations member state) without the sanction of the United Nations Security Council would lack "legitimacy."

- The president charges again that the enemy has weapons of mass destruction and orders its Stalinist leader to disarm or leave his country.

- The Stalinist leader's ambassador to the United Nations answers that "the hand cannot give what the hand does not hold." (Of course, the ambassador did not ask the president to leave *his* country because *he* was known by everyone in the world to have weapons of mass destruction.)

- The Stalinist leader refuses to leave his country.

- With his military leaders promising to "shock and awe" and "massacre" with an attack that "will be lethal, devastating, persistent, lightning and precise," the president, with his "prime-minister-in-tow," massively invades a country that had not attacked *his*, bombing *its* cities, killing *its* people, soldiers and civilians alike. All done in clear contravention of international law.

Webster's defines an aggressor as one in the "practice of making attacks." It cannot be disputed that the president fits the definition. His flying, floating, falling, mechanized, armored, computerized, blistering juggernaut of an apocalyptic force visited massive violence upon the people of a distant country in a mismatch of a dimension so stunning as to suggest the aggressor as a bully, which *Webster's* defines as one "habitually cruel to others who are weaker." When asked how the bombing of the enemy's capital had affected him, the president said that he hadn't "lost a night's sleep."

Great leaders anguish long and hard over decisions that may entail paying the full and horrible human price of war. They do so even when the war is necessary and unavoidable. In the instant case, war was neither necessary nor unavoidable, and the president, who had anything but anguished over his decision, appeared to revel in it, like an eager and insecure boy eyeing some first misbegotten opportunity for manhood. In the wake of September 11, instead of soothing our fresh national fears, the president played to them, as a demagogue would to a frightened mob. And in so doing, he seemed to remember and forget in the same thought that he was the president of a nation whose world-system caretaking responsibilities were equal, at least, to its enormous power. This was the insight, had he happened upon it, that might have provided him at least a rudimentary touch of the wisdom of forbearance.

The president's military people took his reckless cue and talked hotly in the days before the war began about doing what they are trained to do, and that is kill mass numbers of people with administrative efficiency.

The improbable victims in this wrenching, huge-scale, life-and-death drama have to be the undermanned soldiers and people of the country invaded by the president. The president's forces claim to have captured more than three thousand enemy prisoners. The enemy has captured, to date, all of seven of the president's soldiers—and yes, put them on television, thereby likely *increasing* their chances for survival. The president's military leaders are incensed about this, not because the soldiers were humiliated by the enemy, but rather, I think, because the president's soldiers, separated from their machines of war, wore on their faces the unmistakable stamp of naked fear.

The soldiers had not been captured in Oklahoma or Texas or Florida, but in a country far from theirs, whose people the captured soldiers had traveled thousands of miles to kill. And so the enemy put them on television. Could the equities here be more apparent than the indisputable facts make them out to be? This, in the long reach of time, the president cannot turn upside down and inside out.

The president had said consistently before his invasion began that the objective was more political than military, that the real purpose of his action was to "liberate" the enemy's oppressed people and to win their hearts and minds. The people under the president's round-the-clock bombing raids did not seem to believe him. The death toll of innocent civilians killed by the president's bombs and missiles was enormous. Pictures of the bloody carnage appeared on televisions and in newspapers region-wide. The people of the region are now becoming hostile to their own governments for not doing more to assist a beleaguered sister state under attack by "foreign invaders."

Chapter Thirteen

Iraq

Of course this is about Iraq, but it needn't have been. So many disparate peoples across the world are joined by experience in their suspicions of American motives.

Among all the world's leaders, only President George W. Bush could accomplish the outcome likely to be in the offing, notwithstanding what happens on the battlefield. In one cruel and foolish gambit, the president has, in Egyptian president Hosni Mubarak's view, created "a hundred Osama bin Ladens," weakened moderate and "friendly" Arab governments, galvanized an infuriated Islamic world against the United States, and launched into legend, where time forgives all sins, Saddam Hussein, who will be remembered in lore only for his brave stand against the snorting American bull in Iraq's small nook of the global china shop. A dubious David against techno-Goliath, practicing asymmetric warfare—guerrilla tactics, fake surrenders, soldiers in mufti, suicide bombers—to offset the bullying techno-behemoth's advantages for just long enough to win the admiration even of those who have every good reason to detest him.

Allah be praised. Who would have believed that it would be George W. Bush who would provide the sixty-five-year-old Iraqi tyrant with a stage for his grand leave-taking to immortality? Who but this president could have made this Iraqi leader a candidate for canonization from Paris to Amman?

I am an American citizen in good standing. I intend to remain one. For all my troubles, American citizenship, if little more, remains my hard-won property. I pay my taxes. I obey the laws. I am not a Muslim. I am not an Arab. I belong, however, to that global multilingual society of dark hearts where kindred unifying memories fester—memories of ruthless maltreatment and unrespected promises, memories of American hypocrisy and American sponsorship of suffering.

I make no brief for Saddam Hussein. I am glad that he's been toppled from power. But I would have wished him to have been toppled by his own people, and not by a set of overweening foreign interlopers who would look on with crazed horror were such a crushing invasion force ever set so pitilessly and implacably upon *them* and *their* own defenseless citizenries.

I spent twenty-five years of my life fighting against the South African apartheid system that the United States underpinned for nearly a half century with loans, investments, weapons systems, and computer technology for the white minority dictatorship's budding nuclear weapons programs. Never, during our efforts, did I—or Nelson Mandela or Desmond Tutu or anyone else for that matter—counsel the U.S. government to invade South Africa militarily, not that, had we so counseled, it would have made the smallest difference in Washington's support for the Pretoria government. We wanted a changed South Africa, not a slaughtered South Africa. There were flesh-and-blood people living there. The majority of them were black—people my country appeared not to care about any more than it had cared about Nicaraguans under Somoza, Dominicans under Trujillo, Haitians under Duvalier, Chileans under Pinochet, Filipinos under Marcos, Zimbabweans under Smith, Mozambicans and Guineans and Angolans under Salazar, and, nearer in time and place to its current human rights insensitivity, Palestinians under Sharon.

It is this memory, this unremarked deep core *knowing* of pain, that joins all of the subjugated, all of the long-suffering browns of the world in a society of empathy for Iraq's pain, not Saddam Hussein's, but the Iraq of the greater whole, the ageless Iraq of biblical Babylon, the Iraq of cacophonous souks, the Iraq of mundane bustling routine, the Iraq of families and hope and love and pride, and the Iraq of small everyday everywhere life, and now, because of America, the Iraq of brutal sudden death, the Iraq of a child's open, lifeless, gray, dust-laden eyes, bombed-down hospitals, markets, and schools.

What, indeed, is the source of my leaving the country of my birth? Could it be that I, too, believed in science, only to learn that that science had failed me? That I had been duped—duped into believing that all of humankind shared, if little else, a common species? If I any longer believed such to be the case, I would choose, if I could so choose, to resign from that species, to reject its broad brackets as intolerably repugnant, rather than share even that small invented rubric of classification, that academic common ground of *species,* with the likes of George W. Bush, Donald Rumsfeld, Condoleezza Rice, Colin Powell, and all the unsettlingly toneless generals who've allowed their humanity to be trained out of them. For what species member, recognizable as such to me as mine, could put a hand to an implement that could—indeed, would, knowingly would—snuff life cruelly, brutally, violently, randomly from anonymous innocents. And afterward, on the afternoon of the morning of the red nights, go home for supper, to kiss the wife, play with the children, listen to Bach, walk playful, leaping dogs on a green, green lawn.

As for the two of them that are *ours,* I am all the more ashamed. But why should I be? Perhaps it is that no dissociation that I could manage would be complete enough to uncouple me totally from them in so racially conscious a society. How sorry and sad I am that they are black and, no doubt, proud of themselves, at the apex of their public careers. But they are killers, remote perhaps, but killers nonetheless, like all the others, but lower, more cowardly, than the ordinary street types who at least visit the scene of their crimes and accept the scene's risks.

I don't know why it is that I think Ms. Rice is not worth my thoughts, but Mr. Powell, somehow, is. Why would I expect more of him, an army general, trained to do just what he has done? A Ronald Reagan rectal success of a conscience-dead black man is how I see him in my utter helplessness to do anything for the people his bombs are killing around the clock in Baghdad. For a brief period he was the administration's lone multilateralist, only to be warned off his vestigial conscience by the president. Not only has he now joined in the crime, but he has done so gutlessly. To keep a *job*. To play Speer. To be what he has now become for eternity, for review out beyond the petty earthly, where the gods watch.

I guess, as well, that I am embarrassed by the perpetual and foolish surprise of my naive and disappointed expectation of Mr. Powell, somehow thinking stupidly that because he is black, he is going to *feel* something, a commonness of some sympathetic small joining, some perhaps silly notion that the barest faint *Maroon Blue Mountain* memory of slavery is wrapped tightly, but still reposes ever so faintly in his Jamaican genetic instruction.

But clearly nothing reposes there but an ambitious army general in mufti.

I have never killed anyone, attempted to kill anyone, or wished to kill anyone. In a transformed state of mind, I believe that I could kill, however, were I or my family placed in imminent danger, or were stripped of some human right so fundamental, so basic to my essential, consciously self-perceived humanity that my life would stand devoid of all spiritual worth, owing to that stripping. Then, I think, and even hope, that I could, under such circumstances, kill.

Even so, even in such reluctant self-defense, I would wish that for the taking of but a single human life that I would suffer some enduring anguish, notwithstanding the race or ethnicity or nationality or even the mitigating acts of my victim. To kill another human being is either to reduce, by that killing, one's *own* humanity, or to affirm by that killing a preexisting diminishment.

War, by its very nature, is an indiscriminate killer. Knowing this, responsible, secure, and prudent leaders take pains to make certain that war is the course taken last, and then only after every other possible course of legitimate self-defense has been fully exhausted. I cannot cease visualizing children being blown apart by exploding

American ordnance of such shatteringly concussive effect as to destroy their tender, guiltless minds, if not their small, half-formed bodies.

American soldiers, white and black, shot to death seven unarmed Iraqi women and children in a van that failed to stop at an American checkpoint. A dispute ensued over whether or not the soldiers had fired warning shots before loosing a fusillade of rounds into the crowded van. An American army spokesman said, perfunctorily, that the deaths of the unarmed women and children were "tragic," but proceeded apace to blame the tragedy on the Iraqi government, which had promised a defensive wave of suicide bombings.

An elderly conservative black lawyer in St. Kitts who has been in the past an unfailing fan of America, American tourism to the island, and all that that would, unhappily in my view, entail, said to me recently, as if by epiphany: "I have finally come to believe that white countries are different from everybody else in the world." He was appalled by what American soldiers, white and black, were doing in Iraq, but even more greatly saddened by the soldiers' apparent moral detachment from what they were doing. I thought about what he had said as I listened to the army spokesman blame the deaths of the women and children on the Iraqis themselves.

His remote and impassive demeanor of delivery amidst the grieving shrieks of the Iraqi victims of *American terror* had come to typify an American style of explication of the awful and the horrific. The demeanor, cool and flat, bore no relation to the scope of the tragedy inflicted. It was this observation that had caused my conservative *Ameriphile* friend to conclude that *white countries are different*. This is nonsense, of course, given all the madness about. But only white countries are capable of killing so many at one time.

I used to believe it was just the Germans whose souls were cauterized, but now I am not nearly so sure of that. After all, a large majority of the German people believed that they were right when their armies rolled into Czechoslovakia and Poland. As hard as it may be to believe, the American people may possibly have made themselves believe that the regime of Saddam Hussein (who can't put a plane in the air) represents a real and immediate threat to

American freedoms, but I don't for a minute believe this. It could well be, however, that one gets the unexamined result of a "Goebbels Cocktail" when one mixes the self-administered *mantra lie* into the deep vat of American arrogance, and then peppers the powerful stew with ample amounts of racial prejudice.

American generals and their soldiers, I am convinced, actually *believe* they are right, even as they invade someone else's country, rumbling over the terrain in caravans of lethal armor, spread-eagling, handcuffing, body-searching antiquity's locals, flying their murderous sorties, sometimes two thousand a day, bombing all night, every night, bombing not just strategic targets, but a children's hospital and markets and, for some improbable reason, the Iraqi Olympic Games headquarters building.

Still, they blame the victims. It is this peculiar material form of popular American insanity that frightens me. They just don't get it, these chillingly one-dimensional, opaque Americans. They don't get any of what the rest of the world gets easily enough, except their English and Australian blood-mates. You beseech them.

Please read this twice and slowly. There is *no* acceptable justification for killing civilians or soldiers or anybody else when you are *invading their* country. It is *their* country and your reasons for assaulting it are globally assessed as specious. A regime change your president promises with his silly little boy smile. Unilaterally. Eight thousand miles from his doorstep. What nerve. What gall. Small wonder you are distrusted so. Go home, for God's sake. Let some heaven-sent wind of unfamiliar humility fill your tacking sails and blow you there before you wreck the community of nations and its undervalued house of assembly, the United Nations.

Opinion polls in America rose with the tide of our boys' victories in Iraq. Even Massachusetts (the only state in a long-ago presidential election to give its electoral votes to the liberal Democrat, George McGovern) polled its citizens in support of the Anglo-American invasion by a majority of 64 percent. Former president Clinton said that now that America was committed to the war, there could be no question of our support for it. The entire Democratic Party has gone to the ground, its frightened leaders peeking out mutely from crouching positions behind the bunkers of their political futures. They are afraid of some irrational and soulless force that they can feel but cannot see. Nothing seems to deflect it from its course, not even the 108,000 jobs lost this month from an economy sagging toward recession.

On April 5, 2002, a journalist named Kate Zernike wrote in *The New York Times*:

> At the University of Wisconsin at Madison, awash in antiwar protests in the Vietnam era, a columnist for a student newspaper took a professor to task for canceling classes to protest the war in Iraq, saying the university should reprimand her and refund tuitions for the missed periods.
>
> Irvine Valley College in Southern California sent faculty members a memo that warned them not to discuss the war unless it was specifically related to the course material. When professors cried censorship, the administration explained that the requests had come from students.
>
> Here at Amherst College, many students were vocally annoyed this semester when forty professors paraded into the dining hall with antiwar signs. One student confronted a protesting professor and shoved him. Some students here accuse professors of behaving inappropriately, of not knowing their place.

The bungalow peasants are not alone. The ranks of the righteous have lost the *students,* and even at the "better" schools. The androids are winning and nothing seems to matter. That the original justification for the two-hundred-billion-dollar war has dissipated like a vapor, does not matter. That our soldiers are killing innocent civilians, does not matter. That much of the civilized world despises us with much the same fear-driven passion it had despised the Germans with during their *early-Hitler-late-democracy* phase of moral rot, does not matter. Nothing matters. Not even the plans being laid at the White House to install as Iraq's new leader the Iraqi exile who was said to have put the president up to all of this in the first place.

No. Nothing matters. The monster, deaf, dumb, and blind, is loose in the land.

God help us. I feel in the dark for the backstop behind me. It is no longer where it had been. I reach further and cannot find it. I had made certain assumptions and begun to rest too comfortably against them. Muslims are arrested in America and held without charge in solitary confinement indefinitely. The androids wear but two visages, angry and pleased, nothing betwixt. All else is suspicious.

What is next? What where? What they? What us? What *me*?

No one bothered to ask anymore whether or not what the president and his army were doing was *right*. This central and most important question had become irrelevant.

The retired generals wanted to make all this look hard to cover our guys who are just busting up the place, busting up everything.

But this ain't hard. This ain't even a little hard. Teach 'em a goddamn lesson, you know. Teach 'em to fuck with America, you know.

Christ, does anyone remember this was supposed to have been about disarmament?

Man, this ain't about no disarmament. This ain't even about just conquering and capturing the bastards. This is about finding and killing, not capturing, not prosecuting, but killing Saddam Hussein, killing him, killing his sons, and killing all their helpers dead, dead, dead.

In Washington, Donald Rumsfeld, the slaughter's architect who was thought to have been less capable of pathos than even Robert McNamara, suffers as well. Rumsfeld (class of '54) has weathered the removal of his picture from a wall of honor at the Princeton University, not by decision of the school's fathers, however, but rather because the celebrated alumnus's portrait had been damaged by an overzealous, yet-to-be-identified student antiwar protestor.

Now Rumsfeld, once pictured shaking hands with Saddam Hussein *after* the Iraqi president had gassed his own people, will run the Iraq he has only just destroyed out of his Pentagon office, while letting multibillion-dollar contracts be awarded to the administration's corporate cronies to repair the damage he has wrought.

More powerful than Nazi Germany could ever have dreamt of becoming, the United States is now the unrivaled ruler of the world and militarily overwhelming enough to unveil before a stunned family of nations a new concept of global hegemonic leadership, to wit: *preventive war,* pursuant to which, America alone at the pinnacle of power awards *itself* the "right" to attack *any* country that America deems a "potential threat."

How little Americans appear to realize what all this means. How little we appear to have noticed the sea change in our country's behavior. Our undeclared but headlong abandonment of democracy's fundamental underlying values. Ironically, it is likely to have been noticed from the outside first. By the United Nations Security Council ambassadors whose home telephones we had bugged in the failed effort to win a use-of-force resolution. Cameroon. Chile. Others. By the foreign news organizations whose war they described to their nationals was diametrically different from the war our news organizations described to ours. By the Iraqis, whose decapitated children's terrible deaths they grieved, but Americans never saw. By a bystanding world, from whose teeming streets billions watch, wary, angry, helpless—but not quite. By an increasingly lessening number of Americans, democracy's beleaguered, misunderstood, now sheltering patriots. By Ahmad Chalabi, the crown prince of the Pentagon, the delegated would-be ruler, the ground-boss apparent, today's Diem, tomorrow's Shah, the fifty-eight-year-old banker favored by Rumsfeld to figurehead the new American Baghdad oil show, the ambitious Iraqi who speaks English with an American accent and drags home behind him the baggage of a forty-five-year exile. Ah, yes. If Rumsfeld has his way, this would be the jowly, erstwhile Iraqi that he would situate upon the throne while espousing for all who would listen the absurd oxymoron of top-down democracy.

How must it feel to drink the heady water, to postulate any wild and dangerous notion to sullen capitulation abroad and contagiously febrile obedience at home? How must it feel to the wealthy ambitious and hungry *Captains of America* who have arrived at last to unopposed dizzying power after a lifetime of relentless climbing, and surveying from the summit of that unprecedented power the sea upon sea of the camouflaged, half-educated poor, standing ramrod-straight at the duty-shaped ready, like proper zombies, to march under *any* order against other, and even poorer half-educated zombies described to them flimsily by their masters as hostile? How must it feel to *kill* those for whom you harbor no personal animus, those you do not know, can never know, will never know? Those who are poor and powerless like *you,* taking orders like *you,* taking them on small information like *you*? Killing senselessly like *you.* Dying like *you,* but on their own land, on their own soil? How does it feel to be so young, with so little past and so much future, and to risk it *all* at the bidding of a president who would not do then that which he has ordered you to do now? How does it feel to be poor and brave and selfless in service to the rich and cowardly and self-seeking?

"How does it feel? How does it feel?" Column right! Column left! To the rear, march! Dress right! Look sharp! Stay in line! How does it feel? What you mean, how does . . .

It's not that the poor are set upon each other, killing, maiming, for nothing. There are reasons, all right. But those who are called upon to kill and die will never know them.

Societies are fragile fabrics of habit. Owing to the war, Iraqi society will not work again for many years.

Their nations' names are less important for our real understanding than the European stem culture that had shaped their ancestors' social values. They were always going or coming somewhere, but unlike the progeny of many cultures, in the Europeans' case, the travel was usually rationalized by one form or another of wholly self-interested conquest: religious, cultural, military, material, or simply megalomaniacal.

Columbus sought riches and glory for himself and Spain. Owing only to the achievement of these particular purposes, he is celebrated today throughout the white world unlike any other European explorer, including those who actually sighted the Americas, and one, Leif Eriksson, who constructed a settlement on the North American continent hundreds of years before Columbus mistook the Bahamas for Japan.

Beginning with that fateful, world-changing October morning in 1492, Europe would become the planet-wide Great Kahn, but with a euphemizing cover story the brutal, unhypocritical Kahn would never have felt constrained to invent. Columbus did not tell the Taino that he had come to take their lands, their wealth, their bodies, their way of life and, lastly, their very lives from them. In fact, he affected, if impatiently, the diplomatic air of charitable purpose. He had come to do Europe's proverbial ostensible good, as the Pilgrims would later do for the Native American, as the British and French would do for the Carib, as Portuguese rain-forest kidnappers would do for the Wolof, as King Leopold would do for the Congolese, as the white world would do generally for a world that they, for all intents and purposes, would come to claim as theirs, to do with as they pleased. Indeed the list of their victims would include countless poor and ignorant conscripts and volunteers from among their own ranks, puffed up with national pride, willing to die in battles whose real purposes they could have no way of understanding.

In Iraq, President Bush sacrificed American and Iraqi lives to three ostensible objectives: to wage war against Al Qaeda, to destroy Iraq's "weapons of mass destruction," and to spare the Iraqi people from further suffering at the hand of Saddam Hussein. No Iraqi connection to Al Qaeda has ever been convincingly demonstrated. No weapons of mass destruction have been found. And never in America's history has the country gone to war only to relieve the suffering of a people not its own. In keeping with the old values of Columbus, its polestar cultural forebear, the United States never goes to war unless some usually undisclosed narrowly American interest of the privileged is to be served.

This well-veiled inclination toward a particularized selfishness is of a piece with America's European cultural roots. The Atlantic slave trade, for instance, should not be remembered only as a long-standing isolated epoch of race-based human bondage. More thought-fully it should be seen as an event in a chain of events, a discrete and brutal outcome of a European cultural continuum that since time immemorial has prepared its people to ruthlessly exploit others under the color of law and high language.

The broad failure of white societies to ask themselves not just what wrong they have done, but more searchingly, *why* they continue to do them, allows a permanent life for the central flaw at these societies' moral core. The contemporary lie veils the active event, even from the white world's own larger democratic publics.

The facts and dates of the lamentable abuses change, but the basic behavior remains more or less constant, a behavior characterized by insatiable material acquisitiveness and well-rationalized brutality. This is the saddening imprint of white culture upon the world, stretching in its reach from the time before Columbus up until the United States invaded Iraq in the spring of 2003.

The instant question of importance is not what the United States has done in Iraq. That should be plain enough to see. But *why* did America invade in the first place? No one even faintly acquainted with American foreign policy believes that the invasion was undertaken to relieve human suffering. After rising to power in Indonesia in 1966, President Suharto slaughtered five hundred thousand of his own people. This did not disturb America's affection for the new Indonesian dictator. Much of Liberia's current instability can be ascribed to Ronald Reagan, who as president during the 1980s, provided five hundred million dollars in U.S. assistance to Sgt. Samuel K. Doe, *after* Doe had lined up officials of the democratic government he had overthrown and shot them to death on a beach outside Monrovia. Indeed, the United States had been well disposed toward Saddam Hussein *after* he was shown to have gassed his own people.

No, it is not possible that the United States invaded Iraq for humanitarian reasons.

But why, then?

We've only to connect the dots from Columbus to the present

to discover the likely answer. The lines between the dots will depict once again the simple, open, age-old face of Western material greed.

Bill Moyers reported in July 2003 on his PBS public affairs program that in response to a court case brought by the Washington-based Judicial Watch following Vice President Dick Cheney's adamant refusal to reveal the details of high-level meetings between Bush administration officials and U.S. energy sector corporate executives, the court ordered the release of the meetings' documents, which reveal, in part, the following:

Months before September 11 and more than a year before the U.S. invasion of Iraq, Vice President Cheney met with U.S. energy company executives (1) to discuss and study a map of Iraq, focusing on oil deposits and opportunities; (2) to discuss the division of Iraq into strategic areas; and (3) to identify international oil companies that would be invited to "partake" of Iraq's oil possibilities.

Without success, the vice president fought tooth and nail to keep the details of the meetings secret.

At this moment, fifty-nine wars are being fought around the world, at a human cost of forty thousand lives a month. The largest of these wars has been initiated by the United States against Iraq. All of the wars involve, almost exclusively, the poor killing the poor for the benefit of the privileged. In the United States, where the army is 35 percent African-American, the president has cut twenty-seven billion dollars from the disabled veterans fund and planned payments many times that amount to the accounts of the wealthy noncombatants who salivate to rebuild a devastated Iraq.

The American army is all volunteer now, which means it is poorer, blacker, and browner than ever in the nation's history. It is an army of miseducated whites and misled blacks trained into hostility against cultural and racial near-kin. Overall, the army is less well-educated than ever, and for that reason, infinitely more manageable and less representationally democratic. Put starkly, the most privileged in our society recruit with patriotic camp verse the most menial and servile of our ranks to perform for the privileged the menial and servile work of state killing. Aristotle put it squarely: "If there is menial and servile work to be done, there must be menial and servile people to do it." This obtains so aptly in war, with all the risks borne by the menial and servile, and all the benefits enjoyed by the privileged who watch the carnage from afar, while benefiting commensurately from each exploded shell, each burning oil well, each vaporized building. Let's face up to it honestly: The U.S. army is a mercenary force that looks little like the population it presumes to kill for. The ranks of the army comprise American society's most voiceless, while those Americans with the juice to influence the course of American public policy remain safely ensconced at home, largely quiet, with little or nothing personally at risk. A cherry arrangement for the war-makers and profiteers, indeed. No inherent checks and balances here at all. They've all been rather deliberately winnowed out. These are not circumstances of accident.

And now the plunder of one of antiquity's richest troves. The National Museum of Iraq has been ransacked of priceless artifacts that date from the country's Sumerian, Babylonian, and Assyrian periods. The American troops have been guarding the oil fields and not Iraq's cultural heritage. The robbery appears to have been well planned and undertaken by people with an eye both for opportunity and value. The treasures have already begun showing up in Paris. The Iraqi people's memory of their ancient forbears had been stored in the museum that the vanquished government opened little more than a year before. Many of the museum's precious relics have now become casualties of an invasion undertaken by forces that cared more about oil than archeology, that guarded an empty British embassy but not a hospital filled with Iraqi sick and wounded.

On the day that the robbery was discovered in Baghdad, the Bechtel Corporation, with former Republican secretary of state George Shultz aboard, was awarded a six-hundred-and-eighty-million-dollar, eighteen-month contract by the Bush administration to do reconstruction work in Iraq.

*   *   *

There are no checks anymore on American power, either from within or from without; from above or from below. Syria may well be next in line. This likely planned for before the invasion of Iraq. Plans laid then, as well, for, let's say, Iran. Roll out the prepackaged, time-release justifications and Americans will buy them. Sure as shootin'. Democracies don't function with a self-checking balance of authority when their citizens don't.

The authors of the American Constitution understood well enough that no single person or assemblage of persons could be trusted with power uncircumscribed by laws. Thus the Constitution's framers wrote a document that tacitly acknowledged and protected them and us from their own confessed vulnerability to the inevitable toxicity of unlimited authority. They then lifted the document well above themselves and made of it a text of enduring reverence.

One could apply the wisdom of the framers to the modern relationship between the United States and the world at large. We cannot make the rules *by* ourselves and apply them to everyone *but* ourselves. That is virtually what we have done in Iraq, and much of the world hates us for that alone. Nothing can be good for Americans and bad for the rest of the world at the same time. We may well learn this lesson the hard way, and our leaders will have to accept responsibility for their reckless imprudence. No public can be blamed wholly for the extremes to which their leaders incite them, leaders who have information that their publics do not have, leaders who all too self-servingly rev up the engines of their publics' dormant provincial bigotries.

I believe that the United States has committed a colossal long-term wrong with the military invasion of Iraq, a wrong that should have been alarmingly apparent to the American public. Can virtually an entire public be delusional? Or amoral? Or somehow bereft of human empathy? I struggle to explain this disconnect to myself, to reconcile the absurdity of our course with the moral reason we have so clearly taken leave of. I struggle to do this, to understand this, so that I can feel *safe* from public tyranny *in* America. For how could anyone not delusional or amoral or bereft of empathy justify an action tantamount to killing an ant in its own habitat with a nuclear-tipped missile? And my concern is not merely intellectual. Were it so, I might have been able to manage calmer language. I am *afraid*. I am afraid for the world and for myself, afraid of my own country. For if *they* could do so patently wrongful a thing and sell it to themselves so convincingly as *right,* they could do anything—to anybody, anywhere. Lawlessness from the world's ultimate power is imminently more dangerous to the world than the small despotism of a regional petty tyrant. How could the American public miss so plain a point? Or could that public be so woefully misinformed as to have no independent frame of reference by which to measure and evaluate the actions of its government? Can you not, indeed, quarantine *any* public or sub-public and sell it virtually *anything,* from visions of a Thousand-Year Reich in Germany to mass suicide in Jonestown, Guyana? Cannot a public's leaders provide its subjects, even in a democracy, so lightless a space within which to think as to shut down thinking altogether?

Is it that I see the world somewhat differently from the mainstream American public because my career work in international affairs has afforded me broader vistas? I think. I haven't always been able to think outside of the proverbial box, however.

Forty years ago, when I was twenty-two and on orders to go to Vietnam, I would have gone, although I didn't *want* to go, but not because I understood the wrongfulness of America's participation in a civil war nine thousand miles from its shores, attacking people who hadn't attacked America. As it was, I was taken off orders because my date of discharge was too near to send me all the way to Vietnam, only to return in a month or so. Thus, I understand well enough now that publics follow irresponsible leadership oftener than not for no other reason than an inadequacy of accurate information. Hence, the need to raise law above the heads of nations, and especially those that are relatively more powerful. For, when no common consensus standard of law is raised above the world *by all* for blind application *to all,* the condition that results lowers itself to the untrammeled behavior of the most powerful. In effect, might becomes right, but only because might says that it is. This will result ultimately in chaos and the collapse of an international system that depends in essential part on a modicum of demonstrated comity and cooperation.

In 1932, a relatively wealthy and well-educated public democratically elected Adolf Hitler as chancellor of an industrialized Germany still licking its wounds from the humiliation of Versailles. The new chancellor did not tell the German people all that he had in mind for Germany and the world. That would come later, episode by accommodated episode. The new German leader, early on, won high notice at home, and in important quarters across Europe. The German industrial sector liked what Hitler was doing for a recovering *Fatherland*. The general German public glowed under Hitler's leadership with resuscitated pride in their country, and in its renewed military unilateralism as well.

The German people were people like any other people anywhere else in the world. Some were estimable. Others were not. From their ranks had come over the centuries many of the world's great philosophers, scientists, composers, and, indeed, the theologian credited with sparking the Protestant Reformation.

Berlin was widely considered to be one of the world's great cities, cosmopolitan and enchantingly beautiful. The German general public, not unlike other general publics, could not be blamed for falling victim to the blandishments of its inspirational new leader even as the new leader began to expand upon his original writ of largely uncircumscribed powers. The German people were once again proud of themselves, and proud, as well, of Adolf Hitler, the instrument of their patriotic rally.

At least a portion of their resurgent pride was sourced in the very powers that Hitler was busy gathering for himself. After all, this was Germany, and Germany would show the world.

Weak though the Weimar Republic may have been, Germany, for a short time at least, had been a big and complex industrialized democracy, and, as is necessarily the case with all large, advanced states, there was little in the way of intimacy between the governors and the governed. The German people, remote socially from the high councils of power, viewed and listened to their leaders largely through their country's national media organs. They had little idea before it had become far too late that they had elected a madman. For, indeed, how are citizens in any democracy anywhere to know, in time to avert disaster, whether or not the leaders they have elected are, for whatever reason, incapable of distinguishing the desired directly proportional relationship between power and caution in the prudent use of either? The wise rule being: The greater the power, the greater the caution employed in power's exercise.

I thought of this as I watched American bombs rain down on a helpless Baghdad. I thought less with language than with a tumescent sadness. Sadness for a world in which boys of small judgment had gripped fast the reigns of unprecedented power.

The night sky flashed a purplish, blood-stroked red before the massive bomb's report shook the space above the city, rendering fresh, ironic resonance to an old Arab proverb: *Death is the midnight runner*. Well-equipped American soldiers watched the carnage from a safe distance through night goggles that the Syrians had been warned by the Americans against providing to the night-blind Iraqis.

Other than a name here and there, nothing ever changes, or so it would seem. "There had never been an independent Iraq. . . . Now she (the Englishwoman, Gertrude Bell) was not only dividing a country; she was devising its shape and determining its composition: who would lead it, how it would be governed . . . Imperialist and Orientalist both, she was creating an asset for England, constructing an entity for the Arabs. The power was intoxicating, and at the beginning of December 1918, she wrote home: 'I feel at this time like the Creator about the middle of the week. He must have wondered what it was going to be like, as I do.' " —(*Desert Queen*, Janet Wallach)

PART THREE

THE INNOCENCE
OF GUILTLESS
SMALL PLACES

Chapter Fourteen

Hubris

April 22, 2003
US Draws Up Plan to Bomb
North Korea's Nuclear Plant

Sydney (AFP)—The Pentagon has produced detailed plans to bomb North Korea's nuclear plant at Yong-byon if the Stalinist state goes ahead with reprocessing of spent nuclear fuel rods, an Australian report said.

Citing "well-informed sources close to US thinking," the Australian newspaper said the plan also included a US strike against North Korean heavy artillery in the hills above the border with South Korea.

The artillery directly threatens Seoul as well as US troops stationed south of the Demilitarized Zone.

The Pentagon hardliners said to be behind the plan reportedly believe the precision strikes envisaged in it would not lead to North Korea initiating a general war it would be certain to lose.

This is because Washington would inform Pyongyang that the bombing was not aimed at destroying the regime of Kim Jong-il, but merely at destroying its nuclear weapons capacity.

The Australian report coincides with reports from Washington of an alternative US plan which envisages the United States teaming up with China to press for the removal of North Korea's leadership.

The second plan, contained in a classified memo reportedly circulated by Defense Secretary Donald Rumsfeld, argues that Washington's goal should be the collapse of Kim Jong-il's regime. . . .

April 23. Following large demonstrations in Iraq in which Shiites in one location and Sunnis in another demanded that American forces leave Iraq, White House Press Secretary Ari Fleischer said in Washington: "We've made clear to Iran that we would oppose any outside organization's interference in Iraq." This is exactly what the man said. With a straight face. Without the barest hint of irony. Seeing nothing odd or illogical in what he had said to a room of American journalists who saw nothing strange or even comical about the statement. America has never been more dangerous to the world than now. Wounded lion, judgment warped by anger, no longer killing for food alone, blind with the cool, organized rage of the European of the species, serving notice now to the entire planet, shedding all pretense, dispensing with all of its tribe's thin shibboleths about justice and fairness and other such bullshit that great powers talk when great powers aren't angry.

White folks have always been rather flamboyantly invisible to themselves, but never before like now.

Decades before a black army unit, the 369th infantry (or Harlem Hellfighters), bested the Germans in World War I while becoming the first U.S. unit to reach the Rhine River, Frederick Law Olmsted dreamed of civilizing a teeming, fractious New York by building in the center of Manhattan a huge park in which the city's warring social classes could mingle and find, quite literally, common ground. African-Americans, however, were excluded *en masse* from the construction crew of this massive metaphor so as not to offend the Irish. While stories like this would surprise no nineteenth-, twentieth- or twenty-first-century African-American, white folk would likely respond, in so many words, with a slightly bemused, "But what's your point?" The point is they never seem to see what they're doing to people until the hue and cry is loud enough to melt an iceberg. Even then, the wrongdoing, no matter how egregious, never *de-*

stroys a reputation but falls merely into the *Oh, that* bin of back-store history forever.

In high school, I had a French teacher, black of course, who thought it useful to teach a little history along with the language. On one such occasion, she talked about Cornwallis's surrender of his army at Yorktown in 1781 to the combined American and French armies of George Washington and Comte de Rochambeau, the French general. The teacher made of Rochambeau's name an exquisite sound, pronouncing the first syllable more *Wo* than *Ro*, with the *w* followed by a wisp of an *r*. "General Wroshambo," as it slipped ever so easily off her tongue. She told us what our American history textbook had told her. Which was not a lot, certainly not that while soldiering for Napoleon Bonaparte against Toussaint-Loverture's soon-to-be successful slave revolt in Haiti, George Washington's valued colleague had committed monstrous atrocities against Haiti's blacks, once shooting down in a town square the wives of a hundred or so watching black freedom-seekers before slaughtering all of the husbands in a bloody heap themselves.

None if this figured against Rochambeau's standing in the only world he really cared about. Or Frederick Law Olmstead's. Or Robert E. Lee's. Or John Wayne's. Or the standing of any other major white figure who had, in an otherwise distinguished career, at one time or another, rounded brutally on one or more of some other race or religion or *different* somebody elses. You see, the fact is, to the industrialized white societies of the world, *we* don't count. The Iraqis don't count. The Palestinians don't count. Nelson Mandela doesn't count. Nobody counts unless you do what you are told to do (General Powell, King Abdullah . . .) and then you still don't count. Just try to change the course of their conquest events, the hegemony stuff. You'll see.

Blacks, somehow, have an intrinsic understanding of this, as if it were hammered onto the template of their common social experience in America. Three out of five blacks oppose the war in Iraq, while only one out of five whites opposes the war. Blacks, however, are almost nowhere to be found in the ranks of American antiwar demonstrations. Why the discrepancy? Oh *we* know. Know down deep. Know how to husband our stores and shelter our worn flints, how to use our weathered energy. Know that whites don't give a shit what we think. Never did. Never will.

The networks canvassed all of Europe and much of Asia on the war. Who asked the Africans? Who asked the Caribbeans? Nobody, that's who. We black people—Africans, Caribbeans, Afro-Brazilians, African-Americans—should see an opportunity in this to talk *to* ourselves *about* ourselves, to set an unwatched course for an unwatched people of unimportant regard to the angry white lion. And navigate the world from the inside out and not the other way around.

But the lion overlooks little.

The village of Sandy Point lies just ten miles to the west along the main island road from my house. The American soldiers were said to have come there to build a day-care center for the working parents of the village. I saw the two white soldiers standing rock-still on a grassy embankment above my passing car. They wore battle fatigues with a swampy camouflage pattern. They were standing above a curve in the road, looking impassively across it and out toward the placid clear waters of the Caribbean Sea. Both held themselves erect as if they were performing some duty that required stillness. Their soft caps were raked forward, shading their eyes. The soldier on the right stood like an "A" frame with his hands clasped behind him. The other soldier's hands were in front of him and holding diagonally and fast to his chest a very large assault weapon.

Chapter Fifteen

Frauds

Would the war in Iraq have been worth a single life, if that single life were mine?

Ask yourself this question. Answer it, honestly. Just to yourself. Silently.

Before anyone supports war for others, against others, one should ask one's self this question. To measure for one's self the real value of conviction, one must know not whether one is prepared to sacrifice another life's, but whether one is prepared to sacrifice one's *own*. For if nothing else is equal in this world, life, the one precious, irreplaceable—if temporary—window onto its all and everything, is. Certainly one can draw no morally defensible distinction between the value of one life against that of the next. With respect to the simple all-valuable possession of *life* itself, if in nothing else, the Muslim, the Christian, the woman, the man, the soldier, the civilian, the president, and the peasant are equal.

So there the question poses itself again. Would the war in Iraq, in which thousands lost the ultimate everything, have been worth a single life *if* that single life were yours? Mr. President? Secretary Rumsfeld? Secretary Powell? Reverend Robertson? Anyone? Please.

For if the answer conveyed, in but a synapse's involuntary leap, is *no,* and you supported the war, or worse, made it happen for those who died on both sides, then you are the most reprehensible of moral frauds.

Was, indeed, the war absolutely *necessary* and morally *right* as seen against the question raised above? And in a country where citizens declaim their freedoms so ostentatiously, why have such questions, so obvious and central to how we as Americans choose to see ourselves, not been raised and discoursed thoroughly in the various public councils arranged for such? The very failure to do so is disquieting enough to warrant a detailed answer of its own.

The Italian dictator, Benito Mussolini, defined Italy's World War II–era fascism as a merger between the state and business interests. The United States is far from a fascist state, but it does seem increasingly to have taken on some of fascism's more worrying characteristics, one, for example, being the Mussolini-like *marriage* between the state and the imbedded corporate media's coverage of the state's war against Iraq. As a consequence, neither did the administration that prosecuted the war raise these uncomfortable questions, nor did the American news media, which saw its all too literally embedded corporate self reduced to the ignominious role of virtual state collaborator. The American people, in the discharge of their democratic responsibility to debate their government's policies, needed a searching, open, and independent news industry to inform them. The American people did not get this, and hence, crazed with induced war fever, asked themselves few questions about the moral or even geopolitical appropriateness of the administration's course.

There have been propositions of war for which large numbers of Americans, even noncombatant Americans could honestly answer *yes* to the question of their willingness to surrender their own lives in an authentic defense of an authentically threatened freedom. World War II would be such an example. In the short trip from the head to the heart, I think we all know—those who supported the war and those who did not—that the war against Iraq was not such a war. Thus, we have sullied before the world our own moral measure of ourselves. For if we have been afraid to ask questions of ourselves for fear of the answers, we have left ourselves only to free-fall into the moral wasteland of the scoundrel's last refuge: *If we win we are right. If we lose, or even if we suffer great losses in stalemate, we will have been wrong.* Of course, whether the war was right or necessary or worth a single life has nothing at all to do with whether we won or lost.

The trouble is that Americans were never presented the chance to discuss the ethics of their country's behavior, or even to imagine a need for such a discussion. Most of us live our daily lives trapped in a maze of the numbing mundane, where all that we can see in common from our walled-up, unequal vantage points is a flag fluttering high above and a television tube flickering values and *news* in a darkened windowless corridor. Thinking requires a training of the imagination that few of us have the time or the natural inclination to cultivate. In order to think about a world that we cannot see, we need to have that world described to us so that we can understand how to engage it. We need to view with constructive curiosity its palette of cultures, languages, religions, social institutions. We need to know the stories of peoples who didn't look like us, think like us, dress like us, work like us, worship like us, or do much of anything else like us. We need to learn, learn hard, that there is no *better*, no *worse*, but only *different*, wonderfully, stimulatingly, equally *different*, to be treasured, protected, profited from. We need to see the humanity of that strange and distant world as indistinguishable from our own.

The lowest point in the war came for me with a deafening kaleidoscopic explosion that fired red the midnight Baghdad sky and fountained in slow-motion arcs massive slabs of concrete and steel rod upon anyone who'd happened with mortal bad luck into its wide radius. The American anchorman watching the bomb explosion live said with scarcely suppressed joy, "God, did you see that?" hoping without hoping that the question was rhetorical.

Then there was the business about the five-thousand-year-old artifacts stolen from the museum the Americans hadn't troubled to guard. Two hundred thousand pieces. Think for a moment about how Americans would feel were somebody to make off with the Liberty Bell, the Constitution, and the Declaration of Independence, mere infants in an ancient world of ageless treasures.

You see, people need buildings, but buildings, when destroyed, are virtually always replaceable. The furnishings of a people's history, however, are not. All people *need* history, a story, a memory, that gives them past and future, that raises theirs from brief unremarkable, otherwise meaningless lives to indispensable links in the long chain of culture, its living bearers ever so exquisitely able to connect in their tribal consciousness the two ends of time. From memory comes, in a symmetrical arc, foresight. The length of the former governs the reach of the latter. Memory provides us the rich fuel of self-esteem. Foresight, borne of memory, provides us direction and a purpose for living. No worse crime can be committed against any people than to strip from them their memory of themselves. This is far and away the most egregious particular in the long bill against slavery, the long-running culture-destructive crime from which black people have yet to recover anywhere in the world.

In April, The Learning Channel aired *Moses and the Exodus*. After exhaustive archeological investigations, no trace of settlement can be found in the region of Egypt where the Bible tells that Jews settled for forty years after being led out of bondage by Moses. Was the story of the Jewish Exodus then a fabrication? The documentary's narrator suggested that this was entirely possible and that leaders of ancient Israel may have invented the story "in order to give the Jewish people a sense of special history." We shall never *know,* and, perhaps, there is no need to know so long as the people who require the story's psychic sustenance *believe* it to be true.

Black people have well-documented and equally restorative stories from ancient Africa, but virtually all historical accounts of Africa's ancient greatness were stripped during slavery from our memory banks and thus from our everyday religious and social rituals. Modern black people miss badly that which they have no awareness of ever having, a rich five-thousand-year story of themselves. Slavery has left us without a matrix of memory in which to celebrate ourselves, form ambitions for our living, or even see with any expansiveness our future.

From Columbus forward, I know of no sustained contact with Western whites that black and brown peoples and their cultures have survived undevastated, anywhere. From the northernmost point in North America to the bottom of South America, western whites have over time undermined every indigenous culture that they have encountered, with disturbing contemporary social consequences.

From Inca to Inuit, from African to Aborigine, little else do the world's far-flung darker peoples have in common beyond a shared victimhood at the hands of Western whites.

This is the conjoining of sufferings mortared with sympathy, the *circle of browns,* that joins African-American in some otherwise unfathomable sympathy with the people of Iraq. An old Iraqi woman under a black chador screams her lament: "We have our pride," and black Americans *know* her to be a familiar stranger in the world of the unheard.

The mere contact with whites invariably in one place or another has produced for *us* all one plague or another: slavery, colonialism, plunder, conquest, massacre, economic globalization, culture transplantation. I can hear the grieving of my African-American forbears in the plaintive music of Australia's Aboriginal and first people. I can feel the anger of the Congolese whose priceless art treasures rest stolen still in a museum outside Brussels. I can sense even now the lingering humiliation of the Hawaiian people whose last monarch, Queen Lili'uokalani, was overthrown with the help of U.S. Marines and forced to surrender her kingdom to the United States in 1893.

In an interview on November 18, 2002, with John Kampfner of the *New Statesman,* British foreign minister Jack Straw confesses a good measure of British responsibility in the nonwhite world for bollixing and stealing:

> . . . . India, Pakistan—we made some quite serious mistakes. We were complacent with what happened in Kashmir, the boundaries weren't published until two days after independence. Bad story for us, the consequences are still there. Afghanistan—where we played less than a glorious role over a century and a half. . . . There's hardly a country—the odd lines for Iraq's borders were drawn by Brits. The Balfour Declaration and the contradictory assurances which were being given to Palestinians in private at the same time as they were

being given to the Israelis—again an interesting history
for us but not an entirely honorable one. . . . However,
when any Zimbabwean, any African, says to me land is
a key issue . . . the early [European] colonizers were all
about taking land.

It has never failed to hold true. Western whites, once well inside
the place of another's different, less pugnacious, more welcoming
culture, destroy it, root and branch. For inexplicable reasons, they
are seemingly constrained by some aberrant force of nature to dis-
parage all culture, all history, all religion, all memory, all faces, all
life not theirs. They simply cannot come—their soldiers, their preach-
ers, their teachers, their investors, their nobodies—without taking.
The *circle of the browns,* for all of this, had been formed not by
those within the circle, but by those who were not.

I saw in *The New York Times* a picture of Defense Secretary
Rumsfeld signing his name on the white Arabic lettering of a Baghdad street sign. He did this before cameras, surrounded by American soldiers. The powerful manager of America's crushing war
against Iraq had arrived like a rock star in its conquered capital to
signal a crassly banal and senselessly gratuitous final humiliation
with the defacement of a street sign while producing with a flourish of his pen a new anti-American terrorist for each letter in his
name. Was this his intent? An intent to insult *all* Iraqis? To boil
their blood? To ridicule them in their ancient home, see them seeing
him, amongst his lethal men, encircled by a smoking city of
seething eyes, smiling for his smiling men, oblivious? Was this
his intent? Were they, the conquered, owing only to their exotic
swarthiness, fixed for him well beneath any thoughtful conscious
regard? Whatever the case, the gesture was white-Western-old and
territorial—reminiscent of Columbus jangling onto the Taino's beach
and swearing unintelligible oaths to distant monarchs of their New
World possessions.

On May 6, U.S. Senator Robert C. Byrd of West Virginia addressed the Senate on the matter of the president's remarks to the
nation marking the end of the war in Iraq:

As I watched the president's fighter jet swoop down onto the deck of the aircraft carrier *Abraham Lincoln,* I could not help but contrast the reported simple dignity of President Lincoln at Gettysburg with the flamboyant showmanship of President Bush aboard the USS *Abraham Lincoln.*

President Bush's address to the American people announcing combat victory in Iraq deserved to be marked with solemnity, not extravagance; with gratitude to God, not self-congratulatory gestures. American blood has been shed on foreign soil in defense of the president's policies. This is not some made-for-TV backdrop for a campaign commercial. This is real life, and real lives have been lost. To me, it is an affront to the Americans killed or injured in Iraq for the president to exploit the trappings of war for the momentary spectacle of a speech. . . . War is not theater, and victory is not a campaign slogan.

The USS *Abraham Lincoln,* which was ferrying U.S. troops from Iraq, had had to slow down at considerable taxpayer expense in order to accommodate the president's globally televised fly-in. The president stepped down from the fighter jet and walked across the massive landing deck, scarcely able to suppress the childlike little hop that betrayed the adrenaline rush that he felt. He was literally dressed as a warrior with figurative twin six-shooters dragging along the deck. Eddie Rickenbacker. Ace. Boy with power. Fully realized. Chilling.

Toward the end of his remarks to the Senate, Senator Byrd had added: "It may make for grand theater to describe Saddam Hussein as an ally of Al Qaeda or to characterize the fall of Baghdad as a victory in a war on terror, but stirring rhetoric does not necessarily reflect sobering reality. Not one of the nineteen September 11 hijackers was an Iraqi. In fact, there is not a shred of evidence to link the September 11 attack on the United States to Iraq."

Chapter Sixteen

Leaving

I had left America a year and a half before the war began, so the war had nothing to do with my reasons for leaving. The reasons are not easy to organize and write about, scattered as they are in sobering, disillusioning bits and pieces across the changing fields of a lifetime.

All societies have ugly sides to them, I suppose, and it stands to reason that ours, the most powerful of societies, would disport on the hide of its overall behavior a few large and unattractive warts, the most repellent of which being the seemingly unconscious habit of denying that American society is, like all other societies, flawed in the least.

This refusal to examine, to look at itself at all, as would virtually the rest of the world, has produced, or perhaps is produced of, a collective national psychosis, accommodated and protected by layer upon layer of an orchestrated self-adoration that only great power could insulate from effective critical assault.

Why, for example, is Liberia in such a wounded state? Western journalists report on the war-torn country's crisis as if the crisis were solely of Liberia's own making and not, in substantial part, of an America that had used Liberia for the better part of the twentieth century as a vast rubber plantation and regional intelligence hub, manipulating its politics, controlling its economy, installing and exploiting its corrupt democrats and, thence, puppet despots. The Cold War ended, America saw little further use for Liberia, and allowed the society that it had gutted to collapse onto itself. With no consideration of long-term consequence, America stripped Liberia of everything it owned of marketable value, blamed the ensuing carnage on the African victims, and closed the book with the better part of the world none the wiser.

Since the age of Christopher Columbus, *exemplar extraordinaire,* wealthy white Western societies have employed the *exploit, dump, and bury* method as the principal *modus operandi* for engaging a red, brown, and black world they, over a period of more than five centuries, enslaved, slaughtered, suppressed, and stole from. The resultant socioeconomic damage is deep and far-reaching. It would seem clear, at least in the black world, that any repairs of significance would have to begin with a full confession from the modern beneficiaries. Europe. America. And Western whites generally, all of whom are born to relative advantage because all of this happened.

Were whites in critical mass even minimally inclined to honesty, where would truth begin its reconstruction of so sordid a past? Where must you start the Grand Apologia?

Not with the transatlantic slave trade. That would be starting at mid-story. How about starting *our* story where you start yours, six or so thousand years ago. By doing such, you can establish in the statement you have long suppressed, the context in which Herodotus, the Greek historian, your "father of history," appraised advanced African civilizations long before the birth of Christ. Please detail this in your telling. We, being slaves, couldn't hold onto it. So tell it as it actually happened. For we *need* our *African glories* story as much as the Jews need their *Exodus,* invented or not. You'll talk of Kush and Axum, of course, and of the seminal role that Ethiopians (not just Zipporah, Moses' wife) played in the founding of the Christian Church.

You'll have to be insistent in order to undo all of the damage done. When you write at first of *a distant antiquity's incandescent glory,* Man-boy will not know for a while what you are talking about. You must, however, persevere. It will take time, perhaps a lifetime or two, for Man-boy and, particularly, for yourselves, having as much or more than he to unlearn.

Then, you, *Beneficiary America,* official America, (scholars alone will not do, not at all) can tell us what happened during the long night of slavery and the mean Jim Crow dawn that followed it. Where went the stolen value of our toil? Where does it reside now? Numbers, names, dates.

And then tell me what my name is. Memoryless me.

Once I had only needed, as I was malforming in the Old South, to know what had happened and who was responsible. I am a small boy at this point in my petition and no one has explained why *I* alone have been stranded adrift on a shoreless sea of time with no story of myself, America evidently seeing no need that I should be supplied with such. It was then, I think, fifty-five years ago, that I began to form askew in my opinion of America, the country that was always and never my *home.* You say a six-year-old asks no such questions. Perhaps so. But a six-year-old knows well the pain of unmet needs, to which terms attach themselves later, much later, if ever.

Rose Sanders, a strong, black human rights lawyer from Birmingham, Alabama, with whom I attended law school eons ago, told me recently that she had visited a library in Timbuktu and read a fourteenth-century African rejoinder to Machiavelli's *The Prince.* She cried like a baby right there amidst the ghosts of long-dead African scholars, suspended in air like the dry parchment dust that rose from the ancient texts and floated, as if watching from a shaft of sunlight that bathed the old wooden table at which Rose sat, at long last, remembering dark mothers eternal. It was with a great leavening catharsis that she wept. In an exhalation of a breath held too long, with relief and rejoicing, aflood with tears for, oh God, all and everything. Brave, stalwart Rose, who had spent the whole of her career as a rights fighter in mean Selma, Alabama, pored over yellowed, cracked manuscripts in far-off Timbuktu and understood immortality—knew at once that she had been more in her life than a figment of a brave survivalist's imagination, that she had been, was, would forever be, a black woman, an African woman, with a story as old as time.

Damn the sadists, damn even more the indifferent *normal* Americans who knew what they were doing, in doing nothing.

Who did this to us? I, over the sixty years of my life in America, needed to hear some government official just once say who was responsible.

But, in America, no one was ever responsible—for *anything,* then or since. The opponents of justice, the sponsors of my formative pain, sheltered somewhere in the polemics of reasoned disagreement, the wound, mine, every black American's, a blameless condition of nature like bad weather. No need or responsibility to fix then what no identifiably human hand had wrought. The awful unexplained void in me, us. It was not just that they had told this little boy that he had no history worth recalling, but that they had gone further to describe his foremothers and forefathers as savages. Who did this to me? Of course, nobody. Nobody ever does anything—not to us at least. Not in America.

In December 2003, my mother, Doris Robinson Griffin, will be ninety years old. She is one of two extraordinary parents that forged from the odious space of the old segregationist South four successful black children. My mother had finished college at the top of her class, but forsook, as was the fashion in her day, a career in education to rear her children. By the time my father, a high school history teacher, died at sixty-eight, my mother had not worked for a wage in nearly forty years. At the age of sixty, which appears to be the Robinson family age of new beginnings, she learned to drive, applied for a passport, and became the executive director of the Richmond, Virginia, Young Women's Christian Association. For nearly all of her long and optimistic life, my mother had devoted most of her time to her family, her luxuriant flower garden, and the Baptist Church, the trunk and the branch of it.

Though she, from time to time over the years, had expressed directly to me support for my human rights advocacy, one would hardly have thought of her as an activist or even the political idealist my father had been. My impression had been that she saw life in the smaller units of localized right and wrong. On the subject of my church nonattendance, she would say to me equably, "You are serving God in your way, I in mine, and that is good enough for me." If my mother believed in the pan-Africanism that I had embraced, I was not aware of it. Brilliant though she was, she simply had never been one for the articulated *isms,* though she knew them all by family name well enough.

Now, I think that I may have misjudged her while my mouth was running, for I have recently come to believe that she was *I,* or, more accurately, I, *she*—that is, when my mouth was shut.

Not long ago, she called me and said: "I do not want to die without seeing Africa at least once in my life. Three months from now, I will be going to Zambia, Zimbabwe, and South Africa." And this my eighty-nine-year-old mother did with stunning results, about which for months after her return she did not stop talking. She described it as *the* watershed event of her life. She had gone *home* to a welcome she had never gotten at home. "They all called me mama, took me to their homes, made me feel, really made me feel, like a member of their families. I had never before received such effusive hospitality, and to get it in Africa was just so unforgettably special. It exceeded all of my expectations."

Hearing this, I felt like a little boy again, redeemed by indirect approval, vindicated in the professional nonuse of my law degree, and, as well, in my choice of a career that may have seemed something of a reckless rump impulse to many in the stodgy world of Richmond black society. My mother had felt all along what I had felt for so many years, a longing, a missing *something,* a need to go *back,* to investigate a spiritual anchorage, to meet, before it became too late, her *family,* to read the meaning of her long life in the lineal mists of her people's passage on another continent through the millennial corridors of time, to be introduced, finally, manumittally, to that last hidden corner of herself. It is *who was I*? Not *who am I*? That is the question, the former realming eternal, the latter explaining nothing. My mother knew this. For how long, I do not know. Maybe since before she was born.

This *race cross* weighs heavily upon blacks, like broken chainmail armor on weary ancient soldiers bravely retreating from retreat, searching for distraction and never quite finding it. The *race cross,* a near life form, still and mute most of the time now, lodges and lives in the black subconscious, demanding of its host constant attention to its aberrant requirement. The chronic discomfort of unexplained bottomness. More tolerable than the schizophrenic's *voices,* but nonetheless *there,* marking everything that can be seen, felt, and comprehended. Some blacks try hard, too hard in my view, to decoy it, trick it with the self-denial they would be affronted to hear me call self-loathing. But in one form or another, self-loathing is what one arrives at when bottomness is left unexplained, when all of a cause-and-effect story's early foundation chapters have been hijacked. In any case, the tricking, the decoying, is all but always impermanent. We doubt this only because we cannot see inside the heads of the black grandmasters of the craft. Sometimes, however, we almost can.

I have known for years a black woman of my mother's generation whose behavior might help to illustrate this point. For years the woman had been a model of austere self-assurance and steely self-possession. She seemed to hold membership in everything that would give one lift to hover effortlessly above the hoi polloi of the rest of us. She was a *Links* lady, a *Boule* wife, a *Delta* star, a ballet patron, a debutante trailblazer, a skilled snob of considerable graciousness, a wealthy woman who knew well the responsibilities of noblesse oblige and discharged such with generosity and silken ease.

In old age, the society maven of the arts suffered a series of small strokes that often as not pass unnoticed. On one occasion, however, one or more of the mini-strokes produced in her a dementia thick with fear and disparate weeping. Inconsolable, she began an unburdening: "We are slaves! We are slaves!" Within minutes, the episode ended and she became herself again. Either that or the someone else she had always been. Somewhere still in the back-channel circuits of her brain the *race cross* lay with all of its horrific memories. She was rich but otherwise unexceptional. Not unlike the rest of us, she too was little more than another digit in the long, mean, black experience.

*   *   *

I always read a lot, even as a teenager. I read magazines. I read books. I read newspapers. I even read the dictionary. I read the backs of cereal boxes—over and over and over again. I read whatever was presented to me or whatever I knew to try and get my hands on. I liked to read about foreign places. I read about Mount Everest, but never about the Chinese name for their side of the mountain. I read a lot about Hillary, the Brit, but little about Tensing, the sherpa. I did not know that I was reading more or less. I read whatever there was to be read. With an emphasis on the foreign, without knowing it was anyone's *foreign* in particular.

Test me. You say "the defeat of the Spanish Armada." I say "1588." You say "the Battle of Hastings." I say "1066." You say "the Battle of Bannockburn." I stumble but I've heard of that battle. You say "Magna Carta." I say: "1215." I can run across Europe from Garibaldi to Bismarck, from Caesar to Caesar, from Euripides to Shakespeare. I am fifteen years old and black and segregated because of it, but I know these things because I read everything I can get my hands on. I tell a high school teacher that the correct pronunciation is "mickle-angelo" and not "michael-angelo." She says *"Yes, Randall, I saw last night's documentary, too,"* and gives me that a-little-knowledge-is-a-dangerous-thing look. Yeah, but still I know some things, this poor black boy is thinking in Richmond, Virginia, in the 1950s. I know all this about all these great white people and places and events.

You say "Dessalines" and I'm lost, but you won't say "Dessalines" because you've never heard of him, either. Say "Tuareg Magcharen" and I will not know the founder of Timbuktu in 1100 either, or for that matter, "Kante"—not Emmanuel Kant, but Sumanguru Kante, the leader of Soso, the inventor of the *dan* (xylophone) who died in 1235. I will not know the name "Sundiata," founder of the Mali empire, or when to date the Battle of Kirina, in which Sundiata's forces routed Sumanguru's.

I have not heard of these people or of these places. No one I know has. The names appear in no books that I have seen. Nor in any magazine. Nor on the back of my Post Raisin Bran cereal box.

Thus, these people who look like *me,* who have done great things in eighteenth-century Haiti and twelfth-century West Africa, do not exist.

Last week Congressman Tom Tancredo, a Republican from Colorado, quoted Enoch Powell, the British parliamentarian, on the floor of the U.S. House of Representatives and described Powell as a great philosopher and a visionary. That Powell is recognized to be one of the more virulent European race baiters of his era (rivaled only by Jean-Marie Le Pen of France) was of no apparent consequence to Congressman Tancredo, or apparently to the white members present who listened without objection. Ezra Pound wrote wonderful poetry, but Pound was disqualified from broad public appreciation because of his notorious anti-Semitism. I can think of nothing that anyone could say about blacks that would result in a similar penalty.

In America, I do not exist either, not even fully to myself. This has nothing to do with money or prominence or social station. Those are the facile exterior conditions of a black person's unimportant fortune. They are relative like garments we put on and take off. It is the important fortune, the interior defining condition, the ageless, unfed black *self* that cannot flourish within the culturally intolerant space of self-absorbed white America.

I don't know that very many blacks are even thinking about such things, much less talking about them. I have come to feel increasingly isolated, and not just from white America but from black America as well, from whose already-meager stores, energy is siphoned off to fight the smaller side-battles that we thought we had won and iced away.

I sometimes feel as Bill Cosby must feel watching the *Bernie Mac Show.* Social progress undone. Standards established, then disestablished. But the broad ongoing trivialization of American thought and behavior is hardly peculiar to the entertainment industry. It is society-wide.

What would the great writers and thinkers of the American past think of their contemporary counterparts? I am no unambivalent admirer, but what would a solemn and intellectual Abraham Lincoln have thought of a vacuous and preening George W. Bush? What would a brilliant and compelling Frederick Douglass have thought of his modern heirs apparent? What would the eloquent idealists of eras past have thought of the virtual disappearance of their like from these infinitely more perilous times?

Chapter Seventeen

Decline

James G. Abourezk served one six-year term in the U.S. Senate from 1973 to 1979 and refused to run again. In his 1989 memoir, *Advise and Dissent,* Senator Abourezk writes:

> There are men and women who would kill to be re-elected, term after term. I was not one of them. . . . I learned that senators necessarily spend more of their time preparing the groundwork for the next election than running the government. It is the officeholder, not the public, who benefits from this system. . . . The drive to raise money becomes so pervasive that on more than one occasion, I caught myself feeling resentful that my job as a member of Congress intruded on my job as a candidate. But that's the story of politics in today's world.

In a country that just squandered more than two hundred billion dollars on a war of dubious legality, forty-three million Americans—16 percent of the population—are without health care insurance. One in four blacks, including those who need health care insurance most, the poorest, are wholly unprotected.

For more than a quarter century, the U.S. Congress has failed to put in place a health care insurance system comparable to systems available to the citizens of virtually every other industrialized nation in the world, and even small, nonindustrialized nations like my new home, St. Kitts and Nevis, where the United States is using its considerable influence through bilateral and multilateral channels like the World Bank to dismantle this tiny Caribbean nation's institutional compassion. It is not pejorative to characterize the World Bank as a Western front institution. That such is very much the case is evident in the bank's capital subscribership, with the United States controlling the largest block of its votes.

St. Kitts and Nevis has much improved health statistics that compare favorably to much of the industrialized world, including the United States. The World Bank has declined to reflect this progress in its literature, despite repeated requests from the government of St. Kitts and Nevis. Instead the World Bank and its largest power block, the United States (which rates just above embargoed Cuba in World Health Organization rankings), have tried to cause St. Kitts and Nevis to conform *down* to the bank's outdated literature. The bank says to St. Kitts and Nevis: *You have too many doctors.* The country has forty-nine doctors, about one for every 918 citizens. *You also have too many nurses and too many dentists. Get rid of some of them.*

Not all matters of statecraft are complicated. The government of this, the smallest of nations, believes that the first and most important responsibility of any government is, quite simply, to protect the interests of its citizens, something the United States has spectacularly failed to do for *its* citizens in the area of health care for more than twenty-five years. It has preferred rather, with a lightning decisiveness beneficial only to its defense industry, to spend unseemly sums of money on the murderous business of an unnecessary, illegal and dishonestly presented war.

I am not a Communist. It is not that I think communism is evil, but rather that its fundamental suppositions are based upon, as we say in the law, *facts not in evidence.* Communism or a pre-Marxism facsimile of it existed in pre-Columbian traditional societies. People shared everything in common. But not in accordance with the language of an *ism.* The *sharing* in their circular holistic systems of living was as natural as breathing, and just as unremarkable. The Tainos didn't require written precepts from Karl Marx to know how to live in a healthy peaceful harmony.

The *isms* never ever work when you really need them. The Inca lived happily and healthily within a broadly provided institutional utopia until the Spaniards arrived, took a quick look around, and destroyed them. The Inca did not need Karl Marx. And Columbus, the Spaniards, the Americans, let's just say the progeny of Western Europe, would have little use for any man, Marx or any of his like, who naively believed that Europeans would explore, kill, ransack, dispossess, enslave, colonize, exploit, and plunder, only to *share* the booty at home or abroad. I don't believe in communism because, among the cultures of Western Europe and those shaped or corrupted by it, communism cannot work. The greedy will always be greedy, a weakness that not only befalls capitalists but state Communist ideologues as well. Lemmings, comprising the vast majority of America's patriotic and altogether ruly citizens, will always be lemmings, reelable people, pliable as putty in the hands of the greedy. How else could the lemmings have divided their votes between George W. Bush and Al Gore while giving scant support to Ralph Nader, far and away the smartest candidate and the only one who genuinely cared about the interests of the lemmings?

Now, the greeting card companies have come out with *Happy Grandmother Day* cards and *Happy Grandfather Day* cards, perhaps to be followed in due course by *Happy Monday* cards, *Happy Tuesday* cards, *Happy Wednesday* cards . . . and just maybe a *Happy Me Day* card for the friendless and lonely, mailed without a stamp to a return address. The card company capitalists have no cause for worry. Provided a catchy Madison Avenue ad campaign, lemmings will buy *anything*, literally and figuratively. How about a *Happy North Korea* card?

Lastly, on this point, inasmuch as I have no significant capital, I am by definition not a capitalist. Nor likely are you. Thus, we are, you and I, disqualified like all the other lemmings who vote and don't vote, from wielding influence over the public affairs of America, the mirage of democracy where all defensive parapets face outward, lemmings at the ready, watching the wrong hills.

Perhaps there is nothing surprising about the citizen's woeful state of uninformedness. When I was a little boy, America was awash in independent newspapers, and television was not yet peppered with the unambiguous phrasemakers who now do our thinking for us. Only twelve cities are left in the entire country with at least two independent newspapers. News enough, I suppose, and just so *right* to gladden the fascist heart.

How many Iraqis died in the war against Iraq? How many Iraqi soldiers? How many Iraqi civilians? Had the questions crossed your mind? Had any American news organ investigated them? Why is Iraq less stable than before the war? Why wasn't this anticipated? Why is the entire region less stable than before the war? A porous sack of molten jagged rocks it looks to be. Have you any thoughtful idea of what we have wrought in shattering the hard-fired, elaborate ceramic of global cooperation? Poor Oregon, the pride of American state education. Cutting its school week. Laying off its teachers. Harbinger of the times. Flat out of money. No weapons of mass destruction discovered in Iraq or Oregon. No September 11 links. No stability. Just a freaking mess. The death toll mounting. Carnage in Saudi Arabia. And after the war's end. After flyboy George Triumphant alights from his very own hard-won skies upon his very own Plain of Abraham. Did you know that there are sixty million Americans, not forty-three million, who are without health insurance at some point in the year? Democracy. Choices. But not if you can't see them.

You know why we held this war? For much the same reason we don't have health care insurance, you lemming. Nobody in the White House and the Congress, including members and staff, had to fight it. Conversely, we have no universal health care insurance because everybody in the White House and the Congress, again including members of staff, already have it as a part of their package. You mean you didn't know this? Well you weren't supposed to think about such things. Besides, war is very good for the war businesses and health care insurance is not so good for the health businesses. And since you ain't no capitalist because you ain't got no capital, who cares what you think, especially if you ain't think-ing at all, see?

The little boy, cute as a button, was shown to the studio audi-ence on a huge screen by a camera in the green room. The boy, no more than three years old, had bright expressive eyes and an engag-ing smile. The mother had only just been joined by the putative fa-ther on the set. The two of them, halfway through their fifteen minutes of fame, fidgeted in their chairs and smiled nervously at the host while arranging their bodies in attitudes of suspicion toward each other. Right up to this very moment, the two of them had been the unsuspecting child's *parents,* indeed the whole of his world.

Maury Povich, the host, looks at the putative father and asks him if he is ready to find out whether or not he is this plainly happy child's real father. The child, oblivious to fate's unstable tempera-ment, smiles again in the soundless green room.

Povich says something like *okay, here we go.* I turn off the tele-vision set. I had watched about three minutes. Long enough. Too long, in fact. Longer than I had ever watched this particular show, which was, unlike the prurient bile of Jerry Springer and Howard Stern, conspicuous in its cruelty to innocent bystanders. I must con-fess that shows like these amount to little more than an irritant to my spirit, nothing, really, to compare with the lingering tax of the old injuries I've already talked about. But *Maury-Ricki-Howard-Jenny-Jerry* do have a cumulative effect, I suppose, chipping away, as they do, pebble by pebble, at the moral foundation of the gen-eral society. And not just American society. I have to surf this swamp right here in St. Kitts. I have not spoken to anyone here about this, but I wonder what these socially conservative people who are loath to wear shorts in public think when they watch this stuff. Because the product is, you know, *big American stuff,* I won-der what it is doing to traditional thinking here. At first, there must be shock, but after that, what? Robert Llewellyn Bradshaw, the fa-ther of the nation, had warned his country's people of this, but to no avail.

The American sang right through our radios here for the whole little country's consumption: *If I take you to the bed and I use my tongue on you, will you like it?*

One wonders if the conflict of capitalism and democracy is even bigger, at least conceptually, than the conflict between communism and democracy. Indeed, are the very separate and different "freedoms" contemplated here by capitalism and democracy all but mutually exclusive, destructive of each other? Capitalism implies a certain freedom of private capital, but to do *what* and to *whom*? And can such a freedom, indeed, undermine the freedoms that democracy would safeguard? Democracy gives us freedom of political choice. But what happens to the choice-makers, themselves, after they've been treated from birth to a steady diet of *Cinemax* public fucking.

Consider the demeanor of the *Maury-Ricki-Howard-Jenny-Jerry* audience as the guest on the moneymaking sewage-exchange show treats an international public to the lewdest of accounts while devaluing in the process the exquisite mystery of sex and any association it may have had with love.

The audience leers, hoots, and hurls insults at the guest. The bleep machine renders the exchange between audience and guest all but unintelligible. These are the voters, the officerholders' superintendents, the only real democratic authority, Madison's beneficiaries, Jefferson's trustees, those in whom the Constitution of the United States vests the power to govern the most powerful nation in the history of humankind.

Are these people, the people you see in the audience and on the set—and, yes, throw in the host as well, and let's not forget the sponsors, the producers, the executives, the well-heeled investors, the network gang—are these people causes or symptoms of what is increasingly undermining American democracy, namely, the erosion of those ideals of equity and compassion upon which the written tenets of any democracy must necessarily rest? For the common good, are there no limits worthy of imposing on money's untrammeled and often lethal "freedoms"? Can democracy survive unregulated greed? Would not a people's healthy spirit die first and then the democracy that that spirit had once blessed with its radiant light?

The Nobel Prize–winning Mexican writer, Octavio Paz, explores this dilemma in *Itinerary: An Intellectual Journey*:

> The meaning of this word virtue has been argued over many times. . . . but whatever meaning one may choose, the word always denotes self-mastery. When virtue weakens and we are dominated by passions—nearly always by inferior ones like envy, vanity, avarice, lust, laziness—the republics die out. When we can no longer control our appetites we are ready to be dominated by someone else. The market has undermined all the ancient beliefs—many of them, it is true, were nefarious—but one passion has replaced them, that of buying things and consuming this or that object. Our hedonism is not a philosophy of pleasure but an abdication of free will and would have scandalized both the gentle Epicurus and the frantic Marquis de Sade. Hedonism is not the sin of modern democracies: it is the sin of conformism, the vulgarity of its passions, the unconformity of tastes, ideas and convictions.

I sat for a while wondering if years later, the cute little boy with the bright smile would ever learn of the precise moment at which his life had been destroyed on the *Maury Povich Show*.

Spectacle sells. Like drugs, however, the second hit must be bigger than the first. Where will all of this lead? Hard-core pornography on the children's hour? Live murder as an extreme sport? Is this not deadening us? Turning us into "shock" junkies? Heartless bunions? Pain celebrants? People who believe art has to *be* life because they've no memory of a life distinguishable from the low art they watch incessantly, imitatively? Cruel, cancerous, verminous art. So inured are we that shock no longer shocks, that we scarcely notice our trajectory of broad descent, pulling with all of our great power the world into the vortex behind us.

And when the whole thing comes crashing down upon us, when *Headquarters America* becomes downright unlivable, when even truckloads of money won't offset our collective social breakdown, when all hell breaks loose, who will they blame? Yes, I confess that this could be the society-built paranoid speaking, but: *us.* Count on it. They'll blame us. Black people. Isn't that why a young, faceless, nameless white entrepreneur made Snoop Doggy Dog the public face of *Girls Gone Wild*? A skinny, gaudily festooned black man in big dark glasses enveloped by jiggling white tits, eyeballing the half-naked nubile coeds salaciously and sliming the absentee entrepreneur's sales pitch: "Witness the pandemonia." Which means: Buy this video. Which apparently Americans are doing in a big way.

Is all of this just a distraction or a harbinger of American society's terminal disintegration? There are precedents, of course. But I don't know how much they help us. Eight years ago, Hazel, Khalea, and I spent a day in the excavated Roman Empire city of Pompeii, Italy. Fortunately, Khalea, who was five at the time, trailed a little behind us as we walked into the former home of one of the city's wealthy families and found ourselves in a room just off the vestibule surrounded by walls and walls of hard-core, full-color, first-century pornographic art, replete with engorged phalluses, labia, you name it. Shocked, we intercepted Khalea in the nick of time, only to learn as the day wore on that such displays of graphic sex were commonplace in Pompeii, right up until the moment the city was buried by the scolding lava of an erupting Mount Vesuvius in 79 A.D.

Pornography is as old as time, and pre-Christian and Christian societies have vacillated in their attitudes about sex for many centuries. While I don't quite know how or where HBO can find so many well-dressed, non-hooker street interviewees to tell us explicitly on camera just how they like their sex, I am not sure just how much damage this does to society's overall fabric, although, I suppose, more than you'd guess, the trivialization of lovemaking not the least of it. What is of greater concern to me, however, is the less-examined rampant manufacture of unfeelingness in society, the galloping indifferent meanness of strangers, the *bunionization* of the masses, the new voyeurism of pain.

Jerry Springer says to the woman: "Okay, tell your husband what you've come here to tell him." She does. He's crushed. Audience loves it.

Maury says: "Okay, here we go . . . ."

Gratification, instant. At any cost. At any innocent's expense. Money to be made. Lots and lots of it.

At the same time, Ramsey Clark, a former attorney general of the United States and the son of a Supreme Court Justice, forms an organization to circumscribe war-making and racism in the world, and he cannot find a welcoming airway beyond C-SPAN. Ramsey Clark is a very smart, good man of unmistakable integrity. These are the very traits, however, that American society curiously abhors in its prominent people of past and present high position. Unseeable forces have caused us to virtually ridicule those who endeavor to do *good*. The term "do-gooder" was not coined by God-knows-who to be a compliment. When Mr. Clark speaks out, one can all but *feel* a weary old man's stoic acceptance that most of us would perversely prefer to wallow low and glandularly with celebrity sump-stirrers than to listen to calls to help anyone, including ourselves. Nonetheless, the very possibility of global society's long-term survival is borne along only by the very existence and perseverance of the few like Ramsey Clark. The fool never applauds the good and decent. The good and decent, with better vision, come to expect and accept this. It is the price one pays for the richer life.

Materialism does indeed have its quiet, civilized side, like still air in a well-appointed room. My family had lived well in Washington, D.C., in a nice brick colonial house, on a leafy oversized lot on a nice street, in a nice neighborhood, where no one scarcely knew anyone else. The elegant isolation, I think, may have been served by the double-hung windows, which were closed and locked behind the rustproof aluminum double-hung storm windows, which were also closed and locked, in order to seal in the heat in the winter months and the compressor-cooled air in the summer months.

Hazel, even in the frigid winter months, had always wanted to raise the windows, if just an inch or two. I had always resisted this. It was the only incompatibility that we had had to face. She would say *we need fresh air*. I would say, stupidly I confess, *I trust the air that I know.*

And so, the windows would be closed for a while and then opened for a while, even in the coldest months. I never thought much about the possible benefits of the incoming cold fresh air, but only about our expensively heated old stale air making a break for freedom through the cracked windows and onto the alien street of strangers.

Every morning now in a lush land where the days are of near-even length, I rise at 5:30 or so and open wide every door and window in the house. Something close in its effect on me, I suppose, to the first cup of morning coffee to a caffeine lover. The gentle trade wind moves through the house lifting dust covers, tables skirts, and my spirits in line. I never knew before the veritable wonders that air alone could travel thousands of miles to perform. Simple fresh air. *God's caress,* Hazel calls it. She had tried so hard to help me, but I had been stubborn, never appreciating until now the full measure of her loving sufferance. I wonder now how she could have borne it. The very inertia that provides us with a certain social stability also makes the learning hard that there might be a better way to live.

I think of this in an odd place to think of such things and smile to myself. I am sitting in a lounge in the Admirals Club in Chicago's bustling airport, waiting for a connecting flight. The high-armed leather chairs, separated by laminated box-side tables, are arranged, four to a side, in a square. I sit in one facing a massive, hermetically sealed, floor-to-ceiling, double-insulated glass wall that gives onto a runway laid of gray concrete, the color of the low, overcast late-afternoon sky. The air in the room is first still and then drops in a cold mass from a large air register above my head.

There are five men and two women sitting in the chairs opening onto the square. Appearing to all be strangers to each other, they look neither left nor right, but mostly without focus toward the carpeted floor or into the ceiling. They are all white. All talking on cell phones. All with typed reports of one kind or another resting on their laps or on the laminated box tables.

I am reading a book, the only one in this part of the lounge doing so. I am trying with little success to block out what is being said all too loudly into the cell phones around me that appear to have bad connections. The book I am reading is *The Polished Hoe,* a sweeping novel of British colonial atrocities in post-slavery Barbados, by the great Bajan writer, Austin Clarke. Bits and pieces of what I am hearing and what I am reading swim together in unpleasant disharmony and reproduce within the space of the square a briefly sensed microculture of transracial dysfunction and failed communication.

> And talking about Ma's grands strikes me as strange. . . . *Look, how many units can you move to my New Jersey warehouse by . . .* Because we don't go back too far in lineages, not in this hemisphere. I never come across one soul in this village who could say she have a grandmother who was born in Bimshire, to match Mr. Bellfeels bragging. . . . *the whole Southwest region to bring in before we close the quarter. . . .* that he "have family here in Bimshire from the year 1493 A.D."! That bastard! . . . . *Bob, I just can't discount it anymore unless you increase your order. . . .* I don't know one coloured family, or one coloured person in the whole of Bimshire. . . . *I'm hoping we can sell off all the discontinued product before. . . .* perhaps in the whole Wessindies, who could match that claim. . . . *we're all very excited about this new line. . . .* who could lay claim to that claim, and trace-back his ancestries to 1493! You?

I open my zippered, black-leather travel wallet and check again the departure time of my flight home. It is important that I do this. Once I nearly missed a flight while sitting in a quiet lounge far from the departure gate, reading. A U.S. immigration and customs form falls out of the wallet and onto my lap. My eyes alight on line number ten, which I never seem quite certain how to complete. *The purpose of my (our) trip is or was: (check one or both boxes, if applicable)*

☐ *Business*   ☐ *Personal*

There are only two choices, and *business* comes first. Line ten, I think, is a small piece of anthropological evidence evocative of something important about America, but I don't think further about it.

I had come to the United States to give a lecture at a university just last evening. Had this been *business* or *personal*? I had not given the first box serious consideration, if any at all. I had checked personal, as I always do.

Chapter Eighteen

Culture

In early May, Mahalia Jackson arrived in Trinidad for some prearranged concerts, and [Prime Minister Eric] Williams saw that she could be used to blunt the force of the [Black Power] Movement. He said: "Let us give the sister to the Black Power boys." In a hastily arranged supper meeting, Williams offered her three additional public concerts, with additional fees to be paid by the government. This would demonstrate that the government encouraged black culture. Ironically, NJAC [the National Joint Action Committee, an organ of Trinidad's Black Power Movement] also sought political mileage from Mahalia's visit. The Black Power Movement had just gained its first martyr, when police shot and killed a twenty-one-year-old unknown black activist, Basil Davis, near Woodford Square. Davis' parents handed the body of their son over to NJAC, which organized a "state" funeral. The Black Power leaders asked Mahalia Jackson to sing at Davis' funeral. Her response to one of the Williams's advisors was, "what fee should I charge?" When told that she was expected to perform at the funeral without a fee, her response was, "But I did not get this voice for free!"

—Ken Boodhoo
The Elusive Eric Williams

The Trinidadians were stunned. Mahalia Jackson was black, but very much an American nonetheless. Like African-Americans generally, owing to minorityness, she occupied a shifting hybrid cultural space located somewhere between African communalism and European acquisitiveness, perhaps best capsulized by the guru of *effective negotiation*, Dr. Chester L. Karrass: "In business, you don't get what you deserve, you get what you negotiate." Or, as *Newsweek* once more sweepingly put it: "Negotiation is the game of life." Natural, perhaps, to Americans who are largely of a European cultural moorage, but significantly less so to Trinidadians, Caribbeans in general and Haitians in particular, who owe a great deal more of their cultural predisposition to Africa than do their numerically overwhelmed African-American cousins.

I've been asked to speak at functions around the island many times. As far as I can tell, the word "honorarium" is not to be found in the local lexicon. Here, it would be boorish to ask for, and only slightly less so to accept a fee for baby-sitting. Much the same would apply to hair-braiding. These are among the many small services that people extend here free of charge to friend and stranger alike. Although such practices render smaller and warmer the oblivion between strangers, Americans are culturally constructed to find these kindnesses the naive failings of inferiors suitable for exploitation. I don't know how empirically broad such a reading would be, but no doubt broad enough to warrant remark.

But *this* American, however, very much likes the performing unselfish decencies of a Caribbean culture, where no house can be entered without a proffer of hospitality—*please let me get you something cold to drink*—and no conversation can begin, telephonic or otherwise, without a dispensation of serial courtesies: *How is your mother? How is your father? How are your children? How is your* . . . Where one is not *dropped off* at the airport. Where hosts stand and watch from the doorway as you leave their homes until you are out onto the street and well along the sidewalk. "Why are they standing there?" I had asked Hazel the first time I had experienced this. "Are they trying to overhear what we're saying?" Rudeness is blind, first and foremost to itself.

"Wha—" was as far as I got, my mouth hanging foolishly open at my first sighting of the *moko jumbie,* the ancient Senegalese stiltwalker who survived the Middle Passage, slavery, colonialism, and all else to strut alive and proud through downtown Basseterre.

Yes, I like it here. I am at *home* here in this contemporary transplanted womb of the old culture, *ours* it is, part remembered, part made, like no other could ever be, with its black pudding and breadfruit cou cou and bun bun, its warm happy noises, the music of its moving bodies; and the talk, man, the talk about everything everywhere. Radio talk, calypso talk, car-top amplified talk, debating-team talk, Rasta talk, money-ain't-everything talk, little-man-to-big-shot talk, slavery-days-done-me-know-me-rights talk. Culture, the primordial *home* of a people, built across the ages, designed to suit, constructed to last, tailored to fit, buttressed to defend, wrecked by slavery, suppressed by colonialism, and shot back into vivid life by *these* people and their lyrical, sweet-sounding talk. Talk of their *now*. Talk of their *long ago*. Talk of what the St. Vincent prime minister Ralph Gonsalves calls *our Caribbean Civilization*. Talk of things nonmaterial, things I needed but never had. Not in America. Never in America.

Cultures are not to be described as good or bad, worthy or unworthy, better or worse. Cultures simply *are*. They are *different* in ageless ways because they serve people who are *different* in ageless ways. They are plasma to humanity's ongoing drama of march. They succor. They nourish. They train the young, splint the broken, comfort the old. They sing in the wonderfully unique voice of a people's timeless artistic spirit. They are the grand and colorful millennial mosaics of related countless lifetimes. And they have memories. Memories that transfer from the dead to the living. From the living to the distant horizons of an indiscernible future's children. They supercede their fragile living constituents with an answer to mortal humankind's great quest: immortality. They collect the infinitesimal bits of our creative individualities and weave them into the elaborate tapestry of the culture's frontispiece.

And for some like us, a culture saves memories for its excised children, children displaced, transplanted, battered, orphaned from its protective arms by centuries of memory-erasing slavery.

I have come to believe that one can *remember* experiences that

one has not lived or been told of. Or perhaps it would be more accurate to say that one can *feel* experiences that transpired in the
larger life of one's mother culture long before one's actual living. A
little like, but hardly so somatic as, African-Americans finding cold
weather less to their liking than white Americans do. Africa talking
to us still.

Experiences that explain our likes and dislikes, the timbre of our
personalities, the swing of our bodies, the tonality of our speech.
All sourced in an age predating our savage orphanage.

I think such thoughts as I sit through a program in the Washington National Cathedral during Khalea's last year in the National
Cathedral School before our departure from America. The cathedral is an impressive building, vaulting, cavernous, detailed, stony.
It is a huge, echoic space in which souls would unlikely cross to
join. The building was not designed for *me* and my genetic memory
of who I am supposed to be, if not who I have managed, under trying social circumstances, to be. I look about and I see money but I
do not see God in the shadowy corners of sculpted stone or in the
high, darkened pitch of the ceiling. The building seems not to connect the assembled, but to diminish and subordinate them to archi-
tecture that is perfectly and symmetrically mathematical.

It is a reflection of a culture, someone else's, to which I have
proved unable or unwilling to adapt fully. I am the uncomfortable
guest in another's foreign home. I clap lightly as they do. I whisper
as they do. I sit in the cheap seats. Those parents who have con-
tributed ten thousand dollars to the school are seated in the front
row of the cathedral. As they do, I sing from the hymnal with re-
straint in the precise words and notes printed on the page before
me. All space between design and performance has been shrunken
to an imperceptible margin, but seen still as a flaw. I do not know
how to discern whether people are enjoying the service or not enjoying the service. The faces have expressions on them but they
seem scripted like everything else, the building, the speakers, the
students, the parents, the guests, and, of course, me.

I am pretending and I don't like the feeling it gives me. There are
five hundred or so people seated in the long nave of the cathedral.

All but thirty-five or so are white. I look around at the *thirty-five,* which include Indians, Chinese, Japanese, as well as blacks. One of the blacks is Dean Nathan Baxter, the head of the cathedral. This, however, changes nothing in the feel of the place. He is a guest every bit as much as Hazel and I are. He is pretending, too, as are all the rest here who are not white. The whites, I am certain, are not pretending. They are at *home.* What seems like spiceless order-liness to me would be perfectly natural to them. This is *their* cul-ture. I am only pretending to wear it as a garment cut for me. But it does not fit me. That is uncomfortable enough, but that I am *pre-tending* to like it in the same low-key way that the whites are *actu-ally* liking it is in a very minor and manageable way humiliating to me. Thus I do not enjoy being here. Have never enjoyed being here. Not once.

We sing another hymn written and sung in a musical language that my soul cannot understand. Again, it is not a question of whether the music is good or bad. I simply emotionally cannot *feel* it or even know whether or not I am supposed to. Or perhaps it is not the music at all that puts me off. For more than a third of my personal music collection is classical and produced of their culture. I love it, as I do virtually every form of world music. I suspect it is just this place, here atop Washington's highest point, with the sheer arrogance of its soaring spires implying with dishonesty that it was built to honor *God* rather than to slake the extravagant tastes of its privileged white congregants.

> Architecture is merely the embellishment with which we
> hide our deepest needs.
>
> —Jean Le Rond d'Alembert

Hazel and I, as we do most of the times at these school affairs, look at Khalea. She is standing among rows of schoolmates arrayed choir-style across the transept section at the point that it intersects with the longer nave section of the cruciform church, with the fly-ing buttresses that remind one of the Cathedral of Notre Dame on the Seine in Paris. There are forty-seven girls facing us. Five of them are black. Khalea, who started here at five, is eleven now. She has been a guest in this house, a visitor to its culture, for all of her school life. The parties with boys from St. Albans will begin in a few years, and then the walls that were never really down will be fortified—from both sides. There was the time when Khalea's class had been asked to write about a Norman Rockwell painting of their choice. Khalea chose the Rockwell painting of the five-year-old black girl, Ruby Bridges, walking bravely through a sneering crowd of whites gathered at the door of the school Ruby was about to integrate in New Orleans. Khalea wrote that Rockwell in the painting had depicted Ruby's courage, courage that she would hope to demonstrate under similar circumstances, courage in the "proud tradition of Frederick Douglass, Marcus Garvey and Nat Turner," heroes all, described to her in just such terms by her parents. One of Khalea's white teachers had been alarmed by her essay. "You shouldn't have included Marcus Garvey and Nat Turner. They did not help black people. They just made trouble."

It was not that the school's leaders made no effort to attract and accommodate black students. They did this, and from all appearances, in good faith. In Khalea's case the school took pains to recognize her strong academic performance in a range of ways, some public, some not. I cannot recall a single concern of ours that was not met with a constructive response from faculty officials.

Still, one generally comes to feel a bit unmoored living in a cultural house not one's own, even when its welcome is wide and warm, and there is nothing much that the most well-meaning school official can do about it. This is the unsolvable and inextricable mess that the centuries-old global repositing of peoples has left us in, the rather less conspicuous and incidental consequence of slavery, colonialism, and Western global dominance. In a pot, cheek by jowl now, where *nothing* has melted as nothing should ever have been reasonably expected to.

Only children under six, with the prehensile wisdom of their species, see racial and cultural antagonism as a ceremony of the stupid. But small children don't run things, and those first and wonderful insights of theirs bake off like chimerical rainbows under the brilliant hot sun of sobering grown-up bigotries. As a rule, it is around six that they first begin to lean away from those different from themselves and toward the reassuring suns of their like and their like's respective cultures. Once "teams" develop, no one wishes to "play on the road." Trouble is that in America whites almost never have to, and thus cannot imagine the sensation of cultural displacement and alienation. On this point, try as they might, there was little that the school could do for its black students. For by now, history is history, and its various dislocations are simply the way things are.

We say at last to a white mother with whom we have been for years on friendly terms: "We have decided to leave America. We are moving to the Caribbean, to St. Kitts."

The white mother, caring I think, says to us: "But what are you going to do about Khalea? Where will she go to school?"

Had we not known before, we know now. We have made the right decision.

Hazel, incredulous: "In St. Kitts. Where else?"

I follow with my eyes the sounds of the girls' light voices as the sounds climb, flatten out, and roam into the narrow gray fissures of the complicated ceiling work high above us.

Centuries before the *Reformation,* grand cathedral structures not unlike this one dotted the Europe of the Middle Ages. The buildings themselves symbolized both the considerable religious and secular power of the Roman Catholic Church. Surrounded oftener than not by seas of squalor, the construction of these monumental temples to Rome claimed by large margins the greater part of an ambitious host community's resources. The bishop enjoyed spectacular influence. The master stonemason's prestige would likely never reach such heights again.

I think about these things as I look about me. I *feel* nothing, save a kind of academic wonderment, not unlike the sensation I have felt in reaction to the exhibits in the National Air and Space Museum. It is for me less a place of worship than a coldly imposing museum in which one involuntarily estimates in a mind-doodle the cost of construction and appointment, and comes up stunningly short.

I look at the program and see that we have a way to go still. I lose myself again in a thin reverie that is interrupted by a fluttering of light applause, which I join, though I haven't the slightest idea of what I am praising.

Not fifty yards from where I sit stands Hearst Hall, the school's first building. Constructed in the stone tradition of the cathedral and topped with a mansard roof of heavy slate tiles, Hearst Hall bears the name of the school's founder and first major grantor, Phoebe Randolph Hearst, who was also the mother of William Randolph Hearst, the newspaper and movie magnate of the early to mid-twentieth century.

I had asked Khalea once how she liked the school. Never one to complain, she said with neither animus nor affection that she liked the "ambience, the setting, the teachers and, yes, the food, too," which was of restaurant quality.

The organ is playing something Bach-like that is not Bach, but with chords broad and woeful enough to brace the faithless. We pat out our appreciation in a sound you would imagine emanating from a chorus of butterflies, were butterflies noisy travelers.

The school has tried, and I think earnestly. An African song is even on the program. Some of the white parents will complain, but to no avail. The African song stays. As will the Hebrew song and the Spanish song. But, as against the sum of this massive European-ness, there is little toward a useful cultural equilibrium to be gained from a song. I have never known equilibrium and I would like to know what it feels like. I am wary of the tag *subculture*. Who would want to live one's entire life as a *sub* anything? I wish to be for once where ours is *the* culture. I am not of European descent, as are those here who appear to be inhaling this building and its sounds with much, albeit muted, pride. But I *am* pretending. Not to *be* them, but with my every detestable mannerism here, to *be-have* indistinguishably *like* them. To stand in, not out. I feel a fraud for it and that is much of why I hate these programs. But if Khalea, whom I love as I watch, can endure the long presences here, I must be willing to endure the short.

Break a vase, and the love that reassembles the fragments is stronger than that love which took its symmetry for granted when it was whole. As if to relieve me of my deceit, the line written by the St. Lucian poet, Derek Walcott, comes to me from nowhere. I do not say in my head these exact words as I sit here. I remember only the *feel* of them providing me some bulwark, some focus upon *my* purpose, while sitting in a place with quite another, not hostile to mine, but somehow worse. Indifferent. Walcott's exact words I put down later, as I recall then what I feel and how I fight it. *Deprived of their original language, the captured and indentured tribes create their own, accreting and secreting fragments of an old, an epic vocabulary, from Asia and from Africa, but to an ancestral, an ecstatic rhythm in the blood that cannot be subdued by slavery or indenture. . . .*

There has been a correspondence of growing mutual exclusivity between the culture of whites and the culture of blacks. The overpowering national dominance of white culture is underscored ironically by the notice given to us in the month of February and the African song on the program being performed in this, the Episcopalian's signature church. The all-day, everyday culture of mainstream America is white. I am not white. Thus I have a problem, as do the other blacks, Hispanics, East Indians, Jews, third-worlders, and nonwhites generally in this room—the three seated in the apse, the handful singing from the transept, and the rest of them spread thinly across the nave. I don't know about the others, but I suspect that many of the blacks, though they certainly must feel an undiagnosed strangeness being here, do not believe that they have any problem at all, and those who do are stuck here, in any case, wanting as they do the very best education for their children.

The public schools in the District of Columbia are good and better-funded only in city neighborhoods with high concentrations of whites. So public school was not an option for us. We would have liked Khalea to have attended a school with a high concentration of black students. We could not do this, in large part, because the District's funding formula all but guarantees the failure of these schools. Hence, the blacks are here with no place to celebrate themselves, unlike the Jews who have their own full-time academies as well as supplementary weekend schools to provide their children with that which the National Cathedral School will not.

Unbeknownst, I am certain, to the whites here, the vast majority of the blacks sitting here speak two languages: the first, the English we learned in slavery, and the second, the English we learned after slavery, although some, like Frederick Douglass, who taught himself to read while enslaved, spoke during slavery the second English as fluently as the first.

One might say that first English is to blacks what Yiddish is to Jews, Yiddish being the bastardized admixture of German and Slavic languages spoken by the poor and savagely oppressed Jews of Eastern Europe. Society Jews, I am told, are somewhat ashamed of Yiddish, as are society blacks, including those sitting here, ashamed of their first English.

It is very difficult to learn a language at the same time that you are not allowed to learn to read. Worse still is to be forced into this while being stripped of the language of your native birth culture. *Deprived of their original language, the captured and indentured tribes create their own. . . .*

I am not a linguist but it is reasonable to assume that there is something about the phonetic structure of the languages of the West African peoples from whose midst we were stolen that eschews the English language *th* sound. Caribbeans drop the *h* and turn *think* into *tink, thief* into *tief.* America's black descendants of slaves avoid the *th* sound as well by dropping both letters and putting a *d* in their place. *That* becomes *dat. Those* become *dose.* My point is that I am sure that there is a perfectly good reason why black people here and in the Caribbean do this, that a look at Wolof or Hausa or Dogon or any number of other languages would explain how a crushed, faint memory of mother tongues forgotten could turn up in the mandatory learning of the new cruel master's language.

But I am pretending here. Thus, I never say *dem* to *them,* they, following whose every lead, as ever *right,* I pronounce the French word *Detroit* as *Dee-tro-it.* On the dominant culture's say-so alone, I do this while saying all the *dems, doses,* and *deeses* I please at home as if I were sneaking a drink of rotgut from the cupboard. I am sitting here sick of the tyranny of the dominant culture, knowing my center of validating gravity must be located within the circle of my own people. Otherwise, I cannot find peace, which, in the last analysis, is what in life matters most.

I do not defend what I am about to say as a high value of any sort, but for some curious reason I've not yet puzzled out, I do not join easily with blacks who have no knowledge at all of first English, not even an ability to mimic it easily. Or at least the *hey, man* informal tonality of the black idiom. Of course, I would not apply this involuntary screen to a black reared apart from other blacks, let's say, on the moon somewhere. I should say, before going too far down this road, that I am practical enough to know that first English (*Ebonics* sounds like an illness to me) alone, of the ungrammatical stripe, is not the road on which one can travel to mainstream American success. Let's face it. Those with no other English to speak are all but doomed to career failure. That is the indisputable fact of the matter. No, what I'm really talking about here is first English as a kind of linguistic social avocation, a homage of sorts, a bridge to trapped classes of the living, a figurative reminder in our internal affairs of those who were *forced* to speak the language in this fashion as a consequence of racial oppression, a memory of them in appreciation for our relative deliverance, a link to a painful past never to be colored with shame. The language spoken in dark, cold, drafty slave huts, the language with which we soothed our abused mothers and comforted our broken fathers, the language with which we raised our children to face long tomorrows of brutal bondage. The language much like the victims come to speak it, battered, tortured, wrenched out of kilter. To have no memory of how we once had no alternative but to speak is to forswear the whole of the past with all of its sufferings, all of its strivings, all of its long, epic narrative of how we have come to be here in this land and today in this remote, cold, vaulted chamber, out-numbered. *Pretending*.

Culture moves across time like a broad, slow river, collecting, forgiving, leaving behind nothing. Its picture is all that can be said of a people who without its long memory are nothing to themselves.

I would not, sitting here, feel as I feel had America done something more than crack its door to a few of us in self-exculpating charity. Had it uncovered the past it had hidden from us. Had exalted it for universal consumption as an equal partner to its own. Had it shared American culture's panorama of itself with all who comprised it, Native Americans, Hispanic-Americans, Asian-Americans, African-Americans. Had it fairly shared ownership of the *idea* of America with all of its racial constituencies exuberant in mutual celebration, making finally *one* of the whole mottled lot of us.

For I am not at home here and I should be by now, wouldn't you think?

Leopold Sedar Senghor, the Senegalese poet and future president, wrote of such feelings of apartness while teaching in Tours, France, in 1936:

> The Europeans spring
> Makes advances to me
> Offering me the virgin scent of its fields
> The smile of facades in the sun
> And the soft grey of the roofs
> In gentle Touraine
> It has yet to know
> the demands of my imperious negritude

I am of *African* descent, *different* in America. I and the ageless line that I stand in require to be shown and praised on a common plane with all other Americans, though different, one group from the other, yet indistinguishable in the attention paid to any one segment of us by all of the rest of us. I am not so irreparably disaffected because such is a requirement unmet, but rather that such is an end quite clearly unsought.

Chapter Nineteen

Callousness

Notwithstanding race, America as regards government programs may well be the least compassionate toward its own citizens of the world's wealthy industrialized and middle-income nations. The American government spends a smaller percentage of its tax dollar on public programs than does virtually every country in Europe. Every Briton, every Canadian, every Kittitian need only walk into a hospital or doctor's office to qualify for medical treatment. As a percentage of GNP, America lodges parsimoniously at the bottom of the aid-giving industrialized world.

On the private side, American income disparities separating the rich from the poor have widened at an alarming rate over the last few years. Consumer advocate Ralph Nader writes in *Crashing the Party*:

> The wealth of the Forbes 400 in the three years 1998 to 2000 increased on the average for each of them by a total of 1.9 million per day! The economy has more than doubled in per capita output since the sixties, yet the working poor, the working near-poor, and the just plain destitute are everywhere. What has changed is that the rich have become superrich and, unlike the stagnant federal minimum wage, the compensation package of the well-insured and the pensioned members of Congress is keeping well ahead of inflation, thank you.

Some time before his suicide years ago, Mitch Snyder, the Washington-based advocate for the homeless, asked the church leaders of the National Cathedral to open its doors at night to the homeless. The church leaders declined. Little more than a year ago, the National Cathedral School opened on its grounds for use by its students a twenty-five-million-dollar gymnasium.

How does one explain this growing alienation of the privileged from the world around them?

These soaring, fortress-thick stone walls would appear to symbolize this alienation. For what union of spirits could occur *here,* where amplified voices boom and spread hollow into gray nothingness? There *is* here the *form* of Christian procedure, but little more. Scarcely little talk of help for any desperate *living* soul. At least, not that I have ever heard word of in this building, one of the largest of its kind in the world.

These are the people we see every day while dropping off and picking up Khalea. We see them. They smile. We smile. They speak. We speak. This much we manage across the mutually remembered national *experience.* But this is all. All we care, or, at least, safely, all we venture to know about each other. Thus, I know only the lineaments of their faces. Nothing more. By the same token, *they* know nothing of the discontents that harbor in the folds of my spirit.

How strange they seem to me is the exact measure of how strange I must seem to them. In fact, I am likely even stranger to them. They see me less often and even then, less often properly reflected in the public mirror of *their* America.

So far, so good, if the privileged had one, would be their motto.

I could name more than a score of countries, with precious little surplus in their economies, that struggle mightily to apply their meager surpluses equitably toward the protection of all their people. The United States not only makes no effort to do this, but attempts to stop poorer and more humane countries from doing this. Every woman resident of St. Kitts is eligible for an annual Pap smear, free of charge. U.S.-dominated institutions like the International Monetary Fund and the World Bank are harshly critical of this practice. But why? Are economic numbers more important than life itself? In America, the answer would at the very least be a qualified *yes*. Economic numbers quite clearly are more important than the lives of those who neither make the policies nor have voice to influence them. Like the Spartans who hurled their defective newborns from the top of Mount Taygetus, America treats its poor—white, brown, and black alike—with near the same brutishness.

American policy-makers have largely accommodated this coarseness and, calloused now, are oblivious to it. But why would America, with its hot-flint bent against public, programmatic compassion, be so dramatically unlike other majority white countries like Canada or Norway or Sweden or virtually any of the rest of the rest of Western Europe? From whence comes this peculiar pitilessness and spareness of charity? But worse than that, it could hardly be an issue of charity, in any case, when the tax dollars of the uninsured working poor *finance* the huge profits gained by the rich in first blowing up a country like Iraq and then repairing it.

For all of my life, I had wished only to live in an America that would but reciprocate my loyalty, a country that would exhort from the several and diverse mounts of its decision-making authority an ideal of public candor and unconditional compassion, a country that would say without reserve to its disadvantaged, to its involuntary victims, to Native Americans, to African-Americans, to the wretchedly poor of all colors, stripes, tongues, and religions, that your country wronged you, wronged you in separate and discrete ways, wronged you with horrific and lingering consequence, wronged you, in some cases, from long ago and for a very long time, wronged you to a degree that would morally compel any civilized nation's serious and sustained attention.

Were America Norway or Sweden or the Netherlands, I've little doubt that it would behave with a larger and more embracing spirit. Were America more racially homogeneous, were America *white*, were it not riven with the sapping fears and bigotries of *color*, were it not gripped by a sheer meanness given rise to by the seismic aftershocks of racial divisiveness, were it not money's ready catapult, were it not a fiction of its creed, its voters opiate and the demagogue's toy, were it able to comprehend how *race* alone affects, distorts, obscures virtually everything that America does at home and abroad, were it inclined to brave but a short season of *honest* self-examination, I might have remained in the only country I have ever really known and once tried to love.

Hazel and I are not impetuous people. Our decision to leave America and move to the country of her birth and childhood was taken over a considerable section of time. I knew St. Kitts as well as any nonresident could. I had visited twice a year for years, coming the first time not long after Hazel and I were married in June 1987.

Though she is a naturalized American citizen, Hazel had always wished at some point to return home for good. My reasons for leaving America, of course, were different. I had always felt spiritually countryless. I belonged to the black world and not necessarily to America. This quite unremarkable social fact was little more than an unavoidable consequence of an American racial experience that all blacks there are caused to negotiate with varying psychosocial outcomes. Leaving for me was easy.

In any case, neither Hazel's reasons for leaving nor mine were our first consideration. We wanted Khalea to experience at least part of her childhood in a racially freight-free environment that was welcoming, socially enriching, and, above all, safe. Of the three of us, hers was the biggest adjustment to make. At the age of eleven, she was changing countries, cultures, schools, and friends. Hazel and I had agreed before leaving that the decision to stay in St. Kitts or return to America would largely vest in Khalea. Our decision has been firmly vindicated. Khalea has made new friends within a stable and affirming culture where there is no wearying necessity to make of one's race a battlement. As it had in America, her academic performance continues to be exemplary.

For my own part, I have never known before now such inconspicuous, weightless ordinariness, never felt the taxless pleasure of its clear, unfouled space.

In the mind's eye of most white Americans, the *color* of poverty in America is black. A near-latent strain of subsurface racism renders what whites *see* when they look at the several *colors* of America as no more pictorially representational than a mad artist's abstract painting. Thus they literally cannot *learn* as a group through the obstruction or distortion of it that, in absolute numbers, white poverty *exceeds* black poverty. So intent are America's leaders on begrudging the descendants of slaves any special assistance that, in trying to hit poor blacks, the polished policy bigots fire birdshot from a spray gun and strike as many of their own as ours. Thus, because America is less socially compassionate than Western Europe, in degrees directly proportional to the incidence of blackness among its white, whiter, and whitest allies, racism of the virulent and distorting stripe penalizes poor white Americans right along with poor black Americans. Few thoughtful people would doubt that were America as *white* as Sweden, universal health care would have been the law of the land decades ago.

Its upper-deck passengers diverted by movie scenes of a triumphant America at war, I am convinced that America's domestic social ship is slowly sinking. The poor trapped belowdecks in endless internecine racial antagonism see the water line drawing closer to their portholes but can do little about it. Those well above who *can* do *something, do* nothing, oblivious of danger as they have been for far too long, not knowing that the balconied suites that they occupy are nothing more than larger ill-fated berths on the same proverbial sinking boat.

Boat listing now to starboard. *So far, so good,* sung loudly in the ship's ballroom, Wagnerian opera-style.

For the past twenty-five years I have lectured about race on campuses across the United States. For more than a decade, I have given somewhere in America at least one speech on every Martin Luther King Jr. Day. I believe that Dr. King would like to have seen himself first as an American and second as an African-American. However, America never allowed him or any of us that victory, then or since. Across the board, the university audience for the programs that I have addressed on King Day have been roughly 80 percent black. By and large, white students don't come and apparently don't care. They tell us by their absence much about contemporary America.

Relatively few white people will read this book. Judging from letters I have received in response to previous books, I am extrapolating a guess that whites who read black-authored nonfiction books largely read those that applaud or absolve white society of the social dilemmas of blacks. In order to win the white reader's attention, our social difficulties must be written of as unascribable and past-less, even to be of our own essential making. Failing meeting such conditions, black writers suffer from white readers a banishment of subjective nonexistence. They simply do not want to hear about causes and consequences, even when the consequences have serious implications for the well-being of the general society.

Americans tend to see the outside world in much the same way. For those in America who know me, or know of me, in leaving the United States I will have disappeared into thin air. I will continue to exist to them, but the new existence will be technical and unvisualizable. I will have left *from,* but I will not have arrived *to.* At least not to any one place they ever heard of or cared much about.

Left undescribed, *there* to Americans does not exist as anything more than a name in a space on a page, a foreign unfamiliar notation, a cartographer's figment, a schoolchild's forgettable exam fact, a cold, flat, lifeless unit of expendable information. To Americans I am *there,* and only as alive in their minds as the high school classmates they years ago lost track off, suspended in the gray thick overcast of an occluded imagination, not so much forgotten but *gone,* gone to some place in which they have been well taught to have no real interest, and even smaller knowledge.

This is how I believe white America sees black America. What is *here* to us with all that matters is very much *there* to them, and of very little interest. And because whites control the instrumentalities of national, if not global, information, *they* are *here* to *us,* even as *we* remain *there* to *them,* and for the same reasons, too often *there* even to ourselves.

In America, whites have at least ten times the wealth of blacks.

Their homeownership rate is twice ours. Our unemployment rate is twice theirs. Though constituting only 12 percent of the population, we comprise 50 percent of the country's prisoners and 50 percent of those sentenced to death. I can say these data and not offend whites. Data are what *is*. Data are *here*. Such data may even comfort them, I think. But I must not *explain* the data. Explanations belong to *there,* and *there* bores and irritates whites. Thus I cannot speak of slavery and racial discrimination and keep their attention. For the causes of all problems not directly theirs have been relegated to *there,* a place of opaque white American indifference.

"All stand, please. We will now sing with the girls our closing selection found in your hymnals on page 261."

Chapter Twenty

Friend

I had never given the subject much thought before, but now that I think about it, he was rather unlike his peers around the world who seemed dependent for their authority upon the elaborate vestments that they wore and the odd seminarian syntax with which they called out a language at you. I had been told that he was an orator of some considerable power, and perhaps he was when speaking to gatherings of his own people in his and their own language, *Creole,* but you wouldn't know this, as if one ever can, from the look and carriage of him.

He is a small man. Small and, on first appearance, quiet. Upon speaking with him, however, it becomes readily apparent that he possesses a power, not a conferred power, but some personal wellspring power that he had had all of the forty plus years of his life before I met him, just after he had begun his political exile in Washington in the early 1990s.

Perhaps I am even misidentifying this, his most distinguishing trait, but this *power* that he bore from the depths of him was almost certainly borne of that rare wedding in an unmarred soul of absolute self-knowledge and unshakable religious faith. He was a Catholic priest in those days, as well as the democratically elected president of his country, Haiti. He was also a *Christian.* The two, being a priest and a *Christian,* I mean, are not mutually exclusive, but hardly mutually inclusive, either. Indeed he was one of the very few *Christians* that I have ever had occasion to know in my life. By that I mean, he practiced the teachings of Christ in his everyday life, which I should think is a very rare thing for modern Christians. After all, Christians run the modern industrialized war machines. Christians bought and sold slaves. One Christian, Sir John Newton, made his fortune this way while writing Christian hymns on the side, *Amazing Grace* being the most famous of them. Another Christian named his British slave vessel *Jesus*.

Most people in the West call themselves Christians, including those responsible for the bombing of Baghdad and other such unChristian doings. Calling oneself a Christian these days means nothing, so sullied has the *social* faith become, having fallen sway to the blandishments of wealth and power. Easily summoned is the memory of King Herod, the near apostate Israelite who desecrated the soil of the Holy Land with temples raised before the time of Christ to honor the Roman Emperor Augustus. But a self-possessed Christ leaned against the political grain of his time, not into its tempting folds.

Theologian Howard Thurman writes of this period in *Jesus and the Disinherited*:

> In the midst of his psychological climate, Jesus began his teaching and his ministry. His words were directed to the House of Israel, a minority within the Greco-Roman world, smarting under the loss of status, freedom, and autonomy, haunted by the dream of the restoration of a lost glory and a former greatness. He focused on the urgency of a radical change in the inner attitude of the people. He recognized fully that out of the heart are issues of life and that no eternal force, however great and overwhelming, can at long last destroy a people if it does not first win the victory of the spirit against them. . . . With increasing insight and startling accuracy, he placed his finger on the "inward center" as the crucial arena where the issues would determine the destiny of his people.

One is hard put to believe that Christ would be welcomed today into the leadership ranks of the religion that he started, so few and far between are the sincere followers of his teachings. Most of us seem to have somehow forgotten that Christ was preeminently a public advocate for the rights of the poor and the dispossessed. He did not genuflect to Herod's successors or Rome or anyone else for that matter, but rather, frayed the sufferance of the rich and powerful who saw his persistent perorations on behalf of the poor and the powerless to be, in the very least, inconvenient, and, in the final analysis, threatening to the established order of the day. Most of us who identify ourselves as *Christians* are merely *social* church-sitting Christians, and thus hardly *Christians* at all, having never thought that in order to fairly call oneself a *Christian,* one ought to have been leading a life emulous of Christ, the social and political activist who led a small group of men, as poor and undecorated as himself, against the unjust and (what could only have seemed then to be the) invincible governance apparatus of all-powerful Rome and the House of Israel. You *do* see the parallels here, I trust, or else all hope should be lost for America's future. For the only kind of power the put-upon can ever hope to wield is sourced where insight necessarily begins, and that is from the realms *within.* It is this *self-knowledge,* the power of the *inner-directed,* that is, in today's culture of frivolous enticements, so difficult to discover, but once found, all but impossible to halt the contagion of.

I say all this by way of introducing further my friend, the Haitian *Christian* who possessed such power of self-possession, a power that had made him, like his exemplar, an irritant to the established order, in this, the current case, the U.S. government.

While most of us know how to distinguish what is fair from what is unfair, few of us know well enough the information and the people to which we are invited to apply this standard. We know less still when the people and the information reside far from our shores. In the case of my friend, I have the advantage of knowing the information *and* the man, the Haitian *Christian,* very well.

I have never had any illusions about the definition of friendship. My needs in this area have never been great, thus I have been able to afford my standards, which have been more than moderately exacting. Besides integrity, courage, and the various other platitudes the cliché-fiddlers have mass produced into meaninglessness, I require from my friends a melding of social compassion with intellectual independence to think, *as it were,* for themselves, and by compatible extension, for the general good of their people. Such is not an easy task when greater wealthier powers of the world warn lesser poorer people's leaders away from a defense of their *own* perceived interests, to stand down, to look away, to cut a deal, to call *up* down and *down* up. You just can't know what the pressures could be like, pressures applied in small, windowless rooms, inducements and consequences laid forward, side by side, the former there on the table to be personally squirreled away under a cloak of confidence. To really know what this is like, how lonely virtue, how utterly private and thankless morality, is to know, commensurately, how rare is the ability, first, to *know* one's own council, and then, against a gold storm befitting Herod and Rome, to muster, virtually alone, a private decency as hard as crucible steel, to keep it.

My friend had done this, and he and his country had paid, but not nearly so much as would have been the near-permanent case had Haiti sold full its storied proud soul to America.

It was in the late 1990s that I last saw him. I had been invited to visit Lafanmi Selavi, the center for street children he had founded in 1986, nearly five years before he had been elected president of Haiti with 67 percent of the vote, in the country's first democratic elections in almost two hundred years of independence.

He was standing by the front gate when I arrived that afternoon at Lafanmi Selavi ("the family is life"). By then he had been elected president of his country. Having been finally persuaded to stand for the office on the last day of registration, and with almost no time or money for campaigning, he had won all but 33 percent of the vote, despite American support for one of the other twelve candidates who ran hard and lost badly. After decades of harsh, U.S.-backed military dictatorship, the little soft-spoken priest's announcement to run for the presidency had electrified the country. He gave his campaign the name "Lavalas," which means a cleansing flood.

"Welcome back to Haiti, my friend," he said to me smiling. "Please come in. I want you to meet the children. I want you to meet the young people who will one day rebuild our country."

I looked about and drew in the moment. It was something of a political, if not a religious miracle that he was here—indeed, that he was alive at all. By then he had survived at least nine attempts on his life by members and supporters of the military dictatorship that he had spoken out against in sermons to the parishioners of St. Jean Bosco, his church on the verge of "La Saline," one of the largest slums in the capital, Port-au-Prince. On Sundays he spoke passionately in Creole to the wretchedly poor congregants of "hope and human dignity," citing with his gift for lyricism the Haitian proverb, *tout moun se moun,* every human being is a human being. The sermons were broadcast across the country on Radio Soleil, Catholic church radio. His masses were attended by the thousands.

The unassuming priest with the light inside him was at home among the poor, into whose ranks he had been born in the coastal town of Port-Salut on July 15, 1953. He was so unobtrusively self-assured that he appeared equally comfortable in the several radically different settings in which I had seen him over the years. Once, during his two-and-half-year exile in Washington, he had joined me in a press conference following a twenty-eight-day hunger strike I had undertaken to embarrass President Clinton into stopping his repatriation of refugees who were fleeing the Haitian military killing machine that the United States had trained and armed. President Clinton, who had returned many fleeing Haitians to their deaths, had agreed to comply with international law by allowing Haitians a safe haven if I would remove my own looming demise from his public conscience. The press conference had been packed with journalists from all over the world. Wan and weak, I sat beside my friend, the exiled priest-president, and listened to him answer questions in French, Spanish, Hebrew, as well as in English and Creole. I would have been even more surprised than I was had any Italian- or German-speaking journalist asked a question. But none did, and I would learn only later that he was fluent in those two languages, as well as the five I heard him speak that day.

On September 11, 1988, as my friend celebrated mass inside St. Jean Bosco, a group of paramilitary killers riddled the church with bullets. Dozens of parishioners were killed and the church was burned to the ground. The assailants directed a fusillade of rounds at the priest himself, who stood stock-still looking squarely into their faces. He was not touched. Following the massacre, public revulsion was such that it brought down the post-Duvalierist military junta that was at the time led by a faceless army general named Namphy. Rome, or, to update accounts for accuracy's sake, the Vatican, expelled the priest from the Salesian order on the grounds that his advocacy on behalf of the destitute and voiceless had crossed over from religion to politics.

But he was back now, restored to his democratically elected office, to serve out his term, most of which had expired during his exile. I embraced him and looked up at the building for signs of the fire that had been set by more of the same thugs on the eve of his inauguration. Four of the Lafanmi Selavi children had perished in the flames.

So many had suffered. During the three years of his exile, including the time in Venezuela, the military had unleashed a reign of terror. At least five thousand people had been murdered. Hundreds of thousands had gone into hiding. Another fifty thousand had fled into the sea, including those to whom President Clinton would refuse a safe haven.

We started to walk along a balustraded outside hallway toward a courtyard alive with the excited, soaring voices of children, hundreds of them from the sound of it. I had only known the president to wear a suit, usually dark and conservative, with a white shirt and a quiet necktie. Today, however, he was dressed in dark slacks and a white, open-neck dress shirt. No jacket. We turned a corner and became visible to the children assembled in the sun-drenched courtyard.

A man who may have been a Lafanmi Selavi staff person approached and said what sounded like, "Monsieur President," but by then his voice had been overtaken by a spontaneous laughing, calling, shouting roar of welcome from the children. Sounds of musically inflected Creole crossed high in the warm mid-afternoon air above the courtyard. Few words could I carve from the cacophony of laughing voices to distinguish clearly enough for understanding. One I had heard before and knew well to whom it affectionately referred: "Titid . . . Titid . . . Titid!" It was the nickname by which he was known to his parishioners at St. Jean Bosco.

And then they deluged him. Perhaps it was because many, if not most of them, knew that they would not be here, well-dressed, well-scrubbed, well-fed, learning, were it not for his initiative alone, that they would likely not be alive at all had he not salvaged them from the dangerous urban street warrens in which they had scratched to survive. They obviously loved him, and it was easy to see why. He had a way with people that all but never marks the relation of the high to the low. He had about him an openness and a humility only afforded those unbroken souls who grasp clearly the root point of life. His was the most private and least boasted of decencies. Once during his Washington exile, Ethel Kennedy had asked him to dance. He had demurred, quietly explaining that it didn't seem the right thing to do with his people at home in Haiti suffering under military dictatorship. At dinner at our home in Washington, he would eat little of his food. I had thought at the time that he was naturally abstemious. Only years later did I discover that he habitually ate little in exile for much the same reason he had declined to dance with Ethel Kennedy following the wedding of one of her children.

Later, after he had left his priesthood and married, on weekends he would throw open the grounds of the president's home at Tabarre to the poorest of the poor, in much the same way he had opened wide the gates of the National Palace on the occasion of his inauguration as president.

Perhaps it was that I had done so and not known it, but this much at least I can say with certainty: Jean-Bertrand Aristide is one of a very few *Christians* that I have ever known. By a similar and painfully ironic token, he is also one of a somewhat larger but still smaller number of *democrats* that I have known. ". . . [O]ne of the morally transcendent leaders of our time," wrote Jonathan Kozol, putting his finger right on it.

Literally no one inside or outside of Haiti, even those with political ambitions of their own, even the most implacable of his opponents, believes that his overwhelming presidential election victories of 1990 and 2001 were not fairly won, or that anyone in Haiti could come close to contesting his sweeping, well-earned popularity.

Yet the United States has taken relentless pains to destroy his every effectiveness as the democratically elected president of his country, crudely and very publicly occasioning for the Haitian people every imaginable privation. The United States had led the international community in imposing a crippling embargo on Haiti, which denied the Haitian people any of the capital needed by their government for programs that would provide, among other things, literacy training and safe drinking water.

Dr. Timothy Harris, the foreign minister of St. Kitts, was to say of this in a January 2003 interview published in *The Haiti Bulletin*:

> Democracy thrives when governments are able to deliver on their promises. People expect their government to improve their quality of life. When there are obstacles deliberately put in the path of a government being able to deliver, however, it is not just in the existing government that people lose hope, but in the entire system of democracy. Democracy takes time to build, to nurture, to develop to a satisfactory level.
>
> Countries that *truly* believe in democracy should try not to subvert any elected government and they should not deny any elected government access to the very resources needed to fulfil its social contract.

In another issue of the same publication, Dr. Paul Farmer, a professor of medicine and anthropology at Harvard University would add:

> I had worked in Haiti under the Duvalier dictatorship and despite the brutality of that regime, U.S. and international aid flowed freely. Aid also flowed under a series of military juntas famous for their oppression. Granted,

there were brief periods during these three decades in which the violations were so spectacular that we cut off aid. But, ironically, it was really only after these brutal and undemocratic governments were replaced by real democracy that the United States, the OAS, *et al.* decided to ban aid to the Haitian government.

The Pulitzer Prize–winning author Tracy Kidder wrote in *The Washington Post* on August 7, 2002:

> Indeed the United States is actively impeding the flow of foreign aid to Haiti's government, a total of approximately five hundred million dollars, a sum roughly equal to the country's annual budget. We are even blocking illegally, a series of already-approved loans from the Inter-American Development Bank (IDB) totaling one hundred and forty-eight million, designated for improvements in Haiti's water resources, education and public health.
>
> The Bush administration's foreign policy bureaucrats have spun webs of pretexts to justify this shunning of a democratically elected government—"irregularities in vote-counting" in legislative election is only the most ridiculous of these. The plain fact is that our foreign policy establishment despises Haiti's very popular president, Jean-Bertrand Aristide, and wants to make sure his popularity wanes.

They despise this self-possessed, principled black man precisely because he *is* a self-possessed, principled, and decent black man. They despise him because, as any democracy's social contract would require, he listens first to *his* people as they would listen to him, and finally because he has sustained the temerity to represent his country's interests to America before representing America's interests to his country.

We are galled only that he is not a toady. He is a man. What's more, he is a brilliant man, a brilliant, black, honorable man who *is* not, *cannot,* will *not* ever be America's toady. And for this alone,

America loathes him, utterly, shamefully, self-revealingly. Loathes him enough to ignore—no—destroy his democracy and kill his country's children for the collateral mischief of it. And there is nothing the Haitians can do. They've tried everything. They've even paid out millions of dollars that they could ill afford in interest and "commission fees" to the Inter-American Development Bank, but the bank, under pressure from Washington, had refused to release the loan funds that were approved long ago. Even the bank had been embarrassed about how it would publicly explain bank loan ledgers that registered a ZERO for Haiti, the hemisphere's poorest country, a full-fledged democracy—this long after loans had been fully approved for health care, education, roads, and clean drinking water.

Isaac Alfred would have been thirteen at the time that I visited Lafanmi Selavi. It is unlikely, however, that he was there. He was neither an orphan nor homeless. In fact he lived with both of his parents in Cange, which is a considerable distance from the capital. By all accounts, Isaac was a good student and an industrious worker, helping his mother and father with a range of family-related chores.

A little over a year ago, just after Isaac had turned fifteen, he contracted typhoid fever from the unclean water in Cange. Cange had been earmarked for a special water project by the government, but the project had never been started because the funds for its construction had never been released by the Inter-American Development Bank. Isaac could not be treated when the fever struck him because there was no health facility near his home. His parents took him to the nearest clinic, which turned out to be a great distance from Cange, and by the time they reached the clinic with him, the fever had done considerable damage to his internal organs.

It was at the clinic that Isaac and his parents met Ethel Kennedy, who was leading an American fact-finding delegation looking into the human impact of the international embargo against Haiti. Several congresswomen were traveling with Mrs. Kennedy, including Donna Christensen, Jan Schakowsky, and Diane Watson. Todd Howland, the executive director of the Robert F. Kennedy Memorial, said in an interview later that the members of the delegation had been "greatly affected by their meeting with them [Isaac and his parents]. When the delegation returned to the United States, they learned that Isaac had died."

Not long thereafter, the Robert F. Kennedy Memorial brought suit in the U.S. Federal District Court in Washington, D.C., against the Inter-American Development Bank over its Haiti policy. Mr. Howland said: "This action dates back to four loans, totaling about one hundred and forty-six million dollars, that were approved for Haiti by the Inter-American Development Bank in 1998. These loans were for four sectors—health, education, water, and roads.

"On the IDB's website, there are glowing reports about the outstanding work that the IDB is doing in Haiti. What they do not mention is that the IDB never actually funded these projects . . . as a result, Haitians have died. There have been actual deaths linked to the fact that the IDB never disbursed these loans. . . .

"We are taking action in tort and in contract. The government of Haiti acted on behalf of third-party beneficiaries—the people of Haiti. The government signed and ratified loans and also *paid* five million dollars to the IDB in anticipation of receiving the benefits of this contract. Haiti received nothing."

Why?

Why the crude, gratuitous hostility? When America supports abusive unelected governments all over the world, why the spectacular meanness toward a poor, nascent democracy like Haiti's? With its rudimentary health system already compromised by an AIDS crisis precipitated by American and Canadian sex tourists, why would a colossus like the United States notice to trample unprovoked upon the new and unconsolidated freedoms of a people like Haiti's, a people from among whose ranks, a great general, Francois Dominique Toussaint L'Ouverture, had once emerged to fight at Savannah alongside George Washington when freedom's fate hung *here* in the American balance?

In general, one is to wonder what it is in the American bully's character that would have it ration the leaders of poorer, nonlethal countries so little space in which to stand erect, to effect even the pose of self-determination, to raise any but the most perfunctory of voices on behalf of *theirs* who dream much the same as Americans dream, of freedom and the richer life that only freedom affords?

But American hatred for Haiti goes well beyond its general arrogance toward *third-world* countries. Indeed, there is no rational reason to explain the deep-seated institutional enmity with which America has addressed Haiti during the two hundred years that have followed its successful military slave revolt against France and Napoleon Bonaparte. I expect that the real reason marks yet again the yawning divide between blacks and whites in America and elsewhere. It is profoundly *racial,* with its own detailed annotated history, unlike the American full long experience with any other people of the Caribbean archipelago. What black Americans should love Haiti for, indeed what *all* blacks across the hemisphere *owe* Haiti for, official America (which is largely white America) subconsciously and sometimes not so subconsciously has *hated* Haiti for, time immemorial. The Haitians are *different.* They are just not like the rest of us black hemispheric locals—ambulatory bad replicas of our conquerors. This is what Aristide, the decent man that I know well, represents with his impregnable self-possession. Even in these, the worst of Haitian times, it can be seen in the proud spark with which Haitians talk of and remember themselves. They are the *Africans* in the neighborhood whose spirit the slaver never really conquered. They are the inconvenient reminders who remember. And they *remember* all.

Somewhere in the troubled rest of the American subconscious, some *something* that only the Haitians have miraculously retained cuts in the American craw like a sharp, jagged black diamond hewn from stolen earth by the slave sweat of Africa. Some whole, surviving, remembering, ageless personhood that they, the Haitians, hold for us *all* in trust, America simply cannot brook. Aristide is but the living face of an epic Haitian story. He is its trustee, its curator, its griot, his people's muse, their brilliant and brave living champion, their moral grasp and understanding of the long pull. He is the *personification* of the Haitian people's quiet, nonnegotiable dignity.

And America loathes this, as it loathes that vestigial *us,* still faintly decipherable in the old, well-banked fire that flickers and crackles to burn anew in revival of a spiritually long-abused people. Haiti, you *must* see, is the *North Star* of our past and the open window onto our psychic renewal, our joining of a lost past to a found future. *The way out is the way back through.* In this hemisphere, the Africa of the shining ancients lives nowhere as it does in embattled Haiti. Whether America *knows* this or not is of no consequence. It is lodged in its subconscious. It is the only explanation for America's deep and abiding animus toward a people who announce with a watchtowerman's indefatigable sense of duty: *I am a Haitian.* Said just like so. And America hates this with the exponential guilt of a war criminal on the lam from its past.

On countless plantations, blacks in America tried to do what the Haitian slaves had done, but failed. We had some small victory in Jamaica with their *Maroons,* but nothing like Haiti's. Everywhere else we had failed. Denmark Vesey had failed. Gabriel Prosser had failed. Harriet Tubman, Frederick Douglass, Sojourner Truth, and the others managed against *it* about as much victory as there was to be managed in America.

But Haiti, or St. Domingue, as it was then called, had succeeded, succeeded spectacularly. With military tactics studied even today, these Haitians, these black people, *our* people, for god's sake, *defeated* the sixty-thousand-man army of Napoleon Bonaparte, expelled British forces, and sent Spain packing as well, shattering, we had hoped forever, the myth of white strategic, political, military, and spiritual superiority.

On November 18, 1803, Capois Death, so called because of his fearlessness, led the Haitian charge against the French fort at Vestieres. His horse was shot out from under him. He rose and began running toward the thick walls of the fort, pointing his sword toward the French guns mounted behind the parapet and crying out to his men: *"En avant! En avant!"* Forward! Forward! His hat was shot from his head. Again he rose running toward the French guns that exploded the ground around him. Men falling, gut-shot. Blood everywhere. The sounds of agonized dying mixed with peals of bloody thunder. *"En avant! En avant!"* Death screamed, afoot still, but never slowing. This was the battle that turned the corner against French rule over Haiti, that marked the beginning of the end of Europe's stranglehold on the *New World*.

Former slaves had done this. Haitians. It was never to be forgotten. Or forgiven:

> The rebellious slaves of Haiti inflicted grievous military defeat on all who opposed them: The *colons* of the island and their militias, regular French regiments sent from Europe, a significant Spanish army from Santo Domingo, a British army with regular soldiers, and finally, a fully equipped French force fresh from Napoleon's victories in Europe led by the Emperor's own brother-in-law. For many who have recounted this story the victory is made all the more dramatic by the fact that the triumphant slaves, fresh from the debilitating labor of plantation agriculture in the tropics, were able to defeat experienced soldiers. As C. L. R. James put it: "The revolt is the only successful slave revolt in history. . . . The transformation of slaves, trembling in hundreds before a single white man, into a people able to organize themselves and defeat the most powerful European nations of their day, is one of the great epics of revolutionary struggle and achievement.
> —John K. Thornton
> "African Soldiers in the Haitian Revolution"
> *Caribbean Slavery in the Atlantic World*

The successful Haitian slave revolt ended France's dreams of empire in the *New World* and made possible the Louisiana Purchase from France by the United States. For its own part, in answer to Haiti's hard-won freedom, the United States joined with its allies in imposing a global economic embargo against the fledgling black republic that would last until 1862.

It would hardly overstate the case to say that the far-reaching reverberations of Haiti's military success against the powers of Europe changed forever the political and economic landscape of the *New World*.

Simon Bolivar, the Great Liberator, launched from a free Haiti his military campaign to free Central and South America from the clutches of Spain. Haiti's president, Alexandre Petion, provided Bolivar not only shelter twice, but "4000 guns, 15,000 pounds of powder, a quantity of lead, some provisions and a printing press" (Logan 1941:222). Petion also gave him the help of Haitian volunteer soldiers. This infuriated a hegemonic America. Under pressure from the United States, the new Spanish-American republics, created out of Bolivar's success, declined to recognize Haiti or to invite it to participate in the Pan-American Conference of 1825.

> It [Haiti] was "the first of a number of third-world revolutionary societies to become important objects in the politics of hegemonic or core powers, especially those of the United States, and suffer the consequences of diplomatic isolation and systematic attempts at subversion by those core powers" (Stinchcombe 1995:239). Yet at the same time, it also became a positive and hopeful symbol of revolutionary social change for those who identified with its racial project. Without recognition as a legitimate state, Haiti had to build international ties through informal and, at times, covert channels of communication that linked it with those who had interest in abolishing slavery and liberating black people.
>
> —Mimi Sheller
> *Democracy After Slavery*

In the teeth of American economic isolation, diplomatic ostracism, and general hostility, Haiti gave refuge to runaway American slaves. It welcomed both Native Americans and Africans to its door. Writes Sheller: "When black captives being transported from Maryland to Georgia led a shipboard rebellion in 1826, for example, they reportedly demanded that the vessel's surviving crew take them to Haiti."

Haiti was suspected by Spain of having links to the abolitionist movements in its colonies in Cuba and Puerto Rico. Events in Haiti also had a profound influence of blacks seeking freedom in nearby Jamaica. In America, black abolitionists like Martin Delaney and David Walker were inspired by the convulsions that had transfigured Haiti. Another, Henry Highland Garnet, lauded Toussaint L'Ouverture and called for a slave rebellion in America. When John Brown was executed in December 1859, flags across Haiti were flown at half-mast. By the 1860s, Haiti was associated with the antislavery struggle from one end of the Americas to the other.

In exchange for the indispensable assistance that Haiti was to render to Simon Bolivar, Alexandre Petion, the Haitian president, made of the Great Liberator but one request: that upon success, Bolivar would free Latin America's slaves. Bolivar agreed and put his commitment in the form of a published proclamation. However, with the cutting of deals to facilitate Bolivar's primary goals, Petion's lone request was sacrificed to expediency and Bolivar's commitment to emancipate the slaves was forgotten.[1]

This was among the first of many treacheries that the people of Haiti would be caused to endure from whites over the next two hundred years as a price, direct and indirect, of their victory over France and over the interests of slaveholding and slave-trading nations around the world, including the United States of America.

Thomas Jefferson was to write during this period that, "Eternal vigilance is the price of liberty." But the American president, who did so much to globally quarantine the newly liberated Haiti, and who never freed, in his lifetime, a single one of his own slaves, was writing only about the liberty of whites, feeling strongly as he did that whenever necessary, white liberty, anywhere in the world, was to be taken and defended at the very *expense* of black liberty.

Haiti, the world's first black republic, had been *there* for Bolivar. It had not dissembled or quaked or feared of Spain's angry, and

---

[1] Alexandre Petion became president of Haiti in 1807. He confiscated French plantations and divided the land among the Haitian peasants. He also provided them with theretofore unknown freedoms.

likely, costly reaction. It had given Bolivar, a white, the assistance that no one else would give him, not only because it was consistent with Haiti's beliefs in notions of *universal* liberty, but because it was to them the right and honorable thing to do.

Bolivar, however, under pressure from America, Europe, and slaveholding interests in Latin America, was not *there* for Haiti and not for the black slaves chained in relentless misery to Latin American plantations. Despite the promises that Bolivar had made to Petion in order to get from him what he needed, Bolivar proved himself, in the final analysis, clearly more concerned about the views and sensibilities of the world's white power structures than about the requirements of his black benefactors and the suffering of the slaves that his benefactors cared so deeply about.[2]

Of course, President Petion, who met with Bolivar on January 2, 1816, could not have read in time the letter of advice that a twenty-three-year-old writer, Alexander Pushkin, had written to his younger brother, Lev Sergeevich Pushkin, in the fall of 1822. Pushkin, who only once, in a short life of thirty-seven years, set foot outside Russia, was obviously inspired to warn from the Russian in his bloodline (his mother was Ethiopian) that:

> You will have to deal with men with whom you are not
> yet acquainted. Always commence by thinking of them
> all the evil imaginable: then you will not have to lower
> your opinion very much.

There is ample existential evidence to suggest that there exist certain conditioned cultural predispositions to trust or to deceive, to give or to take, and that the distribution of these traits along economic class and/or racial lines, marked from the hour of the landfall in the New World of Christopher Columbus, has favored the propertied whites of Europe at the expense of the people of

---

[2] Five South American countries—Venezuela, Colombia, Ecuador, Peru, and Bolivia—owe their independence to the efforts of Simon Bolivar. His own country, Venezuela, treated him badly for it, not allowing his body back into the country until twelve years after his death from tuberculosis at the age of forty-seven. Some accounts have it that he pleaded with the leaders of the countries he had liberated to free their slaves but failed.

Africa and the indigenous people stumbled upon by Columbus on his first voyage to the Americas in 1492.

> The patience and forbearance of the poor are among the strongest bulwarks of the rich.
> —C. L. R. James
> *The Black Jacobins*

We have given. *They* have taken. They have taken even when we have not given. And they have made us with their power forget virtually all of what has happened, while they have forgotten *nothing*—neither what *they* did nor what *we* did.

While whites tell us that blacks have no long-term history, they remember verbosely to tell us all every detail of *their* evolution as a people—the facts, the fiction, and the mythology. Every calendar day of the year, they gather us in circles around a pile of rocks of suspect provenance in Jamestown, Virginia, and render rote their version of the "American" story. What Italian child does not know the tale of Romulus and Remus and the birth of Rome? What French child failed to participate in the 1996 festivities celebrating the fifteen-hundredth anniversary of the baptism of Clovis I (466–511), thought to be the first monarch to preside over a united France? What Japanese schoolchild cannot recite the belief that the goddess Izanami and the god Izanagi descended from heaven to create the islands of Japan? What first-world nation is without a foundation myth of this kind with which to assert its legitimacy and solidify the collective self-esteem of its people?

No people on earth have a more glorious foundation story (a verifiable history and not a myth) than do the Haitian people, whose forbears sacrificed *all* for their freedom and for ours. What a broadly human disgrace it is that they have little left to show for it but their proud tenacious *Haitianness,* set against a world of endless American-led white revenge and the general ignorance and indifference of blacks in America and, saddest of all, throughout the Caribbean.

In 1789, the fruits of slavery on the West Indian colony of St. Domingue made up two-thirds of the world trade of France. St.

Domingue, whose entire economic structure rested upon the backs of five hundred thousand African slaves, was France's flagship colony and the pride of the French world empire.

In 1791, two years after the start of the French Revolution, the slaves on St. Domingue undertook a meticulously planned and co-ordinated revolt that carried onto every slave plantation in the colony. The fighting would last for twelve years and end with the establishment of the new black Republic of Haiti, constituted of former slaves who by their wits, courage, and tenacity had freed themselves.

> By a phenomenon often observed, the individual leadership responsible for this unique achievement was almost the work of a single man—Toussaint L'Ouverture. . . . The writer believes that between 1789 and 1815 with the single exception of Bonaparte himself, no single figure appeared on the historical stage more greatly gifted than this Negro, a slave till he was forty-five.
>
> —C. L. R. James
> *The Black Jacobins*

On June 7, 1802, and toward the end of Toussaint's and his army's long campaign, the French general Brunet wrote to Toussaint inviting him to meet at Brunet's headquarters. The letter brimmed with expressions of Brunet's good faith and sincerity. Though not well at the time, Toussaint, despite warnings, went to Brunet's headquarters, whereupon Toussaint was arrested, put with his family on a frigate, and summarily embarked for France. Stepping on board, Toussaint spoke the words that were to constitute his last legacy to his people: "In overthrowing me, you have cut down in St. Domingue only the trunk of the tree of liberty. It will spring up again by the roots for they are numerous."

News of Toussaint's arrest did little more than redouble his people's resolve to prevail. Half a century after the revolution, Lemonier-Delafosse, a Frenchman who supported slavery, would record in his memoirs: "But what men these blacks are! How they fight and how they die! One has to make war against them to know

their reckless courage in braving danger. . . . I have seen a solid column, torn by grape-shot from four pieces of cannon, advance without making a retrograde step. The more they fell, the greater
seemed to be the courage of the rest. . . ."

On the orders of Bonaparte, Toussaint was locked away in a
damp, cold prison cell three thousand feet above sea level in France's
Jura Mountains. He would survive only one winter. By the spring of
1803, he had shrunk to a shell of his former robust self. On April 7,
1803, Toussaint L'Ouverture, the former slave whose armies had
defeated Europe's best, was found sitting upright in his chair, frozen
to death. At the hour of his demise, his comrades-at-arms at home
were drafting the Haitian declaration of independence.

In their domestic affairs, American governments, Republican and
Democratic, have always preferred for their favor blacks who stay
roughly to the majority's course of public policy opinion. Blacks
who are personally ambitious and self-seeking, blacks who make
no heartfelt broader brief on behalf of the whole of the black community, are looked upon by the leaders of both parties with some
amount of relieved appreciation. Conversely, blacks who think not
first of their own narrow career lot, but rather of the general condition of their full community are significantly less likely to be invited forward to high public positions. This is quite indisputably
the way things *are* and have always been in America. Thus the
black community, to the extent that it has been represented in the
halls of American power at all, has enjoyed, with respect to its own
long, unaddressed agenda, a mere symbolic race-mute presence at
the policy table, and very seldom anything more.

In any case, America has all but ceased any pretense of effort on
domestic racial and social justice issues. Even the fulsome empty
words of the old promises have disappeared from its public voice.
Still, Republican, as well as Democratic administrations, must anoint
for flattery *leasable* blacks to sit snug to the president in cabinet
meetings, on the condition that no unseemly to-do is made by them
about the general condition of blacks, either the causes of such, or
possible solutions.

In America's foreign policy attitudes toward the black world, a more lethal application of the same selection modality would apply. The case of Haiti is but a troubling example of a larger, more disturbing general American behavior.

First, it must be taken as an axiom that America takes no step toward any country until such step can be seen to serve American interests first. America never *helps* anyone, even the starving, unless its proposed assistance can be tied to an American interest, either strategic or economic, and one cannot always distinguish one from the other. Inasmuch as *business* is the largest unseen gorilla seated at the America foreign policy table, any policy to be promulgated must be fashioned to serve business's interest first.

Business's interest is to make money—for itself and for no one else. Little is as it seems. Free trade is not free. Fair trade is not fair. Foreign aid is not aid.

> Many in the first world imagine the amount of money spent on foreign aid to developing countries is massive. In fact, it amounts to only .03% of GNP of the industrialized nations. In 1995, the director of the U.S. aid agency defended his agency by testifying to his congress that eighty-four cents of every dollar of aid goes back into the U.S. economy in goods and services purchased. For every dollar the United States puts into the World Bank, an estimated two dollars actually goes into the U.S. economy in goods and services. Meanwhile in 1995, severely indebted low-income countries paid one billion dollars more in debt and interest to the International Monetary Fund (IMF) than they received from it. For the forty-six countries of sub-Saharan Africa, foreign debt service was four times their combined governmental health and education budgets in 1996. So, we find that aid does not aid.
>
> —Jean-Bertrand Aristide
> *Eyes of the Heart:*
> *Seeking a Path for the*
> *Poor in the Age of*
> *Globalization*

I know for certain only one other Caribbean head of state who would have written the above. Most, if not all, believe what President Aristide writes to be painfully the case, but few would say so publicly because they wish not to land, as Aristide has, on America's wrong side, which is quite easy to do should you attempt to stand erect in the small space allotted you.

America has no real interest in any poor country's prospect for democracy. In fact, it has no working interest in *any* people's fundamental rights outside of its own to do what it wants to do anywhere it wants to do it. Of course it doesn't come out and say such, honesty being the weak coin that it is. But in seeking advantageous entrée, either business or strategic, to another country it is not hard to see that venal leadership there would be more to America's liking than leadership that takes its own people's interests seriously.

America at home has shown a demonstrable willingness to help blacks who want to help themselves and themselves alone. Blacks with broader, more selfless hopes are invariably deemed angry, strident, outside the mainstream. Violating the new moment's wet-paint orthodoxy, these blacks were the first to arrive to the yawning voiceless hole in which the millions who protested the war against Iraq now live atop them in the racial hierarchy of the ignored.

But this is nothing. Consider the dilemma of Aristide, a good man who has been called by the United States everything but a child of God, this last lie, omission's ironic touch, perhaps the most sadistic lie of them all.

Very serious people have written copiously about what Aristide endures, books, articles, speeches that you likely know nothing of at all, not a jot. America is a *free* country, and serious honest people can write and say all they wish to write and say, but who cares? Nobody much reads. Certainly not Joe Sixpack, who will shoot *the hell outta innybody* he's told to shoot the hell out of. Paul Farmer of Harvard and Noam Chomsky of MIT and Jonathan Kozol of *bestsellerdom* are good men and brilliant thinkers who've written much on this subject. But America doesn't give a damn. America doesn't know that they've written about "that, what, Haiti?" Joe

Sixpack doesn't even know who they *are*! And the rosy-cheek, private-school, policy-wonk sociopaths in Foggy Bottom find the whole sight sidesplitting.

What was it that C. L. R. James wrote way back in 1938 in his classic study of the Haitian Revolution, *The Black Jacobins*?

> But today as then, the great propertied interests and their agents commit the most ferocious crimes in the name of the whole people, and bluff and brow-beat them by lying propaganda.

I'll try to make this as painless as possible, but Americans really must learn that one needs to know, at least, a little of what went on in the past to have any chance at all of understanding the present. Between Toussaint's heroic rebellion of 1791 and Aristide's stunning election in 1991 (with 67 percent of the vote to the U.S.-supported candidate, Marc Bazin's, 14 percent), the United States has done documentably some quite awful things to the people of Haiti:

- During the rebellion itself, the United States joined European powers in aiding France's violent suppression of the slave uprising.

- The United States blocked Haiti's participation in the Western Hemisphere Panama Conference of 1825 and did not recognize Haiti until 1862, when President Abraham Lincoln thought of Haiti as a convenient repository for freed American slaves. Said Senator Robert Hayne of South Carolina in 1824: "We never can acknowledge her independence. . . . The peace and safety of a large portion of our union forbids us even to discuss it."

- Placatory toward France, the United States accommodated its European ally as France pressed Haiti for 150 million francs to be paid in reparations to the slave plantocracy for losses suffered in the slave's successful quest for freedom. This served early on to destroy the new black republic's fragile economy.

- During the American military occupation of Haiti, which began under President Woodrow Wilson on July 28, 1915, and lasted for nineteen years, de facto slavery in Haiti was reinstituted; Haiti's constitutional system was dismantled; 226,000 acres of Haitian soil were given over in concessional lease arrangements to American corporations; fifty thousand peasants were dispossessed in the North alone; workers were forced to toil for twenty cents a day, and the U.S. Marine Corps' "pacification" efforts claimed up to fifteen thousand Haitian lives.

- In 1937, three years after the American occupation had ended, Rafael Trujillo, ruler of the neighboring Dominican Republic, ordered his troops to undertake a massacre of Haitians that claimed eighteen thousand to thirty-five thousand lives. Afterward, Cordell Hull, the U.S. secretary of state, said: "President Trujillo is one of the greatest men in Central America and in most of South America."

- President John F. Kennedy provided the murderous Haitian dictator Francois "Papa Doc" Duvalier with broad military assistance, in the words of Noam Chomsky, "as a part of a general program of extending U.S. control over the security forces in Latin America, a long-standing project carried a long step forward by the Kennedy intellectuals, who recognized that 'in the Latin American cultural environment' the military must be prepared to remove government leaders from office whenever, in the judgment of the military, the conduct of those leaders is injurious to the welfare of the nation."

- Under Jean-Claude "Baby Doc" Duvalier, the ruthless dictator's ruthless son, the United States funded efforts to establish American assembly plants in an environment of terror and pittance wages. Chomsky: "The consequences were profits for U.S. manufacturers and the Haitian superrich, and a decline of fifty-six percent in Haitian wages through the 1890s."

- The United States provided the post-Duvalier National Council of Government (NCG) with $2.8 million in its first year, a year in which the NCG killed more Haitian civilians than Jean-Claude Duvalier had killed in fifteen.

*   *   *

I take with a grain of salt much of what I read in newspapers. Michael Manley of Jamaica had been one of only two Caribbean prime ministers to attend his inauguration. The rest had been chilled away by the United States. I called my old friend in Kingston hoping he would justify my excited hopes.

"I think he is all that is said about him. The Haitian people love him. That, in and of itself, says a lot. It's been a long time since they've had a leader who cared about them."

"I'd like to invite him to Washington to address my annual dinner, but I, of course, don't know him, and I doubt that he's heard in Haiti about what we've been doing here. Will you intercede for me?"

"I'd be happy to call him for you and get back to you in a few days."

I respected Michael Manley and valued his opinions as well as his friendship. To me, the priest seemed to have come out of nowhere, but of course this wasn't so. The Haitian poor, who were getting their first democratic opportunity after decades of U.S.-assisted tyranny, knew him quite well. They were not at all surprised by the drubbing that Marc Bazin, America's handpicked candidate, had received.

The military coup, of course, changed everything. It may have been more than a year later when I finally met President Aristide as I sat next to him on a stage before a packed house that he was to address at Howard University in Washington. It wasn't hard to see the reasons for his huge popularity at home. He wasn't a politician and, from what I could discern from the English segments of his speech, he didn't sound like a politician. In any case, the pro-democracy, Creole-speaking Haitian audience liked what he had had to say.

Over the months that followed, he shared with Hazel and me his despair over what was happening at home in Haiti. Scarcely a morning arrived without the *bodies*. Some had had the faces sheared off. Some were without arms or legs. Those that were not riddled with bullets bore the unmistakable grisly signature of the machete hacked hard against the head, the extremities, the torso, the angle and interval of the wounds suggesting that the victims had been forced to die slowly, watching with terror the glinting arc of the long sharp blade slicing through the out-turned palms of their pleading hands and into their horrified faces. Long rents of veiny extruded tissue lipped open onto black skin. Bodies curled into a last and futile fetal defense. Men, women, children. Most suspected simply of supporting democracy, Aristide. Some simply married to sympathizers. Children, simply there at the time, one supposes. No one really knows.

The sun found the dead at dawn virtually every morning. In the open sewers of Cite Soleil. Along roadsides. Floating in reddened streams. Everywhere.

All knew this to be the work of FRAPH, a paramilitary band of armed thugs operating at the army's behest. Many of them had once been members of the now defunct Tonton Macoutes, the dreaded killing machine that had done similar wet work for Duvaliers, papa and son, in years past.

Between FRAPH and the army that had overthrown Aristide's democratically elected government, more than five thousand civilians had been slaughtered. At daytime rallies, FRAPH members, on their leader's signal, gave the Nazi salute, right hand in the air, palms forward. The leader, a tall man with a moustache that curled at the corners of a cruel mouth, exhorted his charges in broad daylight: "If Aristide were to return, he would die."

The leader's name is Emmanuel "Toto" Constant. He often walks in public with an Uzi or a .357 Magnum tucked under his shirt. He is the son of the late Gerard Emmanuel Constant, the army chief of staff under Francois "Papa Doc" Duvalier. The son is universally feared.

Armed with M-16s, Uzis, pistols, machetes, tire irons, axes, his men break into homes at night and drag out the victims. A woman told Human Rights Watch: "One guy took me by the hands and led me to the front porch. . . . He said 'Lie down. If you don't I'll split your head open.' . . . He pulled his pants down to his knees, and lifted up my nightgown, pulled down my underpants and raped me."

Before FRAPH, before Emmanuel "Toto" Constant, the man the Haitians call "the devil," rape was unknown in Haitian society.

By mid-1994 thousands had fled, many into the forest, into the sea on makeshift boats, rafts with small chance of making safe landfall ninety miles to the north. By now even FRAPH trainees have begun to flee from their fellow members. "When they kill and rape people, we are forced to sit and watch," said one.

Earlier the CIA analyst for Latin America, Brian Latell, had visited and followed with a report: "I do not wish to minimize the role the military plays in intimidating and occasionally terrorizing real and unsuspected opponents, but my experiences confirm the [intelligence] community's view that there is no systematic or frequent lethal violence aimed at civilians."

FRAPH had waited at the docks to identify those who had fled and been returned by President Clinton, who must have known that his repatriation of the refugees was tantamount to a death sentence. No one knows how many Clinton condemned in this fashion to FRAPH and the military's bloody disposal. At least, hundreds.

My hunger strike had changed all that. Now, the president was screening refugees. Those seen to have a well-founded fear were protected in Jamaica and Guantanamo. The refugees continued trying the sea, with half of them perishing there, the other half flooding into the refugee centers by the thousands. And then there was no place more to put them save Florida, whose electoral votes Clinton needed to win a second term. Florida wanted white Cuban refugees. Florida did not want black Haitian refugees.

In September 1994, the United States undertook a full-scale military invasion of Haiti. FRAPH members were rounded up and arrested. The "devil," however, whose whereabouts were well known, remained untouched. Months later on Christmas Eve, Constant walked over the border and into the Dominican Republic, from which he boarded a flight to San Juan, connecting there for New York.

*   *   *

The terrain of the Delmarva Peninsula is table-flat, distinguished only by tall pines that dot the narrow spine that separates the Chesapeake Bay to the west from the Atlantic Ocean to the east.

I am all recovered now from my twenty-eight-day hunger strike. I had lost from my six-foot-five-inch frame a great deal of weight. Toward the end, my blood had become too thick for my heart to pump at its own normal rate of exertion. My pulse had begun to gallop. My blood pressure had spiked, landing me in the hospital with severe dehydration. The fast, however, continued to the apparent alarm of the White House, whose soon-to-be national security advisor, Samuel Berger, a law school classmate of mine at Harvard, paid me a bedside visit in order to reach some understanding of terms that would satisfy me and President Clinton. No need to reprise here what I have already written about in a previous memoir. Suffice it to say luckily I sustained no permanent heart damage, which is what the doctors had feared. Democracy had been restored to Haiti. President Aristide had gone home to lead a country that, though already the poorest in the hemisphere, had been made a lawless bloody shambles by the military and FRAPH during the painful years of their reign.

Hazel and I own a modest retreat on the bay in the southernmost, Virginia part of the three-state peninsula. On Fridays, as often as twice a month, we make the 196-mile drive east and then south from our home in Washington to the tiny eastern shore town of Exmore, Virginia, where we turn west toward the bay. Khalea was six months old when we opened the house. She is now five. We have driven the route so many times that we mark the time we are making by the little towns we pass through but know little else about. Easton, Cambridge, then south toward the largest, Salisbury, before leaving Maryland for the forty-mile drive through the narrowing Virginia section that ends at the bay's mouth, some eighteen miles wide, with Virginia Beach, Virginia, situated due west of the peninsula's toe on the mainland Virginia coast of the United States.

The smallest of the towns have Native American names: Onancock, Nassawadox, Wicomico. Only Wicomico, as I recall, wasn't the name of a town but of a Maryland county. In all the years of passing through it, all I could see as evidence of an established settlement was an ugly blockish building surrounded by a tall, razor wire–topped anchor fence situated to the west of the road in the far reedy flat distance, and a road sign that informed motorists this was the Wicomico County Detention Center. I had sped past it a hundred times and paid it no particular attention. But this time, the next, and the next after that would be different. As we pass, Hazel and I look together at the squat building in the distance and shudder ever so imperceptibly.

He is there. The monster. The "devil." Toto. Haiti's Hitler once apparent. The killer who saw blood and was stirred by its sudsy flow, its peculiar metallic odor. A man who drank in the looks of naked fear on the battered faces of trussed-up torture victims. He was to me something more than a human rights event. He was a sick curiosity, like Al Capone or Pol Pot. An irredeemable sociopath who smirked with diseased pride of handiwork. I had seen him on *60 Minutes*. He had been pathetically transparent, the petty tyrant so wanting to be noticed. A cruel, small, murderous fool.

At one time or another, the killer had said revealingly of himself, "I have one-on-ones with the greatest reporters in the world. All of them. I've met all of them. At one point I was the most interviewed person in the world. I was one of the most important. . . . I was incredible. . . . A leader has to know how to play with the army, the power, and the people."

Unalloyed megalomania, armed and dangerous, under color of small but lethal power, bloodying the night.

And he is just over there. Across this field of tall grass and behind that fence. The man whose henchmen had horribly disfigured the young, pretty face of a woman I knew. The man who had gutted families and, like the archetypal brute's coward, fled his country awash in rivers of blood.

Haiti requested of the United States his extradition for trial. In March 1995, Secretary of State Warren Christopher wrote to Attorney General Janet Reno: "Nothing short of Mr. Constant's removal from the United States can protect our foreign policy interests in Haiti."

Shortly thereafter, Constant revealed that he had all along been an employee of America's unelected, secret, all-powerful sub-government, the CIA, which had employed him, in part, to derail the Clinton administration's efforts to restore democracy in Haiti. He then threatened to divulge the full details of U.S. covert activities in Haiti.

He was never deported. He is a free man and now lives under U.S. protection in New York City, where the former butcher of Port-au-Prince sells real estate.

"Bay kou bliye, pote mak sonje." ("Those who give the blows forget, those who bear the scars remember.") A Creole proverb.

But what else could the victims do other than remember? Nothing, it would seem. Not and remain who and what they are. Here and there he is sighted in New York by Haitians, but they do not kill him. They stare after him and loathe him but they do not kill him. Is this due to inhibitions born of some interior Haitian morality? Or is it because they, too, citizenship notwithstanding, are *guests* in America and, therefore, equal only in status to the monster guest whom they loathe? Yes, of course. It is the common person's math of *realpolitik*.

Thus they must concede the obvious. America is the whole earth's heavyweight champion of ever since. America is the judge, the jury, the book, the gun, the patron saint of safe choices, the arbiter of everything everywhere.

America is a democracy because America *says* it is a democracy. America is godly and good and perfect because America *says* it is godly and good and perfect. These truths must be truths because America's voice is the only voice America hears. It is self-evident that America has all the power. Therefore it follows that America alone issues all the truths—about anything, about anywhere, about anybody.

Bill Hemmer and colleagues reported *ad nauseam* this morning on CNN that a Boeing 727 had disappeared "from Africa." Never would it have been reported that a plane had disappeared from Europe or South America or Asia. These continents have countries, and the plane would have been reported as having disappeared from one or another of them, perhaps with the city and airport thrown in. To wit: "A plane has disappeared from Paris's Charles de Gaulle International Airport." But Bill Hemmer's, and therefore America's, Africa has no countries. Thus the plane could not have disappeared from Angola, from Huambo, a provincial capital I have visited, because Bill Hemmer's Africa, America's Africa, has no countries, no cities, no languages, no cultures, no schools, no families, no past. This, on one Bill Hemmer's say-so alone. Clark Kent telling us the way it is. Every morning. *Later in the hour. Americans favor invading Iran should Iran not. . . .*

Desperate people made crazy. No place to stand. No public prize to win. No cranny of their own left to govern. No published truth that they can recognize as embraceable. No *name* even to hear rightly pronounced if to hear it pronounced at all.

Prep prick erectus. Alias: Anonymous Van Buren. Bob's second boy. Cornell '95. *Cum laude.* End of hall, fifteen-by-fifteen, windowless, memo factory. Room 3305, United States Department of State. Laminated ID on neck chain. Typing pool. Fourth-tier bureaucrat. Fifty poor countries fear him. He is the faceless face of the power that can sustain or destroy. His passport has not yet fallen due for renewal. His condo lamps have just recently moved from milk crates to end tables.

Emmanuel "Toto" Constant is safe in America. Though he is responsible for countless gruesome killings of innocent civilians in his country, he will never be brought to book—here, there, or before the international bar of justice for crimes against humanity. He is free. Anonymous Van Buren as much as said so. This must be true because Anonymous Van Buren has no need to lie; vast inequalities of power as such require no balm of hypocrisy. It is well known by now that whatever Toto's egregious crimes are, they are America's egregious crimes. Inasmuch as America can commit no crime, nor can Toto acting on America's behalf. Thus he is free to preen *Queens,* rubbing his off-track American marriage in the very faces here of those who fled his whistling, blood-smeared machete in Haiti.

This is new in the long history of the nation-state. Where a thing is right because a single nation says that it is. Where no behavior is illegal; where no act is *ultra vires* or beyond the charter because a single nation *is* the law *and* the charter. When whatever it elects to do supersedes all other laws and charters, including the United Nations Charter.

Wealthy nations can survive in fluid coexistence with America, but no small government dare persist in principled disagreement. It simply could not survive. The people, yes, but the state, no. No invasion indicated. Anonymous Van Buren, the fourth-tier U.S. State Department bureaucrat, can manage its economic meltdown from his windowless office.

Guerrilla warfare tactics had been the poorer, weaker world's first answer to the vastly superior military technology of the industrialized West. But the industrialized West had found, in any case, other, more effective ways of compromising the flags of the poor, economic globalization being the most recent of them. Leaders not bombed can be bought. And those who cannot be bought can be squeezed as Aristide is being squeezed by the powerful international financial institutions that America all but controls. The American idea is and was, in its staked-out spheres of the third world, to control every decision of consequence, to devolve upon democratically elected poor-country leaders none save the most ornamental of functions.

Let's not mince words. The United States is strangling the democratic government of Haiti. The government of Haiti, for its part, is doing everything within its limited powers to serve the people of its country, including making gestures to the United States of virtual state obeisance that no democracy should ever be called to make to another.

In early 2003, the U.S. government, after blocking the previously approved loans to Haiti, requested of President Aristide that he replace his police chief, who the State Department had said was "unsuitable." *God, what hubris. Unmetabolized anger. Where does one put it? I am, I'm afraid, neither priest nor saint.* President Aristide acceded to the State Department's request and named a new police chief, whom the State Department again found "unsuitable." *Beneath the palaver of self-praise, America is indisputably an unfeeling country.*

President Aristide then accepts the *American* candidate for the job and Jean-Robert Faveur is named as police chief. In a gambit designed to further humiliate Aristide, the new police chief—two and half weeks after being named and already armed with a U.S. visa—goes into exile in the United States. The political opposition, which by all accounts is tiny and ineffectual but enjoys the politically ineffectual support of the United States, then claims that elections cannot be held because the country is not secure and cites the flight of the police chief as evidence of this condition. *The judge, the jury . . .*

What is it in the character of a nation that would cause it, over so long a period, to punish a people, generation upon generation, for having done nothing other than pursue their freedom from bondage along the only course open to them? Assisting first the sustainment of their enslavement. Then, upon its ending, smothering the economic spark from their newly free republic, followed later by military occupation and sponsorship for delegated tyranny.

Jean-Bertrand Aristide, a passionate democrat, is one of the finest human beings that I have known. His is not the character of the middling decent, but of the most exemplary of the human family. I suppose there are others to compare evenly to him. But I have not known them as I have known him. Thus, the example of his life has become for me a reliable standard by which to measure the gravity of America's broad moral crime against the whole of the black world. I do not say these things about him because he is my friend. It is rather the case that he is my friend because his character would warrant from us the highest regard.

No nation can do what America has done to him and to the Haitian people and deserve the respect of any afforded the vantage position of witness, firsthand, to the cruel coarseness of America's long-term behavior.

How could the matter be clearer?

From the presidency of Thomas Jefferson through that of Abraham Lincoln, from Woodrow Wilson through to the unfinished work of George W. Bush, Haitian blood stains American hands. Blood spilled by a people who would wish only to solidify what Americans claim to cherish—democracy.

As no one questions Aristide's broad popularity at home, no one questions the magnitude of Emmanuel "Toto" Constant's brutal crimes inflicted upon his own defenseless people. But Constant, having done, all too well, the nasty bidding of his benefactor, walks free in America. Meanwhile children are dying in Haiti, no longer at the hand of FRAPH, but now, more directly than before, by the policy pen of the President of the United States.

As a moral man, I must, in every way that I can, stand for what I think to be *right*. As a black man, I am constrained to hold a higher loyalty to Toussaint than to any American who would abridge the hard-earned freedoms of his descendants. For two hundred years after the one slave revolt in modern history that succeeded, I and millions the world around remain in Toussaint's debt.

It may well be that the vast majority of black Americans (not to mention white Americans) do not know who Toussaint L'Ouverture was or much of anything about the heroic and unprecedented slave revolt that he and his armies accomplished two hundred years ago against the sixty-thousand-man French army of Napoleon Bonaparte. Toussaint's victory changed the face of the New World and set in motion social and political forces that accelerated the end of the transatlantic slave trade and indeed, the institution of slavery itself in North and South America.

And yet African-Americans know almost nothing about the man whose name should be more familiar to them than George Washington's. We know much of Napoleon but little of the gifted former slave whose black armies destroyed Napoleon's dreams for a world empire.

Why is this so?

Much of the reason is obvious, subsumed under the general rubric of race discrimination. Generally speaking, the white world prefers its blacks meek and provincial. Toussaint, like his colleagues in revolt, generals Jean-Jacques Dessalines and Henri Christophe, was anything but. It was in neither America's nor Europe's interest at anytime since 1791 to commend figures like these men to the general attention of the world. Thus, in death, Toussaint's final punishment for his wonderfully brilliant gall has been an obscurity as complete as the industrialized information powers could manage to make it. This obscurity has served another American purpose more odious, I think, than the first. Under a broad blanket of popular ignorance, the United States has hidden not only the epochal event of the successful slave revolt itself, but all of America's actions toward Haiti that would follow in its train from that day to this, as well.

Actions that cannot be publicly defended must not be publicly learned about. Behind this veil of utter shamelessness, the United States has done everything, save launch a third invasion, to destroy Haiti's first real chance for democracy in the two hundred years of its independence. If nothing else is clear, President Aristide, like Toussaint L'Ouverture two hundred years before him, has earned America's unwavering enmity for no other reason than the seriousness with which he takes the solemn democratic obligations of his sworn oath to *his* people. That he is loved by *them* is reason enough that he be hated by America.

America. America. Land of my birth and erstwhile distress. Hypocrite immemorial. My heart left long ago. At long last, I have followed it. Trying my very best, how could I, in good conscience, remain *for* a country that has never ever, at home or abroad, been *for* me or *for* mine? I can remember in my forty years of social activism no occasion where American policy was instinctually consistent with America's stated creed of freedom. On too terribly many depleting public policy occasions—segregation, reparations for slavery, apartheid, militarizing tyranny, Ethiopia, Nigeria, Western Sahara, Cuba, South Africa, Namibia, Mozambique, Angola, food, medicine, AIDS, education, trade, police brutality, Haiti—I have fought for and with America's creed—*against* America. For had matters of public course been left alone to the pragmatic discretions of America's *leaders,* South Africa would be ruled today by a white minority. Portugal's colonial empire in Africa would remain profitable from forced African labor. Namibia would not be independent. An enslaved Haiti would be the crown jewel of the French world empire, still. That these outcomes did not eventuate is no tribute to America, but rather to those who fought for so long, so tenaciously, *against* America. I am all but spent by the effort. A life now near used up contesting a fraud.

In January 2004, the world will join the people of Haiti in celebrating the two-hundredth birthday of the Haitian Revolution. I have agreed to serve on the executive committee of Ayiti Oui,[3] or, "Haiti Yes," a nongovernmental event-planning organization, because I deeply believe that as Haiti has, at great continuing cost, done much for us, we must remember publicly our indebtedness to her. In so doing, we serve to remember *ourselves*. All of ourselves. Over the long centuries and across the contemporary world. America will never tell our people's story, fully or accurately. That we must do for ourselves.

After the military coup of September 30, 1991, that drove President Aristide from power, the United States continued to train and arm the Haitian military. There had even been rumors of American complicity in the coup.

Almost a decade later, with Aristide restored to office and the Bush administration in power, fifteen Caribbean foreign ministers met in the Bahamas with Secretary of State Powell to impress upon him the inhumanity of America's obstruction of the loan that had been approved in 1998 to Haiti from the Inter-American Development Bank. The foreign ministers forcefully described to the secretary the human suffering in Haiti occasioned by the American position.

---

[3] Prior to the arrival of Christopher Columbus and other Europeans to a land they called Domingue, the indigenous people had called it Ayiti—"Land of Many Mountains." After the death of Toussaint L'Ouverture, when Jean-Jacques Dessalines and his slave revolutionaries won their war of independence against France in 1804, they paid homage to the land's original inhabitants, long since killed off by the overwork and disease brought by the European powers, by renaming their new republic "Haiti."

Powell was unmoved by their appeal.

At the June 2003 Organization of American States Summit in Lima, Peru, Powell again took a hard line against Haiti and recited certain nonnegotiable conditions that impinged upon the Haitian government's prerogatives of sovereignty.

Powell then laid down a deadline for Haiti's compliance: September 30, the anniversary of the 1991 military coup that overturned Haiti's first ever democratic election. The message of the date of the deadline was less than subtle.

In July 2003, five years after the loan had been approved, the Inter-American Development Bank finally began to release some of the funds to Haiti. The partial release came as a result of enormous pressures that were brought to bear upon the Bush administration by a long list of prominent Americans, including Senator Christopher Dodd; Ethel Kennedy; Congresswoman Barbara Lee; Jeffrey Sachs, the Harvard economist; Joseph Kennedy, the former congressman; and Paul Farmer of Harvard Medical School.

I met Mr. Powell at a Clinton White House occasion for President Aristide, not long after Aristide had been restored to office. Powell had been warm and engaging. Over time, I've come to learn what little this reveals about blacks who feel constrained to prove their mettle and fealty (at the expense of their own) to those to whom they are beholden for their careers. The behavior, sad though it may be, is hardly new.

Once I went with a small group of prominent blacks to seek a grant from a major New York–based foundation. The foundation's black vice president received us warmly, endorsed our project, specified the amount that was within her power to approve, and, indeed, vowed that she would. We then drafted a formal proposal that conformed with the vice president's suggestions and submitted it. Shortly thereafter, we received from the vice president a terse two-sentence form letter stating that the foundation funded nothing of the sort that we had proposed. Months later, a member of our group discovered what had happened. It seems that the foundation's presidency had unexpectedly come open, and the black vice president wanted the job. It was thought that her chances would be enhanced were she to demonstrate a willingness to be "tough" on blacks.

The stratagem did not work her for. She did not get the job. It *has* worked, however, spectacularly for Mr. Powell. The idea behind the notion is simple enough. America is still very much a racially divided country, and blacks who wish to speed up the mainstream ladder understand early on that the more they make the plight of fellow blacks a working term of their public advocacy, the less likely they are to accomplish mainstream American success. America has progressed to not caring that Mr. Powell *is* black, so long as Mr. Powell himself makes no persistent brief for blacks who are put upon and disadvantaged because of their race. Should he ever betray the smallest such sympathy, for person or country, mainstream regard for him will wane commensurately.

Chapter Twenty-one

Morality

May 2003

I don't know what causes this, but the place now feels like a foreign space, like what used to be *here* has become *there*. I am in Room 405 of the Georgetown Inn on lower Wisconsin Avenue in Washington, D.C. I have a strong desire to go *home,* back to the *here* that once was *there*. I lived in this city for twenty-five years, and all but ten of the balance of my years one hundred miles south in Richmond, Virginia, where I was born.

Now I know without dwelling upon it that I no longer belong here. Perhaps it is the room, appointed in worn early-American with looping, heavy, brocaded brown drapes, that depresses me, or it could be that spring has failed to arrive in Washington by this late date of May 19. Coming here from Dulles, the driver said that the sun hadn't been seen in a week. It has been raining since I arrived last night.

The room is cold. The sky is gray. In the middle of the night I call down to the front desk and complain that there is no heat in the room. They tell me that the heat had been turned off throughout the building because it is spring. The temperature outside is fifty-three degrees. There are two windows in the room. They are double hung and built of replacement-window metal mullions, dispelling all impression that Thomas Jefferson had checked out shortly before my arrival. The windows are hideous but do the job of sealing out drafts of the unreasonably cold, wet air.

The desk clerk on the phone tells me that the hotel's space heaters have been distributed to guests earlier in the evening and that he will send up a heater when one becomes available. I find a synthetic blanket on the shelf of the closet to match the brown one on the bed and pull the faux velvet refuge snug up under my chin. I must try to sleep. Just a few blocks from where I am staying is Georgetown University. There, at two o'clock tomorrow afternoon, the president of the university, Dr. John J. DeGioia, will bestow upon me the degree of Doctor of Laws, *Honoris Causa*. I have received many honorary degrees. Still, this occasion was important enough to have had me travel from St. Kitts here for the commencement exercises. A number of black faculty members, so I have been told, had made this happen. Dean Everett Bellamy, who'd been arrested with me in the eighties in front of the South African embassy, had nominated me for the honor. Professor Charles Lawrence, who together with his wife and fellow law professor Mari Matsuda had worked with me on the slavery reparations issue, will read aloud at the commencement exercises the citation that he has written: *Trained as a lawyer, you have made the politics and the transactions of the struggle for racial justice your career and the most oppressed citizens of the planet your passion. Your commitment to the practice of speaking truth to power has been unyielding.*

I am cold under here. Still, I must confess that I am looking forward to tomorrow's ceremony. I do this even as I wonder why it is that we honor those who care and not those cared about, those who do the suffering. It seems always to be a ritual of a certain circular selfishness, where those who care are noticed by those who care rather less, both promising to honor an unspoken pact of polite silence.

Professor Bellamy calls me in the morning and tells me that a campus policeman will collect me at 12:30 and take me to the president's office, where the commencement speaker, the former *New York Times* columnist Anthony Lewis, and the other honorary degree recipients are to gather with faculty.

It has stopped raining. But it remains soddeningly chilly, the sky the color of slate. Nonetheless, I feel good, the euphoria no doubt caused by some mixture of pride that tricks honest self-appraisal like a fun-house mirror, and the expectation of visiting with family and friends following the ceremony.

The room-service waiter arrives with breakfast and a copy of the Sunday *Washington Post,* which I do not open until fifteen minutes before I am to be picked up.

On page six of the Metro section, in a picture above the fold, my eyes catch the sight of two smiling men dressed in academic regalia. The man on the right is Georgetown University president John De-Gioia. The man on the left, acknowledging applause from the graduates of Georgetown's School of Foreign Service, is George J. Tenet, the director of the Central Intelligence Agency. I read the article that covers the top third of the page, look at the picture again, and read the article a second time. Although Director Tenet has been an ardent architect and exponent of the president's war against Iraq, there is no evidence of any opposition to his role from the graduates whose vigorous salute he is returning.

In an instant, the ceremony that is to begin in a little over an hour has lost its value to me. I know what I will do, but not how I will do it. I wish very much that I could talk this over with Hazel, but she has remained in St. Kitts to care for Khalea, who had not wanted to miss tomorrow, Monday, a school day. I can call, of course, but somehow I am uncomfortable about discussing the matter on the phone as well.

For what seems a long time, I stare at a wall of busily floral wallpaper. I have no desire to be what the English novelist Robert Barnard calls a "comic irritant," but I have no taste for choral thinking either. We may never know how many Iraqis (uncounted and unaccounted for) American soldiers pushed into shallow mass graves. I juxtapose in my mind images of the red horror of bomb-lit Baghdad, the screams, the flying body parts, the eyes of children, vacant, catatonic. I juxtapose this with the picture of the two smiling men for whom all is rosy and well on the manicured hilltop campus of Georgetown University, the Jesuit school whose early buildings had been constructed by black American slaves. Although not pictured in the photographs above the fold, the text of the article implies that everyone on the grounds of the university at the time that the picture was taken had been smiling at the director of the Central Intelligence Agency, the man who bore much responsibility for the American blitzkrieg against the lightly defended Iraqi legatees of a seven-thousand-year-old Mesopotamian civilization.

Sometimes, however, it is easier to be brave than an annoyance—particularly, I must confess, a lone, black post-segregation annoyance, burr, disturber, malcontent in a sea of smiling, upper-crust, guiltless white faces who wish to confer upon *me* as evidence of their much-prided newfound kindness some transferable *something* of their perfect validity. Dead Iraqis are not here today. On this campus. Marring the high feelings of the gathered about themselves. *That* needed to happen and it happened. It's over. Okay? Done. It does not belong in *this*. On *this* day.

In the picture, the director of the Central Intelligence Agency appears to render to the young graduates a military salute. What are they thinking, if anything? Who *are* they? What had Iago said: *I am not what I am*. Indeed.

Moral quandaries are usually contained in moments, small private interior moments. No one in the indifferent crowd much cares, except about inconvenient rocks dropped in placid ponds. The space one stands in, the small, lightless space against which the prevailing winds blow cheerful discouragement, one stands in *alone*. One must decide the moment knowing that the *right* decision will likely be punished, if only with isolation, and the wrong decision will be rewarded, smiled upon, borne along to greater acceptance. All that, at least.

Fully dressed, I sit on the very edge of the bed and begin to write on a pad that Hazel had given me to use on the plane during the nearly four-hour flight from San Juan to Washington. By the time I have written, crossed out, added in from above, and rearranged language, a Georgetown police sergeant has arrived to take me up to the campus.

David Bellamy stands waiting in front of the handsome administration building. The circle is difficult to negotiate. Gowned graduating students, faculty members, and close relations jam the driveway, oblivious of everything save the high promise of the occasion.

I get out of the car and push through the happy mob to greet Dean Bellamy at the base of the building's impressive entry stair. Once inside, I ask Dean Bellamy as we walk, "Will I have a chance to say a few words during the exercise?" He says, "No." This in my experience, is always the case, or at least almost always. Months before, upon receiving an honorary degree from the University of South Florida, I was asked, completely without notice, if I wanted to make a few remarks, to which I had replied, "No," having been taken off guard.

"Can we find a place to talk privately?" I say to Dean Bellamy. I want this very much to be over. To leave this place and these happy foreign faces. But I do not want to offend this man who has done me the honor of his nomination and support before school powers, which I suspect did not care very much, one way or the other.

We sit beside each other along a tall wall in the large formal foyer outside the president's office. I describe my concern and follow with, "I cannot accept the honorary degree." He is an assistant dean whose life at the law school I regrettably have just complicated. Nonetheless he understands and arranges meetings with the school's dean, Anthony Lewis and Professor Lawrence, all of whom appear to understand my decision. Lewis, an old acquaintance, photocopies my brief statement and asks me: "What are you going to do with this?" I say, "I don't know." To which he responds, "Of course it only just happened?"

The following is much of the statement I would have no opportunity to deliver. And perhaps it is just as well. In the flush of passion, I am prepared to read a statement that includes a name for the serious crime I believe the president and other administration officials, including George Tenet, to have committed. Although I believe my characterization of the president's and his colleagues' behavior to be accurate, naming their crimes as I have written it out in a bold, blue longhand would likely cause much of the celebratory audience to become annoyed and cease listening. Here it is, minus the incendiary passage:

> I wish to begin by apologizing to all of you if what I am about to say on your day causes you discomfort.
>
> I have fought all of my life against social injustice. I have opposed unjust communist regimes and unjust capitalist regimes. I have fought against unjust white regimes and unjust black regimes.
>
> I do not live in the United States anymore. I live on the tiny democratic Caribbean island of St. Kitts. I only learned this morning that George Tenet, the director of the Central Intelligence Agency, was to be the speaker at your School of Foreign Service exercises yesterday.
>
> I sincerely believe that in the years ahead, the entire world will come to accept that the United States has committed in Iraq a great crime against humanity, a crime against innocent Iraqi women, children, and men, indeed, a crime against our own men and women, who have paid and will continue to pay with their lives for the greed of America's empire-makers.
>
> In my view, President Bush, Secretary of Defense Rumsfeld, Secretary of State Powell and Mr. Tenet are little more than [deleted]. There are no weapons of mass destruction in Iraq, and they knew this. There is no Iraqi connection to 9/11. There was no legal justification for a war in which we have not even bothered to count the Iraqi dead.
>
> America has committed an awful wrong. In the sight of God, I trust in time that this will be the prevailing verdict of humanity.
>
> In any case, you have chosen the wrong person this morning. I should not have come. Indeed, I would not have come had I known before what I learned this morning when I opened the newspaper.
>
> Americans must choose. They must choose between decency of course and empire, between morality and [deleted], between truth and deception.
>
> Mr. Tenet has the right to speech protected by our

Constitution. But that right should not be exercised on a platform so broadly respected as yours.

I cannot accept your honor. For in my view, Georgetown University yesterday disqualified itself of the moral authority to bestow one.

My candle lights little other than the interior of my own conscience. But for me, for all of my life, that has been enough.

I leave the grounds of the Georgetown campus before the exercises begin. Although my name is printed in the program as a recipient of the degree of Doctor of Laws, *Honoris Causa,* no explanation is given for my absence from the podium during the course of the commencement program.

Chapter Twenty-two

Arrival

August 2001

I have landed safely in the youth of old age. I am sixty. I have come with Hazel and Khalea to live on a tiny island that only a small percentage of Americans seem to have ever heard of. Though it is arrestingly beautiful here, with a sharp spine of lush green mountain rising above a warm jeweled sea, we did not come for the vistas alone. Nor was it only because Hazel had grown up here and had never forgotten how the place had shaped her before she left at sixteen on the long journey north to college in Halifax, Nova Scotia. No, I suppose there were larger reasons, some of which I have yet to puzzle out. One tiny thing seems clear enough however. We wanted to leave America with as much conviction as we wanted to come here.

We arrived just three weeks before the World Trade Center towers were destroyed.

Hazel and I were in the post office in downtown Basseterre when we learned about it from a postal clerk who had heard the story moments before on the radio. Taking the transistor down from her ear, "Have you heard about this?"

"About what?" Hazel asked.

"New York. What's happened in New York. A plane has just flown into the World Trade Center. One of the buildings has collapsed."

We were, of course, stunned. More than a little bit incredulous as well. The three of us had visited the observation deck atop Tower Two a little more than two months before. We had been taken around by a very nice black docent who had read one of my books and recognized mine as the face on the cover. She looked to be twenty-two or so, with a smile whose wattage had survived adolescence intact.

As we sat in our Honda CRV in front of the Washington Archibald High School waiting for Khalea to come out to go home for lunch, we debated whether or not to wait until the end of the day to tell her what had happened. We did not want to upset her in the middle of her school day. She is twelve and in first form, which is equivalent to the seventh grade in America. We decided to tell her at lunch, preferring that she learn the horrific news from us as opposed to learning it from school friends returning from home for the afternoon school session. At 11:45 sharp, seven hundred students ranging in age from twelve to seventeen poured out of the yellow masonry courtyard building, the girls gaily dressed in pleated plaid skirts and white cotton blouses, the boys in white shirts and khaki twill trousers.

The day was warm and cloudless. The students who walked past the open windows of our car spoke numberless *good mornings*.

Africa's genetic imprint is more apparent here than in America. Skin color is more darkly uniform. Hair texture is very seldom tinkered or tampered with. Khalea was smiling brightly as she threw her backpack onto the backseat. *She hasn't heard.* After lunch at home in the dining room we told her. She received the news calmly and then asked if CNN had run footage of the carnage. We told her *yes* but we didn't think she should see the pictures if she could possibly avoid them. She saw the wisdom in this and went for a while without speaking. Then a piquant something occurred to her and she started to cry.

"The docent, Mommy, the nice docent. Is she dead?"

"We don't know, darling."

Khalea continued to cry quietly. Hazel put her arms around her.

"Her shift probably hadn't begun."

This was the best that we could manage. We had no way of finding out what had happened to the docent. We had not remembered her name.

Although the news from New York swept the island instantly, afternoon classes proceeded seemingly unaffected. Mr. Jones gave the French test he had promised. The debating club chose topics for an upcoming competition. In math, students drilled on modern math, the rules of which I couldn't, had my life depended upon it, distinguish from Sanskrit. No one mentioned to Khalea what had happened in New York. On a tranquil island that America had scarcely bothered to know existed, life went on as usual.

Well, not entirely as usual. America is a very powerful country. Not to be provoked. Not even to be left to interpret in her wounded state silence as a provocation. Prime Minister Denzil Douglas gave a full-length address on television in which he sympathized with America and condemned terrorism. Days later, the Minister of Tourism invited twenty New York City firefighters to visit St. Kitts and Nevis, all expenses paid. And twenty New York firefighters managed to get their hands on the helpful fellow Rand McNally and show up with their families for their first, and likely last, visit to the little Caribbean island called the golden rock. A smattering of T-shirts bearing an American flag intertwined with the flag of St. Kitts and Nevis popped up here and there.

Running under this current of proper solidarity was a tone of unofficial counterpoint. A panel of scholars on a radio show broadcast from the nearby island of Antigua suggested that what happened in America should have been expected and went on to rake up a long list of injuries administered to the third world by the United States. I thought the show would incite a storm of local protest, but it did not.

Still, it would be at the very least simplistic, and probably just flat wrong, to suggest that the leaders here feel one way about America and the general public another. This is a tiny place and tiny places have to do what tiny places have to do. My guess is that what you see here is a certain practical *recognition* of America's wealth, power, and size that falls short of affection. Realized authority results in many things, awe and imitation among them, but seldom in affection. The radio academics are free to say what they please. The government, however, signals us in direct response to them by its silence.

All of this, however, is impressionistic. I haven't been here long enough to see through to the core of things as yet. As you would expect, because I have moved from one cultural experience to another, my first, quite involuntary, impulse would be to compare the new experience to the old. For instance, owing to its size and power, America overpraises itself without fear, or even thought, of rebuttal, which, in any case, it would not be inclined to notice. Thus America has rendered itself all but constitutionally unable to learn anything about anything from anybody. On the other hand this island does not even appear on many maps. I am guessing that because it is small and has no power in the world to speak of, it tends to underpraise itself, even in those areas where its social health is quite remarkably superior to America's.

Unbalanced power poisons introspection. In its vacated space lay living society's imperative questions, unseen, unphrased, unasked, unanswered.

In the long history of human society, has there evolved a minimalist code of humaneness, an ever so slowly rising expectation of extrasexual moral behavior, one person, one society, toward another? Is this not a central purpose of all the world's great religions, Abrahamic and non-Abrahamic? Writes Karen Armstrong of three such faiths in *A History of God:* "In all three (Abrahamic) faiths, he [God] has inspired an ideal of social justice, even though it has to be said that Jews, Christians and Muslims have often failed to live up to this ideal and have transformed him in the God of the status quo."

What is democracy? Is it not more an ideal than a schematic? Thus, is its measure to be taken more in the genuineness of its social strivings than in the mechanical performance of its expressed constitutional requirements? Does it imply for its beneficiaries something beyond the right to *participate,* beyond that which one is protected *from,* as opposed to the minimal social awards one should be entitled *to?* Not just the right to elect, but the right to require, indeed to command? What is the relationship between the requirements of *democracy* and the ideals of social justice that we acknowledge in our religious beliefs were inspired by God? Are we, in fact, Christians? Are we *democrats*? Are we Godly? What, indeed, *are* we? What, if anything, are we trying to become? Toward what ideal state are we trying to advance?

What responsibility does the Christian bear toward the poor, the dispossessed, the less fortunate? The Christian nation? The democrat? The democratic society? The wealthy Christian democratic society? Does maldistributed privilege cauterize the rich and disempower or, effectively, disenfranchise the poor?

Why, in a democracy, would one quarter of the world's prisoners be ours? Why would half of them be black? Are we safe? From them? From our leaders? Is our justice system *just*? Why would three quarters of those on death row be black and Hispanic?

Where is the *whole* of all that has happened? Have we doctored the record? Shredded the past? Destroyed our chances? Hidden the victim, both from our sight and from our consciousness?

Does a nation contravene universal notions of basic human morality by making unilateral war against another nation that poses no direct and immediate threat to the aggressor nation? If not from the family of nations, on what moral authority could such a decision rest? Who gets to decide? Is it not so that what one nation can unilaterally decide, all nations may so decide, and be, by definition, equally justified or *right*? Or is it that we have conceded in the absence of reflection the nominalism of our democracy? A lie not to be looked upon? Unreviewable. That we are *right* only because we are powerful, hence the irrelevancy of all questions of the rightness or wrongness of our decisions and edicts?

In an interview, Republican Senator Chuck Hagel said, "America owns Iraq," and provoked untold new millions of migrating Muslim enlistees to privatize their war against America. Which of the two wars is more just? Ours against them? Theirs against us? Has a higher, broader moral or political authority sanctioned either?

Why do Americans look upon the United Nations, and not NATO, with such concentrated contempt? Is it that NATO is the redoubt of the white and the wealthy while the United Nations is the house of assembly for all of humanity—all races, all classes, all religions, all predators, all victims? What does America's distaste for them say about America? Its Christianity? Its democracy? Is it not the darker neighborhoods of the world that America and Europe have simultaneously exploited and detested since Columbus set sail, since Africans were stolen, Victoria grew fat, and America rose to empire with clumsy insouciance?

Would not Americans fire missiles into the United Nations headquarters building were it not situated in the heart of New York and shielded unwittingly by America's United Nations white member allies?

Do the public leaders of our democracy elevate us and the practice of democracy by publicly raising such questions? Do they even ruminate over such? If not, how else can democracy ever be truly realized? Are we so blind, in the last analysis, to all awareness, even to an awareness of our very blindness?

I think that it may be the case virtually everywhere that the working class *keeps,* for good or ill, a society's core social values. The rich may contaminate the currents with their particular unseemly excess, but it isn't until twenty poor white women pop up to bare their breasts to the nation on the *Jerry Springer Show* that you know for certain that the whole society may be in more than a spot of trouble. There are no firebreaks any more, not with the Internet and global television. Tasteless behavior spreads across international frontiers like an Arizona wildfire.

Still here, in this new old traditional place, life is lived much as it has been lived. With quiet decorum and unassuming compassion.

I had done some reading about the history and life of the Caribbean before coming here with Hazel and Khalea to live. A passage of something I had read came to mind once as I was sitting through one of the Washington National Cathedral's stony services. The passage is from the Caribbean novelist Earl Lovelace's *The Wine of Astonishment*. In it, Lovelace describes a worship service of a poor Trinidadian congregation forbidden by the British during the colonial era to worship as they were traditionally accustomed to worshipping. The members had been jailed for following in their worship practices the dictates of their Africa-based culture and not mimicking the liturgy of the Church of England. Given the Church of England's *cousin* church where I recalled the passage, it is easy to see how it would draw in my mind a distinction that describes the material and spiritual values of the two cultures I was transiting:

> We have this church in the village. We have this church. The walls made out of mud, the roof covered with carrat leaves: a simple hut with no steeple or cross or acolytes or whites priests or Latin ceremonies. But it is our own. Black people own it. Government ain't spent one cent helping us to build it or to put a bench in it or anything; the bell that we ring when we call to the Spirit is our money that we pay for it. So we have this church.
>
> We have this church where we gather to sings hymns and ring the bell and shout hallelujah and speak in tongues when the spirit come; and we carry the Word to the downtrodden and the forgotten and the lame and the beaten, and we touch black people soul.

A young neighbor of ours, an elementary schoolteacher here, died a few months ago after giving birth to her second child. The doctors had warned her before, when she had problems with a previous pregnancy. But she elected to take the risk. Her husband, who owns a small landscaping business, had been overseeing the construction of their new home, which was all but finished when she died. They were not a part of the island's upper class, just nice decent people who'd helped us to settle in here.

The funeral was held in a village church of medium size. (Unlike Lovelace's church, the walls were not made of mud. There are no such buildings here.) By the time Hazel and I arrived, the mourners had spilled out of the packed church and across the whole of the large lawn. The chairs that had been set up outside had all been taken and there was scarcely any standing room left on the lawn.

After a service marked by that special grief evoked for the dear who die young, the coffin was carried out, followed by our neighbor-friend and his close-knit family. Following in the recessional column walked Prime Minister Douglas and the members of his government. And then out poured the general congregants, ranging from the island's wealthiest to the very poorest.

In a village church, on the occasion of a good and common soul's homegoing, the entire society had arrayed itself with no element of it left unrepresented.

That which makes life something more than a pastime, something rich and ennobling, is never to be found among or in the measure of one's worldly goods, but rather in the simplified uncluttered space of one's spirit, a spirit that has seemed far easier to navigate here than it had in GNP America, where spirits lay weary, encumbered like real estate holdings.

Hazel needed a pharmaceutical that the drugstores in St. Kitts were out of. She called over to Nevis and found what she was looking for in a drugstore in Charlestown.

Kenneth is the owner of Kenneth's Dive School on the Bay Road just east of downtown Basseterre. He owns and operates two catamarans and a V-bottomed powerboat. We know him, but only to greet. We do not dive, I'm afraid.

Hazel told the pharmacist on the phone in Nevis to hold the product for pickup sometime later in the afternoon. She then called Kenneth. They exchanged greetings for a period longer than one would in the United States.

"Are you going to be taking a boat over to Nevis this afternoon?"

"No, all my boats are hired out for the day. How can I help you?"

"Do you know anyone else who might be going over today?"

"No–o–o, I can't think of anyone—but, wait a minute. Let me check with the people in the store."

Kenneth did this. He then went to the front door, which was open with a view to the long arcing harbor against which Basseterre

nestled. He said to a young man standing beside the sma
stair, "Do you know anyone who's taking a boat over today?"

Hazel could not hear the answer. Only the sound of footfalls

"Hello, I'm David. Maybe I can help." Hazel explained wha
she was trying to do.

David said, "The last ferry leaves Nevis at four P.M. I work for a
man in Nevis. I can call him and ask him to go to the drugstore and
get your package. He can put it on the ferry for you. It should be
here at the dock by four forty-five."

Hazel does not know David's boss. She does not know David,
either. He had just happened to be standing at the time near the
front door of Kenneth's Dive Shop.

David's boss went to the drugstore and paid eighteen dollars for
the package that was being held for Hazel Ross-Robinson. He
wrote her name with a marker on the bag and then took it to the
dock and put it on the four o'clock ferry.

Before going to the dock in St. Kitts, Hazel stopped by Kenneth's
Dive Shop with the eighteen dollars. Kenneth looked at her with
surprise.

"You didn't have to bring any money. We can take care of that
any time."

Hazel then went to the dock to meet the ferry. After the boat
had docked and lowered its steel vehicle tray, Hazel walked onto
the boat behind a young man she saw examining the packages
stacked against the gunwale. His name was David. He had come
down to the dock to make certain things had gone as planned.

Later, when Hazel called David to thank him for arranging
things, he said simply, "It makes me feel good to help."

A member of the white American family that owned and operated the small upscale hotel on the slope said that some money of
hers was missing. She had the hotel's Kittitian staff workers body-
searched. Nothing turned up. She then persuaded the police to
search their homes. Again, nothing was found. The innkeeper later
discovered that she had merely mislaid the money and that no theft
had occurred. This she never told the invaded employees.

...mon in several islands particularly in St. ...ves to be branded with the initial letters ...name; and a load of heavy iron hooks ...necks. Indeed on the most trifling oc- ...re loaded with chains; and often instru- ...of torture were added. The iron muzzle thumb screws, &c. are so well known, as not to need a descrip- tion, and were sometimes applied for the slightest faults. I have seen a negro beaten til some of his bones were broken, for even letting a pot boil over.

—Olaudah Equiano
I Was Born a Slave

Up until the 1640s tobacco had been the principal crop of St. Kitts. By then the original Carib population had been slaughtered and erased from the island that had on May 13, 1627, been for- mally divided by treaty between England and France.

In 1648 Dutch refugees from Brazil introduced a new crop, sugar. In twenty years' time, tobacco production had ceased. By 1650, large tracts of virgin forest had been cleared to make way for sugar and cotton production. Planters first relied on indentured Eu- ropean laborers to do the work, but soon found it advantageous to bring in slaves from Africa. By the mid-1660s, the island's popula- tion had climbed past six thousand. More than half of them were slaves who toiled unremunerated in the hot sun on English and French plantations.

Slavery in St. Kitts, as evidenced firsthand by the testaments of slaves like Olaudah Equiano, was said to have been as brutal as any form practiced anywhere in the New World.

The stories of their suffering are never far from our thoughts here. The reminders are everywhere. Independence Square is lined with the frame and stone buildings in whose lower quarters slaves were shackled and pinned, and through whose doors were issued for sale and separation from kin and family. The landscape is dot- ted with the soaring remnants of the round stone-and-mortar mills where harvested sugarcane was once ground.

Clearing the land to build our house, we dredged up ceramic evidence of that terrible time—some undecorated fragments of a slave's coal-pot stove and a few colorfully painted bits and pieces from a long-gone English slave-owner's great-house meal service.

We now live on land that was once part of a massive slave sugar plantation. The plantation's sugar mill, restored years ago by Hazel's father, can be seen from our bedroom window. We never look at it, never set foot on the ground around our home, without thinking of those who had involuntarily wrung from this very earth the stolen wealth of the white world, and, just as involuntarily, surrendered back to it their all-too-brief, pain-laden lives.

The slope-side upscale hotel that is owned by the American family has been troubled for some time by a high rate of turnover among its staff. Although Americans have a difficult time understanding it, and all too often place upon it an offensive construction, employers here cannot wield the wage like a sword over the worker's head. The worker does not suffer insult gladly. The worker will walk. And the worker will remind you. Quietly. But with resolve.

Slavery days done. As of 1834, in fact.

There is a legend here that is reenacted every year during Carnival season. Men don bull's-head masks and charge through the streets, evoking from children peals of laughter.

It seems that in the early 1900s, during the era of British colonialism, there was an English planter here who was said to have imported a prize bull. The legend goes that the planter's bull fell deathly ill and could not be roused. The planter engaged the services of doctors and vets from near and far but to no avail. The bull would not move or stir or open its eyes. Finally, a doctor concocted a powerful potion and administered it to the comatose bull with astounding results. The bull stirred and rose unsteadily to its feet. It snorted frightfully and pawed at the soil while frothing rolls of suds poured from its lolling head. The planter and the potion doctor retreated a step, smiling over the slow onset of fear.

And then the resuscitated bull charged. It charged wildly at a steam-emitting clip straight into the planter's beautiful great-house.

It knocked over his priceless china. It smashed to splinters his hand-rubbed mahogany furniture. It shattered his fine English crystal into sparkling shards of countless pieces. It then charged out of the wrecked house and onto the gallery and through the hand-carved balustrade, before plowing through a score of poorly constructed, thatch-roof workers' huts.

The bull then paused briefly and snorted out ropes of foam that swung from its huge enraged head like poisonous white snakes. It sighted on the planters' unharvested bumper fields of cane, pawed the soil twice deeply, dropped its massive head and charged. Straight through the planter's bountiful crops it bore, this way and that, back and forth and back again, mauling and mashing every stalk of the sweet cane standing upright in the sun. By the time the prize bull had spent its strength, the English planter's crops had been completely destroyed.

Every year without fail this free-flowing street theater of the English planter's prize bull is performed to countrywide merriment.

The world community established an International Criminal Court as a permanent forum for trying those charged with genocide and assorted crimes against humanity. The court represents the culmination of the assembly of nation's long effort to bring persons charged with mass and extrajudicial killings to justice. Over ninety countries signed the treaty establishing the court.

On July 1, 2003, the United States suspended all U.S. military assistance to thirty-five countries that refused to pledge an exemption for any American who might be called before the court. The United States, however, waived the penalty for its European NATO friends and other major allies like Israel, Egypt, Jordan, South Korea, and Japan.

Hubris of unfathomable dimension.

Perhaps there is new science here to be found. The DNA of nationality. Or more narrowly, American DNA. Getting right to the heart of it, white American DNA. Arrogance socialized too long. Absorbed into the genes. Then there would be no hope. The victim can't understand. I mean the victim really *cannot*. It can't do transpositions. It has a dyslexia of empathy. Many will die on both sides because the other people can't understand that the victim just *can't* understand. Genetically, I mean.

America owns Iraq. The outside onlookers thought it was an aberrant musing of a single unbalanced senator. But it wasn't. It was as epidemically, hegemonically American as the Monroe Doctrine. Americans, I am convinced, literally cannot understand that they don't own Iraq, or any other non-NATO country they decide to own, for that matter. *What you mean, we don't own it?* Americans pulled out of Vietnam only because too many Americans were being killed there by the awful North Vietnamese. Before that, few Americans wondered, even privately, what we were doing, killing and carrying-on smack dab in the middle of a distant country's *civil* war.

There are Americans, the other white people, the Japanese—who get a money exception—and then everybody else. Four sets of people. Four sets of rules. Americans don't know *how* to be equals. No, I am not referring to the less important vagaries of material difference, economic or military, but rather, to *human* equality, that essential equality of the *self,* foreordained as God and nature's democratic idea for all who make up the human family. The American mind cannot absorb, cannot wrap itself around notions like this; hence Americans, including black soldiers who are little more than agents of the American empire, feel just fine about doing anything to anybody. They do not believe that they are being attacked in Iraq because they no more belong there occupying someone else's country than Iraqis in tanks and full battle gear belong on Pennsylvania Avenue. But you hear Americans talk—Republicans, Democrats, rich people, poor people—and you come to understand that Americans, many of them otherwise the nicest of people, literally believe—no, *know*—that they cannot, by the psychotic power vested in them by the state of themselves, do *anything* wrong.

They don't care how many Haitians die from unclean drinking water. They don't *see* Haitians.

Considering America's new hyperpower status in the world, this national genetic illness of America's should make the world very nervous.

Here in the Caribbean, it appears strongly to me that such is not the region's natural cultural reflex to know viscerally what it will need to know to survive America with any meaningful independence to show for it. The Caribbean is socially attractive because it has among its people an unsung thoughtfulness that America does not have. In its relations with America, however, it is precisely this characteristic that puts the Caribbean at such a significant disadvantage. Like Christopher Columbus five hundred years ago, Americans have seen the breathtaking Caribbean and now wish to own it. For Caribbeans, the past lies directly ahead, the warning of it obscured only by complaisance and the natural tendency of the decent to trust as the healthy and breathing evening meal would the lion. Ask the Native Americans. Ask the Aboriginal people of Australia. Ask the Hawaiians. Ask the Tainos and Caribs, if there are any left to ask. Ask the sad remnants of owners past, all made over into tragicomic ornaments on the land of their ancestors' sacrifice. And the records kept in the North will not show what happened.

This sweet Caribbean will need to bolster the protective shell of it; to define the political and cultural defense of it, to survive. It will need to depend on itself, look to itself, protect itself or it will be gone, never to be returned in recognizable form to those who had suffered and fought to make it special for them and attractive to predators.

Unless the region's leaders are vigilant, America and Americans will make its lands over into a region of salaried waiters with little choice but to serve the exquisite table its people had once owned. The Americans are coming. They are coming to *acquire*. Silkily. They will be involuntarily constrained by the habits of their history to destroy—even those very characteristics that had first caught their eye.

> (Americans) are insensible to the wonders of inanimate nature, and they may be said not to perceive the mighty forests which surround them till they fall beneath the

hatchet. Their eyes are fixed upon another sight: the American people views its own march across these wilds—drying swamps, turning the course of rivers, peopling solitudes, and subduing nature. This . . . image of themselves does not meet the gaze of the Americans at intervals only; it may be said to haunt everyone of them in his least as well as his most important actions, and to be always flitting before his mind.

—Alexis de Tocqueville
Democracy in America

A very rich, white American named R. Allen Stanford held a press conference here recently with the prime minister and members of his government. Mr. Stanford is a Texas developer and an international banker who is said to have under the management of his company, Stanford Financial Group, some fourteen billion dollars. The press conference was called to announce Mr. Stanford's plan for investment in St. Kitts.

Oh, God. Careful now. Please. You think you know them but you don't. You can't.

Mr. Stanford said that one of his companies, Stanford Caribbean Investment Fund, planned to invest two billion dollars in the region. Mr. Stanford already owned two regional airlines, Caribbean Star and Caribbean Sun, and was building their twenty-five-million-dollar headquarters building next to the St. Kitts airport. He also was exploring the purchase of American Eagle, the largest regional carrier, which would put the Texan in control of all but a small share of commercial air traffic in and out of St. Kitts when Leeward Island Air Transport (LIAT), the airline that the Caribbean governments owned, was allowed to die as expected.

Mr. Stanford said that he would consider investing in schools, roads, piers, and sewage treatment facilities. "In the long term, we can help change the world economic landscape so that St. Kitts as a second-world nation can jump into first-world status."

It was there, on his own view of the desirability of "first-world status," that he tripped over the contradiction of his own making, de Tocqueville's very observation about Americans made so long ago. "The New Yorks and Londons of the world are not nearly as nice a place to live as it is down here. . . . ," continued Mr. Stanford, telling the people here, warning them indirectly himself.

Fernand Braudel had written of Columbus, the first European businessman to invest in the Caribbean, that only Europe " 'needed' the rest of the world, needed to venture outside its own door," its own world having been so badly despoiled, according to Sale. More recently Caryl Phillips observed more of the same: "I saw old Andalucians looking bewildered as men and women in skimpy beachwear cavorted past."

". . . There are so many built-in pluses—the people; then there is the geographical location; the climate; the advantages now, post–September 11, of the safety of this part of the world. You really have a climate here for investors to come in in a significant way and reap *big* [Mr. Stanford's audible emphasis] rewards."

God, he is straightforward about who is to reap the rewards. He says nothing about benefits to the country beyond sixteen clerical jobs and two hundred temporary construction jobs.

"But it will take someone to come in and invest serious money. This is not, unfortunately, a mom-and-pop–type operation to reap big rewards. This is serious money. And we have the financial strength, the history and the connections to pull this off."

He then appears to throw all caution to the wind, lecturing the region's leaders on how they should be behaving toward him and other foreign investors.

"The biggest failure of the leaders of the region in their quest to bring foreign capital to the region is their failure to require investors to perform."

But he does not define the word "perform." Nor does he say anything about how the region will benefit in exchange for the access given him. Will the government participate as a majority owner of the planned projects? Or is it to be an owner at all? Will the government benefit from a tax on Mr. Stanford's profits? Will there be bookkeeping transparency? How will it be done? How else will the people who are providing Mr. Stanford the use of their country benefit quantifiably?

Here he is telling the citizens, in effect, that he is here because his own country has been rendered undesirable by its own people, that he plans to reap big rewards here. He then scolds them for not requiring him to perform, but does not describe, publicly at least, beyond the creation of a limited number of service jobs what his performance is supposed to produce, if anything.

He had already made his approaches to the island of Dominica, and their government had found itself in a difficult position from which to negotiate.

I know something about what happened there. As an American who'd worked on these issues, I could connect the dots.

The American government, as I have said, *works* for American business. In the words of President Calvin Coolidge, "The business of America is business." American business gets American governments elected. American governments help American businesses remain profitable.

At the behest of American business, President Bill Clinton used the instrumentalities of the World Trade Organization to dismantle the Caribbean banana-trade regime with the European Union. In so doing, he wrecked the economies of several banana-producing Caribbean countries, including Dominica, which received 85 percent of its income from the export of bananas. Hence, Dominica, desperate for jobs, is in no position to drive a hard bargain with R. Allen Stanford.

African-Americans love Clinton and know little to nothing about Dominica. Speaking at the funeral of former Atlanta mayor Maynard Jackson, Clinton said to the largely black audience that, "People want to know why black people like me. They like me because I like black people." The audience loved this from the American president who did much to destroy the economies of the Caribbean in a way that would now directly serve the business interest of Mr. Stanford, who has arrived to "reap big rewards." America is a club of economic privilege in which the members, politicians, businessmen, and assorted others arrange to promote each other's interests—

and only each other's interests. They connect all the dots, worldwide. We in the black world don't. We don't even know where the dots are, or that there are dots to be connected. This we must learn, and quickly, to defend ourselves.

In an article that appeared on March 5, 2002, in *The Wall Street Journal*, Peter Fritsch wrote:

Antigua in the Shadow of R. Allen Stanford

St. John's, Antigua—This sun-drenched Caribbean island . . . is fast gaining another reputation as the personal fief of R. Allen Stanford. . . . (who) owns Antigua's biggest commercial and offshore bank, a local airline, Caribbean Star, and Antigua's biggest newspaper . . . consider the recent discovery made by an independent commission investigating official corruption in the building of the new hospital. In the course of its investigation, it found that Mr. Stanford's Bank of Antigua was being repaid a thirty-million-dollar construction loan with money coming directly from the island's social security system. One angry commission member asked Bank of Antigua's president, Kenny Byron, whether the government "was being taken to the cleaners" in the deal. Mr. Byron told the commission, "Yes."

In an interview, Mr. Stanford says he doesn't lend money to the government "without an absolute guarantee of getting paid." He gets those guarantees by having government airport-exit taxes, property taxes and landing fees signed over to his bank. "It's like one of those automatic debit-card deals," he says.

The story of Mr. Stanford in Antigua, in the very least, should inspire the circumspection of Caribbean leaders in their dealings with him. He has advised as much himself. Even Ronald Reagan, considered by almost no one to be a friend of the black world, had something to say of relevance to the instant matter: "Trust, but verify."

Before proceeding further along this course of reason, I must set

out my considerable discomfort with the wh[...]
pression I make of emboldening to advise [...]
how to regard American overtures. For who am [...]

I am an African-American guest of St. Kitts and N[...]
Caribbean region in general. I am but the cousin and n[...]
Nevertheless, I feel a great urgency about these issues, whic[...]
been my life's work. They do not begin and end with the boundar[...]
of the spaces into which we, the descendants of slaves, are fortu-
itously born. They run as a set across the whole of Africa, the Caribbean, Latin America, and black America. Those in the world who
exploit *us* see the world as a single but differentiated commercial opportunity. Those of us who resist can ill afford to see matters more
provincially. We must help each other, but only in ways deemed ap-
propriate by those behind the rampart of their own soil's defense.

Nonetheless, the zeal to do right often overwhelms discretion.
And this may be the case with me. If so, you may attribute much
of it to the alarm of my long experience in America.

I know America, my country, well. As well as you know yours.
It is only for this reason that I urge you to look to the behaviors of
its past to understand its contemporary tendencies and how it cov-
ets what you now have and it does not.

In 1938, the spearhead of Kenyan independence and Kenya's
first prime minister, Jomo Kenyatta, wrote in *Facing Mount Kenya*:

> When the missionaries arrived, the Africans had the
> land and the missionaries the Bible. They taught to pray
> with our eyes closed. When we opened them, they had
> the land and we had the Bible.

Any outsider, either private or government, who puts forward to
the Caribbean a business proposition does so necessarily on terms
that lopsidedly favor the interests of the proposing outsider. Such
would seem self-evident. It would then follow that those who author the gospel of economic globalization and liberalized trade
would be those who would principally benefit from that adhered-to
gospel:

The fact that trade liberalization all too often fails to live up to its promises—but instead simply leads to unemployment—is why it provokes strong opposition. But the *hypocrisy* [author's emphasis] of those pushing for trade liberalization—and the way they have pushed it—has no doubt reinforced hostility to trade liberalization. The Western countries pushed trade liberalization for the products they exported, but at the same time continued to protect those sectors in which competition from developing countries might have threatened their economies.

—Joseph Stiglitz
Nobel Laureate for Economics
Globalization and Its Discontents

President Clinton favored globalization and trade liberalization. Yet at the behest of Chiquita Brands, he used the office of the World Trade Organization to destroy the Caribbean banana-exporting industry, which at its peak claimed no more than 2 percent of the world market. Cruel? Yes. But dispassionately, idly so. American.

It is my profound conviction, no doubt shared across the region, that given the smallest opportunity, the United States will gobble up the hard-fought relative independence of the Caribbean. There is, of course, nothing new in this insight. What may surprise the Caribbean is that it has many friends and potential friends—millions—living amid its "friendly" nemesis, the United States. The Caribbean, for its own survival, must cultivate this strength and put it to work inside America with the same quiet resolve with which the American industrialist has perennially cultivated the involvement of the *America First* political establishment. American foreign and domestic policy is produced from the organized pressures of American public lobbies. There should be such a force representing to the U.S. government the interests of the Caribbean. Without this the region cannot hope to safeguard itself from American indifference.

In protecting itself, the Caribbean has certain existing structural defenses that African-Americans, owing to their "subness" in American society, are relatively without.

> There is an evocation here of a permanent Caribbean spirit which is the essence of our civilization. The transience, and inappropriateness, of every newly minted "Washington consensus" which permeates much of our region is at odds with the core of our values shaped through the fever of our history.
>
> —Dr. Ralph E. Gonsalves
> Prime Minister of St. Vincent
> and the Grenadines
> April 23, 2003

> We are peoples with an identity and a culture and a history—the parliament of Barbados will be 350 years old in 1989. We don't need lessons in democracy from anyone. However severe the economic difficulties facing the Caribbean, we are viable functioning societies with the intellectual and institutional resources to understand and grapple with our problems. Collectively, we have a heritage of exquisite natural beauty entrusted to us. The Caribbean is, after all, a civilization.
>
> —Errol Walton Barrow
> Prime Minister of Barbados
> November 20, 1986

Perhaps it is the very existence of this Caribbean Civilization and its psychic tonic that would explain at least in part why black families in America of West Indian descent enjoy a median income more than eleven thousand dollars higher than African-American families. Conversely, this disparity would also seem to prove the enormity of the psychosocial and material cost to African-Americans of the post-slavery American experience. The cultural, social, political, and economic successes of the Caribbean arguably qualify it as the healthiest quarter of the black world. It is our jewel to be relished and protected, small but exquisite, unboastful but luminous.

Afterword

July 9, 2003

I have lived my life within the innermost of concentric circles; my comfort, my protection, my psychic security provided by the bold unbroken line of the smaller of the rings. Two *countries,* one within the other. The outer, official, distant, alien, unaffirming, hostile. The other, safe for my spirit's function, respectful of my long-sequestered story, loving of my *me*.

The country of my recorded birth. The country of my heart. How I once wished them one and the same.

The larger of the two, powerful and world-beating, is literally and technically a real country. It has borders and bureaucracies and ladders of well-described authority. The smaller of the two is really not a country at all. It has no borders, no organs of operation, no recognition of it anywhere as a sovereign entity unto itself. It is not even a place, but many places. Yet it is indivisible. It is wherever black people live, joined into *one* by a common historic event and, thence, by a common consciousness. This, the figurative country of my *race,* is that to which America has prepared me over time to owe my first allegiance.

Thus, I have only left *America,* and not the *country* that I love— the *country* of Africans in America where my mother lives; the *country* where my friend in Haiti remembers everything; the *country* where crumbling manuscripts in Timbuktu defend my ancient identity; the *country* of unprepossessing civility where I now, for the first time, *live,* spiritually free as never before; the *country* of obsidian splendor and post-slavery privation; the *country* of the whole of Africa's issue and their story, then, now, and forever.

Like an opportunistic infection, a mindless fealty to any flag numbs that part of the human heart set aside by nature at the beginning of life for self-esteem.

I tried to love America, its places, its well-ordered marrow, its surplus appurtenance. But I could not *love* a place. I could not *love* things. No one in good health can. Imagine a world of material wealth devoid of people. What's to *love?* Nothing.

I tried to love America, its people, the dominant majority, their depiction of me, their treatment of mine.

I have tried to love America but America would not love the ancient, full African whole of me. Thus I could not love America. I had come to *know* too much of her work.

I tried to love America, its credos, its ideals, its promise, its process. But these things could mean no more to me than they had to those who had conceived them, written them, recited them, and, ultimately, betrayed then.

Then I stopped trying to love America. I have not despaired the moment. For with it has come a measure of unexpected contentment. It settled upon me like an ancient ancestor's ceremonial robe. Warm and splendid and as old as time. Mislaid but valued all the more for its belated retrieval.

Acknowledgments

As has always been the case, I could not have written this book without the unstinting participation of Hazel Ross-Robinson, my wife and alter ego, who undertook much of the research for this book, commented insightfully upon the manuscript, and, not least, introduced me to the special and exquisitely beautiful twin island nation of St. Kitts and Nevis.

I am also grateful to Marie Brown, my literary agent, and Brian Tart, my editor, for their useful observations which significantly improved the manuscript.

Finally, I should like to thank Jacqueline Bryan who typed the manuscript against a demanding deadline.